God's Purpose for Hell

A compelling probe of
God's love for the lost

Second Edition

D. Robert Pike, Ph.D.

DEDICATION

To my deceased and beloved brother Dennis, who is now in the loving presence of our beloved Savior.

This book is also dedicated to our great God and Savior, the Lord Jesus Christ, (Titus 2:13) who for reasons which I do not yet know, would not leave me alone until I finished my research and put it together in the pages of this book.

I would also like to dedicate this to those who are living in fear, those living with regrets, those who are living in pain, and those who are depressed. The purpose of this book is to provide evidence to you that indeed, God is Love, and if you put your trust in him, you have no reason for anxiety. Acts 16:31 "Believe in the Lord Jesus, and you will be saved," Proverbs 3:5,6 "Trust in the LORD with all your heart, and do not lean on your own understanding. In all your ways acknowledge him, and he will make straight your paths."

Other Translations used in this volume.

CEV – Contemporary English Version

KJV – King James Version

NASB – New American Standard Bible

NIV – New International Version

ROTH – Rotherham Emphasized Bible

WEB – World English Bible

WNT – Weymouth New Testament 1912

YLT – Young's Literal Translation

Other Books by Rob Pike

The Lamb of God Victorious!
The Keeping of the Revelation Promise

God's Promise of Redemption
a story of fulfilled prophecy

Jehovah's Witnesses
Modern Day Arians or Not

The Great American Divide
How we got here and what we can do about it

Find them at Amazon.com or at your favorite book store.

Also, for video content on the above titles and more,

visit Rob's website at:

www.truthinliving.net

Contents

Acknowledgments

Introduction · 9

Prologue · 16

1 The Salvation Promise · 21

2 The God – Man Relationship · 35

3 The Depth of God's Grace · 55

4 Do you Really want to be the Judge? · 68

5 What about This Place Called Hell? · 81

6 Do the Wicked Perish? · 104

7 What is that which is Truly Eternal? · 132

8 Every Knee Shall Bow! · 157

9 The Potter and the Clay · 182

10 From Christ to Augustine · 201

11 Rewards! – God's Promise for the Believer · 227

Epilogue · 243

Appendix I – Objections · 261

Appendix II – The Resurrection · 292

Scripture Index · 329

About the Author · 337

Acknowledgments

First of all, and repeatedly, I thank our great God and Savior, the Lord Jesus Christ, (Titus 2:13) for pushing me so hard to do a second edition of this book.

I thank those who helped me make this book a reality, first of all, my beloved wife Ida who is my constant source of encouragement. I thank God for my proof readers for the first edition, including Ron Workman, Rich Ligthart, Julie McAllen, Shelley Studdard, and George (now deceased) and Carol Dannenberg. I would like to also thank those who have written on subjects similar to this before me, both alive and dead, of whom I most certainly **do not** agree with on everything. Some of their writings will appear in quotations from their publications, and referenced in my footnotes.

Introduction

There is a Christian song entitled "Reckless Love" by Kranthi which states the love of God so aptly with the words of the Chorus

"Oh, the overwhelming, never-ending, reckless love of God Oh, it chases me down, fights 'til I'm found, leaves the ninety-nine. I couldn't earn it, and I don't deserve it, still, You give Yourself away Oh, the overwhelming, never-ending, reckless love of God, yeah!"

What a powerful message of the love of God!

This is taken from the passage in Matthew 18 where Jesus is speaking. Notice his words:

See that you do not despise one of these little ones. For I tell you that in heaven their angels always see the face of my Father who is in heaven. What do you think? If a man has a hundred sheep, and one of them has gone astray, **does he not leave the ninety-nine** on the mountains and go in search of the one that went astray? And if he finds it, truly, I say to you, he rejoices over it more than over the ninety-nine that never went astray. So, **it is NOT the will of my Father** who is in heaven **that one of these little ones should perish.** (Matthew 18:10-14)

With this, I must ask the question:

Is God Sovereign or not? Does God get what he wants, or not?

Or does God just say: "oh well. . .I tried," and accept a position of defeat on this issue"

When I decided to do a second edition, I was torn as to whether to rename the book or not. I was so repulsed by the fact that we are stuck with the word "Hell" which is a **mistranslation taken from a Pagan name** and concept that I wanted to rename it. But after much thought, and as pointed out to me by Dr. Boyd Purcell, I decided not to rename it because if I used the name Gehenna (the name used by Jesus instead of Hell) very few people would even know the meaning of the term.

In addition to a new chapter on judgment, I have also expanded several chapters, and included an appendix entitled "The Resurrection," which explains this often mis-interpreted subject. The content of this book addresses a much-ignored subject. Although there are many who want to talk about God's love and grace, few want to simultaneously talk about the purpose for the judgment of the lost. As you read, you will find that this book will **challenge** the wooden rigidness of traditional Christianity, the creeds, and their preachers. **Why would I want to do this?** Consider this passage of Scripture:

> The brothers immediately sent Paul and Silas away by night to Berea, and when they arrived, they went into the Jewish synagogue. Now these Jews were more noble than those in Thessalonica; they received the word with all eagerness, **examining the Scriptures**

daily to see if these things were so. (Acts 17:10-11)

The Apostle Paul also wrote:

. . .but **test everything**; hold fast what is good. (1 Thess 5:21)

This seems to be the banner that I have been assigned by God. Perhaps it was my upbringing into a cult-like religious organization. Perhaps it is just a burning desire within me to get at the truth. However, I would like to make it clear that whatever conclusions I did reach in the writing of this book, even though I am very confident of the findings, are what I would have to term **a well-researched opinion.** Without a doubt, our salvation is through Christ alone! Without the sacrifice of Jesus, we are all lost.

Since this subject is important, I would encourage you to **do your own research.** Also, I would encourage you **NOT** to disparage those whose view on this subject differs from yours. The scripture above is clear. "Test everything," don't just accept what you are told. It is your responsibility to check it out, but at the same time, some of these matters are difficult. So, show respect to those whose view differs from yours!

Yes, **truth is important**. The Lord Jesus said:

"If you abide in my word, you are truly my disciples, and you will know the truth, and the truth will set you free." (John 8:31-32)

If you are diligent in your research, you **will find** things in the process of your research that will challenge your traditional beliefs. The question is, based on what you have learned and tested, do you have the courage to make a stand that is unpopular, or will you shrink back in fear?

And in the prayer that he prayed that encompasses the entire chapter of John 17 he said:

> Now they know that everything that you have given me is from you. For I have given them the words that you gave me, and they have received them and have come to know in truth that I came from you; and they have believed that you sent me. I am praying for them. I am not praying for the world but for those whom you have given me, for they are yours. All mine are yours, and yours are mine, and I am glorified in them. (John 17:7-10)

So, what is truth? How important is truth to you? Truth is often defined as **an indisputable fact, proposition, or principle.** But it seems that many times today people **don't want the truth.** Why? There are two reasons:

1. Because the truth is sometimes painful to accept.
2. Sometimes learning the truth will compel someone to do something they do not want to do.

But as Jesus stated above, the much over-looked fact is that with truth comes freedom. Jesus told Pilate:

> For this purpose I was born and for this purpose I have come into the world to bear witness to the truth. Everyone who is of the truth listens to my voice. (John 18:37)

Yes, Jesus was standing on deaths door, and this is what he said his purpose was . . . to tell the truth. In fact, **he died for it,** as we know. But Pilate asked him, "What is truth?"

Jesus did not answer him at that time. He had already proclaimed the truth, and for Pilate this was a rhetorical question anyway. What was this truth that Jesus died for? In fact, what is this truth that Jesus felt so strongly about that he was willing to not only die for it, but even to die bearing the sin of all of humanity past and present. He then had to watch his heavenly father turn his back on him. This is because in order to fulfill his commission, Jesus, on the cross, took on the sin of the world as the prophetic "Lamb of God" (John 1:29,36). But Jesus was much more than that, and he summed it up in the famous seven "**I am**" statements written in the book of John. He said:

I am the bread of life. (John 6:35)

I am the light of the world (John 8:51)

I am the way, and the truth, and the life. No one comes to the Father except through me. (John 14:6)

I am the good shepherd. The good shepherd lays down his life for the sheep. (John 10:11)

I am the resurrection and the life. Whoever believes in me, though he die, yet shall he live, (John 11:25)

I am the door. If anyone enters by me, he will be saved and will go in and out and find pasture. (John 10:9)

I am the true vine, and my Father is the vinedresser. (John 15:1)

Yes! Our Lord **gave his life** for this very truth! So now the questions for each of us include: How does this impact me? What do I need to do about this? What possible impact could what he did over 2000 years ago have on my life now?

Jesus also gave us the answer to that question. And make no mistake about it. There is **only one way** to the Father, and that is **through Jesus Christ**, the Lord and Savior!

Notice the following. Jesus said:

> Whoever believes in the Son **has** (past tense) eternal life; whoever does not obey the Son shall not see life, but the wrath of God remains on him. (John 3:36)

Do you realize **the powerful the impact** of that statement? Yes! That's right! As we shall see in the pages that follow, this has profound consequences. That means it is more important than anything else we could possibly do in these few years we are given on this earth. Here are some other things he said that confirm this:

> Truly, truly, I say to you, whoever hears my word and believes him who sent me **has** eternal life. He does not come into judgment, but **has** passed from death to life. (John 5:24)

> Truly, truly, I say to you, whoever believes **has** eternal life. (John 6:47)

The Greek word for believe here is πιστευω (pisteuo) which literally means to put your trust in him.

Yes, that means we do not have to wait! We can have eternal life **NOW** spoken of by God now if we believe in and put our full unwavering trust in Him as our Savior. Are you willing to do this? The reward is great for obeying, but the punishment for disobeying will result in a great loss, regardless of what we think about God's love. His judgment is inevitable.

Yes, this is truth. Is it a truth worth living for? Are you willing to do what you can to bring truth to light? This requires that we need to start with the Word of God!

The Lord Jesus said it best in John 8:31, 32:

> If you abide in my word, you are truly my disciples, and you will know the truth, and the truth will set you free.

Notice what Jesus said was the way to understand the truth. **Yes!** It was by **abiding** in his word! So in effect he told them:

> If you abide in my word, you will really believe. You are really born again. You are the ones who **have passed** from darkness to light (5:24). You **will not die** in your sins (8:24).

Yes, that is what he told his disciples, and it is still true for us today. Our wonderful gracious Savior even prayed for his disciples saying, "Sanctify them in the truth; your word is truth." (John 17:17)

The subject of God's salvation is wonderful. It is truly good news. It is lifesaving. But the truth about the judgment of the lost is equally important. Is there a place called **Gehenna** (inappropriately named **Hell**)? If so, why does it exist? Is it just an outlet for the wrath of God, as many have proposed? This book looks at these questions and provides answers in a straightforward a manner in accord with the research of the author. Be assured that the work of this book has been bathed in prayer. Thank you for being willing to look at my research and reach your own conclusions. And may God bless you as you seek **HIS** truth.

Prologue

The following scenario is **NOT** factual but an improvisation. However, it does involve facts of history. Please consider it carefully and give me your thoughts about the outcome.

======================

The date is July 25, 1942. Your name is Eli. You are a Jew and have been in a Nazi concentration camp for 3 years with your wife Sarah and your two children. Your family has been living a hellish existence under the realization that you are considered as garbage by the operators of the Nazi regime, unfit to live. You have watched as you and your beautiful wife and children have become so skinny you are merely a shadow of your former selves. You are being transported from your camp along with your family like a herd of cattle to a place called Auschwitz-Birkenau in Poland. You are pressed on all sides by people. Conditions in the boxcar moving you to your destination are so bad that eight very weak, sickly people have already died during the trip. You cry out to God: "El Shaddai, please! What have we done to deserve this? Have mercy on us!"

Of course, no officials are in the boxcar to deal with this, so there is great weeping and crying by family members as the train pulls to a stop. Upon arrival you and your family are separated. The dead ones are taken away. You and other somewhat healthy men are sent to one area, and the women and children are sent to another. Despite the hell that you have already been through over the past three years, it is now even worse. You weep as your family is now separated from you. You do not know if you will ever see them again.

You think back to the days when you were working in a small butcher shop with your friend Ben. You would work hard together, then come home at night and enjoy your family. Ben was a Christian, and he would talk to you about Jesus. You and your wife Sarah have discussed it and decided the idea of Jesus being the Messiah was not supported by the Tanakh. Unfortunately, Ben had a beautiful blond-haired blue-eyed wife, and one of the SS officers who lusted after her had them separated. He was able to do that because Ben was of Jewish decent. When Ben fought back against the officer who was removing him, he was shot in the head. "So much for any protection from Jesus," you think "And now El Shaddai also seems to have forsaken us."

You are told by the SS officers that you have been separated from your family in order to examine each person to determine their fitness to work. After the SS doctor looks quickly over each one, some were directed to the right. These ones were determined to be fit for work. The rest were sent in another direction. You are told that since your family is not healthy enough to work, they will be taken to a farmhouse where they will be cared for while you work, and that you will see them later. It is a lie. Those declared unfit for work include those who were sick, (about half of the people) pregnant women, mothers with children, and people too old to work. As you look at your group, it is very small.

As your family is taken away, you struggle to wave goodbye. Sarah looks back, screaming and crying as they drag her and your two children away. Your heart is broken beyond imagination. Every step further away they go, your hope of ever seeing them again lessens. They are taken away in groups, once again being transported like cattle to wherever they are going. You were right in your assumption. Despite what you were told, you will never see them again.

These people, who were deemed unfit for work including Sarah and the children, finally arrive at their destination. Upon arrival they see a beautiful secluded cottage. There are flowers blooming all around and the place looks serene. Perhaps a slight feeling of comfort goes through their minds. But next they are taken to a series of huts where they are told that they must undress in order to be given a bath for the purpose of disinfection. Once they undress, they are led to the farm house. After the humiliation of this passes, many become suspicious because too many people are going in there. **It's not that big!** Those who try to cause panic are led away, and are quietly taken to the back of the building where they are shot in the back of the head.

Those who entered the farmhouse see that it is very different looking on the inside. They are crammed into a room that could not possibly allow them to shower. Once the shower heads are turned on, there is no water coming out, but gas! It was Zyklon B in the form of small lumps of diatomite soaked in prussic acid.

"OH NO," they are screaming. Immediately people start vomiting and dropping like flies. Those closest to the shower heads, the sick and the children die first. Within 30 minutes everyone in that "shower" room are dead. When the doors open, the corpses, which covered the entire floor of the gas chamber, show a half-bent position. Their bodies are smeared with excrement, vomit and blood. Their skin is pink. As the soldiers get over their extreme revulsion to this scene and begin to remove their corpses, they are transported a few hundred yards away to a deep pit. There their bodies are thrown in like garbage, and eventually covered over.

Not knowing any of this, you are sent away to work, but one year later, after overwork and lack of nutrition, you too become too sick to work, and you too are shuffled off to this place called "Red House" where you suffer the same fate.

========================

"So much for any protection for Ben from Jesus," thought Eli "And now El Shaddai also seems to have forsaken us"

========================

Soon after Eli was executed in this matter, the gas chambers were expanded and automated, and many more were executed by the SS regime. This was the fate of millions of Jews, as they were executed during World War II. If you are like most people, you cannot help but feel violently mad and sickened by such inhumane treatment of fellow humans. It is appalling that anyone could treat human beings in such a horrific manner.

But now for the purpose of the subject at hand, we know that Eli has been exposed to the message of Christ. After a discussion with his wife, and because of their religious beliefs, they rejected that message. We know that Hebrews 9:27 tells us: "it is appointed once for man to die, after this, the judgment."

Let us consider that the children are safe in the arms of God. Consider also that Eli and Sarah, who were believers in the faith taught to them by their family have made an **honest mistake** in their choice to reject the words spoken to them by Ben of Jesus being the Messiah. So now we must ask the question: According to your belief about what happens to the lost, what happened to Eli and Sarah, in the afterlife?

Chapter One

The Salvation Promise

Four years ago, he was a lowly unknown fisherman in Israel plodding about, struggling to get enough fish to make a living. Less than a year ago, he was a coward, even denying that he knew Jesus. But now as we look at this message given by the Apostle Peter, we find one of the most charismatic characters in the Bible, one endowed with a most amazing boldness by the power of the Holy Spirit as he spoke to those present. Most people would have been thoroughly intimidated. Why? Present among these people were some of the most powerful religious leaders in Israel. Yet Peter spoke with authority. A man had just been healed. Peter was used by the Lord Jesus to do the healing. But now the High Priest was questioning Peter as to where he had gotten his authority. Now notice Peter's response:

> Then Peter, filled with the Holy Spirit, said to them, "Rulers of the people and elders, if we are being examined today concerning a good deed done to a crippled man, by what means this man has been healed, let it be known to all of you and to all the people of Israel that **by the name of Jesus Christ of Nazareth, whom you crucified,** whom God raised from the dead—by him this man is standing before you well. This Jesus is the stone that was

rejected by you, the builders, which has become the cornerstone. And **there is salvation in no one else,** for there is **no other name** under heaven given among men **by which we must be saved."** (Acts 4:8-12)

There is no doubt; the religious leaders **definitely noticed** the change.

Now when they saw the boldness of Peter and John, and perceived that they were uneducated, common men, they were **astonished.** And they recognized that they had been with Jesus. (Acts 4:13)

Yes, Peter made it clear that salvation is only possible because of Jesus. But where did it all begin? For that, we have to go back to the book of Genesis. It all began with the covenants.

Yes, through the covenants God has revealed his plan for the ages. A covenant is basically a contract between parties. Sometimes, when we go to work for a company, we have to sign a contract with certain stipulations. I personally have signed such agreements. One such agreement stated in the contract that any discoveries or inventions that I made would become the exclusive property of the company, not my property. This was an oath, or a promise on my part, stating that I would not try to take anything I would discover while they were paying me and sell it, or give it to a competitor.

One of the most significant covenants we will ever sign is the covenant of marriage. In this covenant, we make an oath that we will stay with that person forever, no matter what may occur. This probably qualifies as the most broken covenant of all time.

We can relate such covenants as these to biblical covenants, but there is one distinct difference. The biblical covenants involve something much more important than any covenant which two people may form together. Biblical covenants are **promises of God!** As such, it is God who makes the terms of the covenant, and unlike covenants made between men, God **always keeps his promises.**

We could say that the Bible is a historical document, because it does contain a historical chronology of the Jewish people. But it is much more than that. Some have called it "redemptive history" because the main theme of the Bible deals with the redemption of mankind from the death sentence that was pronounced upon man when he decided to disobey God. This death sentence was previewed by God in the book of Genesis:

> The LORD God took the man and put him in the garden of Eden to work it and keep it. And the LORD God commanded the man, saying, "You may surely eat of every tree of the garden, but of the tree of the knowledge of good and evil you shall not eat, for in the day that you eat of it you shall surely die." (Genesis 2:15-17)

Although it is not spoken of as such, this was a covenant that God formed with man after he was placed in the Garden. But we know that the Hebrew concept of covenant was not yet in effect. But it was, nonetheless, a covenant. Man had the choice of living and walking with God, or being dead in the sense that he was dead in his trespasses. We know this to be true, because God told Adam that if he ate of the tree, he would die **that day.** Since man chose to disobey, the result was spiritual death. Thus, when God told Adam he would die that very day, it did happen. He died spiritually. He was separated from God. The fact that he did this was not a surprise. The omniscient (all knowing) God, knew that this entire scenario concerning the disobedience of Adam and Eve would happen. How do we know this? Because God made provision for it as the Apostle Peter stated in his first epistle. This was written under the inspiration of the Holy Spirit. Note the following words concerning the Messiah:

> He indeed was foreordained before the foundation of
> the world, but was manifest in these last times for
> you. (1 Peter 1:20 NKJV)

Yes, as we stated earlier, there was an unspoken covenant in the Garden of Eden. When we think of the concept of covenant, the Greek word διαθηκη pronounced as diatheke, or *diathaykay*, comes to mind. It is used in the New Testament to relate the Hebrew concept of covenant, although its meaning is slightly different in that the **diatheke** could be revoked if desired by the one making the covenant. I guess we could say this makes it more like a last will and testament for us today. Of course, God does not die, and he never revokes his covenants, so in those respects, it is different.

Thus, from all of this we understand that **diatheke;** can be translated not only as the word "covenant," but also as the word "testament." This is perhaps the reason some have been confused into believing the idea that the Old Covenant means the Old Testament, and the New Covenant is the New Testament. There is a difference.

It is important to emphasize that when God initiated a covenant, it was always a very serious agreement. These agreements have long range implications because they are life and death agreements. In our next section we will consider one of great importance to all of mankind, a very unique agreement called the Abrahamic Covenant.

The Abrahamic Covenant

As the twelfth chapter of the book of Genesis opens, we see a complete change of venue. The end of the eleventh chapter has the chronology leading to Abram. Then as chapter twelve begins we see a departure from the Semites, as well as the other branches of the human family. From this point forward, we are confined to the events surrounding the life of Abram. It begins as follows:

> Now the LORD said to Abram, "Go from your country and your kindred and your father's house to the land that I will show you. And I will make of you a great nation, and I will bless you and make your name great, so that you will be a blessing. I will bless those who bless you, and him who dishonors you I will curse, and in you **all the families of the earth** shall be blessed." (Genesis 12:1-3)

This man Abram (later changed to Abraham) was chosen by God. As to why, we are not told. We do know that he was a pagan from a pagan family living in the land of Ur of the Chaldeans. He was most likely the firstborn of Terah, although it does not specifically state so there. We know that God reads hearts, and perhaps this was why he chose Abram to go forth. But for whatever reason, this man Abram was about to embark on a journey of greatness because of the promise of God.

So, he was obedient and as verse 5 said, at the age of 75, Abram left everything behind as he was instructed. This included his home, his family and his country. He did this simply trusting in God for a good result. The writer of Hebrews calls attention to the fact that this was a huge act of faith on the part of this servant.

Note the words:

> By faith he went to live in the land of promise, as in a foreign land, living in tents with Isaac and Jacob, heirs with him of the same promise. For he was looking forward to the city that has foundations, whose designer and builder is God. (Hebrews 11:9-10)

As the narrative in Chapter twelve of Genesis said, Abram settled in the hill country between Bethel and Ai and built an altar to the Lord. But sometime after Abram entered the land, there was a famine in the land, and Abram sojourned to the land of Egypt. To make a long story short, he prospered through all of this and when the famine subsided, he returned to the land near Bethel where he had built the altar years earlier. But having been blessed by God, he was very wealthy as the account said:

> Now Abram was very rich in livestock, in silver, and in gold. And he journeyed on from the Negev as far as Bethel to the place where his tent had been at the beginning, between Bethel and Ai, to the place where he had made an altar at the first. And there Abram called upon the name of the LORD. And Lot, who went with Abram, also had flocks and herds and tents, so that the land could not support both of them dwelling together; for their possessions were so great that they could not dwell together, (Genesis 13:2-6)

Yes, the blessing of wealth bestowed upon Abram and Lot was so great that they had to part ways. As the account of this continues, we find that:

Abram settled in the land of Canaan, while Lot settled among the cities of the valley and moved his tent as far as Sodom. (Genesis 13:12)

As the narrative concerning the life of Abram continues, we find Abram in the presence of Melchizedek, the King of Salem. Melchizedek, who was said to be both the King and Priest of the city of Salem, reiterated the blessing God bestowed upon Abram.

And Melchizedek king of Salem brought out bread and wine. (He was priest of God Most High.) And he blessed him and said, "Blessed be Abram by God Most High, Possessor of heaven and earth; and blessed be God Most High, who has delivered your enemies into your hand!" (Genesis 14:18-20)

As Genesis chapter 15 began, Abram was in the midst of a vision from God. God promised that he would reward and protect him. But Abram mentioned to God that he had no heirs and one of his servants would have to be his heir. At this point God said to Abram:

And behold, the word of the LORD came to him: "This man shall not be your heir; your very own son shall be your heir." And he brought him outside and said, "Look toward heaven, and number the stars, if you are able to number them." Then he said to him, "So shall your offspring be." And he believed the LORD, and he counted it to him as righteousness. (Genesis 15:4-6)

To sum it up, Abram trusted God despite the fact that he was aging beyond normal childbearing age. Almighty God, who read hearts could see this, and "counted it to him as righteousness."

So, then the covenant was formalized by God. This chapter of Genesis specifies the ceremony of cutting up of the carcasses and passing between the pieces. It was one of the customary forms of binding a covenant which men had used. That God would agree to adopt a mode designed by man of pledging himself to men speaks of his love. God wanted him to understand that this covenant was solemn, and this way made it plain to Abram.

The covenant that God made with Abram was simple, yet profound. First, God promised Abram that he would possess the land which would be named later as Canaan. Next, God promised that Abram would become a great nation. Third, Abram was promised that "in you **all the families of the earth shall be blessed."**

Did you notice anything that is missing in the covenant God made with Abram? What about the conditional requirement? Yes, that's right. **There were no conditional requirements.** Therefore, it was going to happen whether Abram liked it or not. Now, by this statement I am not implying that Abram resisted. In fact, the next several chapters in the book of Genesis bear out that he was completely compliant. But the point is that this was God's plan and **he was intent** on making it happen.

The most amazing part of that covenant was the promise in verse 12 where he says: **"in you all the families of the earth shall be blessed." Yes!** The profound significance of this statement to Abram was that God was promising here that this would happen through him and his seed. And from the chronology behind the birth of Jesus in both Matthew and Luke that the seed of Abram did indeed lead to the promised Messiah. And of course, that Messiah was none other than the Lord Jesus, the Son of God, born of Mary in Bethlehem.

Now from this promise to Abram, we need to fast forward to the time of Jesus. The Bible writer Luke records the time, the date, and who was reigning at the time. A prophecy was being fulfilled. It was a prophecy which was originally given by the prophet Isaiah in chapter 40, verses 4-6 of his prophetic writings. And here in the third chapter of Luke's synoptic Gospel, after an introduction, he repeated Isaiah's words:

> during the high priesthood of Annas and Caiaphas, the word of God came to John the son of Zechariah in the wilderness. And he went into the entire region around the Jordan, proclaiming a baptism of repentance for the forgiveness of sins. As it is written in the book of the words of Isaiah the prophet, "The voice of one crying in the wilderness: 'Prepare the way of the Lord, make his paths straight. Every valley shall be filled, and every mountain and hill shall be made low, and the crooked shall become straight, and the rough places shall become level ways, and **all flesh shall see the salvation of God.'**" (Luke 3:2-6)

Yes, it was finally time for the promised Messiah to soon appear on the earth. And the forerunner chosen to announce his coming was John the Baptist. He was in fact 6 months older than Jesus. Indeed, he did announce the coming of the Messiah with those words recorded above in

Luke 3:6 where he says plainly, "**all flesh** shall see the salvation of God." What a powerful proclamation. The question is: What did John mean when he said: "all flesh shall see the salvation of God?" Does he really mean "**all flesh**" meaning every single person? Or is there another meaning to this term? How far reaching is it?

That is the subject of this book as we consider God's promise of salvation. And how can it be that all families of the earth will be blessed when we have been taught about this horrific place called hell, a place of suffering?

These words recorded by Luke are the culmination of the prophecies given in the Old Testament. Of these proclamations of a coming Messiah, there are many. One such passage is recorded by the prophet Isaiah 700 years earlier when he said:

> For unto us a child is born, unto us a son is given: and the government shall be upon his shoulder: and his name shall be called Wonderful, Counsellor, The mighty God, The everlasting Father, and The Prince of Peace. Of the increase of his government and peace there shall be no end, upon the throne of David, and upon his kingdom, to order it, and to establish it with judgment and with justice from henceforth even forever. The zeal of the LORD of hosts will perform this. (Isaiah 9:6-7)

That prophecy was ready to be fulfilled. The Son of God was walking on the surface of the earth. His appointed forerunner had arrived to announce his presence and preparing the hearts of the Israelite nation. But what follows John's proclamation that all flesh will see the salvation of God does not seem to be good news, but something very terrifying indeed. For next he says to them:

> He said therefore to the crowds that came out to be baptized by him, "You brood of vipers! Who warned you to flee from the wrath to come? Bear fruits in keeping with repentance. And do not begin to say to yourselves, 'We have Abraham as our father.' For I tell you, God is able from these stones to raise up children for Abraham. Even now the axe is laid to the root of the trees. Every tree therefore that does not bear good fruit is cut down and thrown into the fire." (Luke 3:7-9)

Yes, that's right! John blasted those ones from the very beginning that have come to visit him for this baptism. The Jews thought they were a favored nation, that God held them to a different standard than the other nations. Wasn't it true that they were held safe from judgment because they were the offspring of Abraham? But the question we are forced to ask is this: Do we find John telling them that this privilege that they had cherished so dearly for hundreds of years meant nothing now? Note the words:

> And the crowds asked him, "What then shall we do?" And he answered them, "Whoever has two tunics is to share with him who has none, and whoever has food is to do likewise." Tax collectors also came to be baptized and said to him, "Teacher, what shall we do?" And he said to them, "Collect no more than you are authorized to do." Soldiers also asked him, "And we, what shall we do?" And he said to them, "Do not extort money from anyone by threats or by false accusation, and be content with your wages." As the

people were in expectation, and all were questioning in their hearts concerning John, whether he might be the Christ, (Luke 3:10-15)

As we read this, we cannot help but realize that there is something special about this character named John the Baptist. And there is something especially powerful about what John is saying. How do we know this? Just look at the response! The Israelite people who are normally skeptical of everything are responding to this relatively unknown man with a powerful spirit of conviction!

They are earnestly hearing his strong words to them, and instead of their usual response, they seem to be cut to the heart, wanting to know what they must do to be saved! And John minces no words in telling them in very specific terms what they must do. In fact, as the scripture points out here, they were so moved as to even wonder if this man standing before them who was obviously imbued with an unexplainable power and charisma might just be the promised Messiah!

But John quickly dispels any such notion by the following pronouncement:

> John answered them all, saying, "I baptize you with water, but he who is mightier than I is coming, the strap of whose sandals I am not worthy to untie. He will baptize you with the Holy Spirit and fire. (Luke 3:16)

So, John is **NOT** the Messiah, but now we find John saying something very strange indeed. What does he mean when he says "He will baptize you with the Holy Spirit and fire?" He gives us a clue in the following words:

His winnowing fork is in his hand, to clear his threshing floor and to gather the wheat into his barn, but the chaff he will burn with unquenchable fire." (Luke 3:17)

But what is meant by these words? Is this a response that is meant to be a prelude to the Messiah sending a message to them, that unless they straighten up, they will be **subject to eternal torment? NO!**

Here we must conclude that these words that John is speaking of is the work that the Holy Spirit would accomplish in the hearts of these people, a work that would be similar to the separation of the chaff from the wheat, or similar to the refining process of gold, a refiners fire that would penetrate to the very depth of the soul. It would thus **invigorate and restore** that person **in the power of God's refinement!**

The account of Luke concerning John stops after this, because he was arrested. John would not mince words, even in the presence of Herod, and this got him arrested.

But before he left the scene, he performed his most important task, and that was the Baptism of the Lamb of God, Jesus.

Now when all the people were baptized, and when Jesus also had been baptized and was praying, the heavens were opened, and the Holy Spirit descended on him in bodily form, like a dove; and a voice came from heaven, "You are my beloved Son; with you I am well pleased." (Luke 3:21-22)

So, it was with this start that Jesus began his ministry. But this gives rise to a bunch of questions. How was Jesus to accomplish the meaning of the words of John given in verse 16? How would it be that "all flesh" would see the salvation of God? How would Jesus baptize with the Holy Spirit and fire? Was God's promise of salvation one which had a catch?

Later the Apostle Paul would further expound on this promise which was to be fulfilled through Christ. He said:

> Therefore, just as sin came into the world through one man, and death through sin, and so death spread to **all men because all sinned**- (Romans 5:12)

And then:

> Therefore, as one trespass led to condemnation **for all men,** so one act of righteousness leads to justification and life **for ALL men.** (Romans 5:18)

One of the most important questions we need to answer is this. How was it to be that **ALL families of the earth would be blessed** by this promise? And how could this lead to justification and life **for ALL men?** And what about what John said earlier in Luke 3:6: "all flesh shall see the salvation of God?" How does this play out with regards to what we have been taught about people suffering in hell? This raises lots of questions to explore.

Chapter Two
The God – Man Relationship

From our last chapter we learned the profound significance of the promise to Abraham. For here God said, "**ALL** the families of the earth would be blessed." And we know from looking at the chronology in both Matthew and Luke that his seed would lead to the promised Messiah. That Messiah was none other than the Lord Jesus, the son of God, born of Mary in Bethlehem.

This gave us good insight concerning the nature of God's relationship with man. We learned that from his dealings with Abraham thousands of years ago, **it was God's desire to bless** those to whom the promise was made. That promise was made because of God's love. This is borne out in the words spoken by Jesus. In the four New Testament Gospels, there are 43 passages which mention the word love, and 40 of those passages are words which are spoken directly by Jesus. Two of the other three are repeats of his words. Thus, we see the love of the Father reflected in the Son while he was on earth.

It is true that God did bring evil upon the descendants of Abraham when they broke the conditional covenants, the first of which was the Mosaic Covenant given at Mount

Sinai. This is because God promised them that he would do this if they did not obey him. Here it is:

> Now therefore, **IF you will indeed obey** my voice and keep my covenant, you shall be my treasured possession among all peoples, for all the earth is mine; and you shall be to me a kingdom of priests and a holy nation. These are the words that you shall speak to the people of Israel." (Exodus 19:5-6)

Did you notice the word **IF?** Now notice the response of the people.

> So, Moses came and called the elders of the people and set before them all these words that the LORD had commanded him. All the people answered together and said, "All that the LORD has spoken we will do." And Moses reported the words of the people to the LORD. (Exodus 19:7-8)

They sealed the covenant with their words.

> And the LORD said to Moses, "Behold, I am coming to you in a thick cloud, that the people may hear when I speak with you, and may also believe you forever." When Moses told the words of the people to the LORD, (Exodus 19:9)

God came to them in a cloud. This was often his normal motif. It reminds us of what Jesus said in his greatest prophecy:

> And then they will see the Son of Man coming in clouds with great power and glory. (Mark 13:26)

The Biblical records regarding these covenants **confirm to us that God keeps his promises,** both good and bad!

The record is clear regarding God's love. You can see the heart of God in the writings of the prophet Jeremiah. Israel was in captivity to Babylon after the first destruction of Jerusalem.

God told them:

> For thus says the LORD: When seventy years are completed for Babylon, I will visit you, and I will fulfill to you my promise and bring you back to this place. For I know the plans I have for you, declares the LORD, **plans for welfare and not for evil, to give you a future and a hope.** Then you will call upon me and come and pray to me, and I will hear you. You will seek me and find me, when you seek me with all your heart. (Jeremiah 29:10-13)

Despite the fact that his people were disobedient, and likened to the adulterous wife of the prophet Hosea, God still loved them. The Old Testament established the fact that the Israelite people were stubborn and disobedient. But God loved them anyway. And later on, as seen in the New Testament, God expanded his love even to the Gentiles. The Apostle Paul explained it this way to the church at Galatia:

> So then, the law was our guardian until Christ came, in order that we might be justified by faith. But now that faith has come, we are no longer under a guardian, for in Christ Jesus you are all sons of God, through faith. For as many of you as were baptized into Christ have put on Christ. There is neither Jew nor Greek, there is neither slave nor free, there is no male and female, for **you are all one in Christ Jesus.** And if you are Christ's, then **you are**

Abraham's offspring, heirs according to promise. (Galatians 3:24-29)

This was God showing the determination of his promise to Abraham, and in so doing, from this point forward the Gentiles who believed were included in the promise. What a powerful example of the love of God, and **continued proof** of God's intention to keep that unconditional promise.

This is significant considering the background of the Galatians. Like the inhabitants of the surrounding country, they were pagans. Their religion was detestable to God. These people worshipped something called a mother of the gods. Albert Barnes reports in his commentary that they were called by others such as Callimachus, in his hymns, "a foolish people." But here we saw God including them as a part of the seed of Abraham, a testament to the fact that he would keep his promise to Abraham.

A few years later, while in Corinth, Paul wrote his letter to the Church in Rome, a Church made up of Jews and Gentiles. And these words written to Galatia also applied to the Romans. But notice what Paul told the Roman church.

> For while we were still weak, at the right time Christ died for the ungodly. (Romans 5:6)

This is followed by:

> but God shows his love for us in that while we were still sinners, Christ died for us. (Romans 5:8)

Later in chapter 14, we find:

> For if we live, we live to the Lord, and if we die, we die to the Lord. So then, whether we live or whether we

die, we are the Lord's. For to this end Christ died and lived again, **that he might be Lord both of the dead and of the living.** (Romans 14:8-9)

Notice what these passages state**: "Christ died for the ungodly," "while we were still sinners,** Christ dies for us," and finally "that he might be Lord **both of the dead and of the living."**

Yes, it is true that his power extended over both worlds. Since he was given "All authority in heaven and on earth" by his Father as he stated in Matthew 28:18, he holds the power over life and death. But doesn't it mean that **he is still** the God over those sinners that have died without knowing him? That **IS** what he said!

We also have from the Old Testament a paradigm of how God handles judgment. Without question, the method we see through the Torah is that **the punishment must fit the crime.** Notice how the people were to judge the crimes committed in their day:

> Whoever takes a human life shall surely be put to death. Whoever takes an animal's life shall make it good, life for life. If anyone injures his neighbor, as he has done it shall be done to him, fracture for fracture, eye for eye, tooth for tooth; whatever injury he has given a person shall be given to him. (Leviticus 24:17-20)

One more principle we must add is this:

> For I the LORD **do not change;** (Malachi 3:6)

Now looking at this standard that was set by the Law of God during the days of Moses, let's compare how most people have been taught of God's judgment of those who die without Christ.

Isn't it true that most people believe that those who have died as unbelievers are turned over to Satan in a fiery miserable place called hell where they will reside forever? In this doctrine, it is said that those unsaved ones will be given over to a state of **endless horror** from which there is no possibility of escape, **and for eternity.** In other words, after a thousand lifetimes, those undergoing this torment process which is said to be by a loving God will be no nearer to the end of this horrific process than they were at the beginning.

To top it off, it is said by those who would purvey this heinous form of punishment that **THIS IS** the fate of **the majority of mankind.** One of the passages they refer to for support is taken from the words of our Lord:

> Enter by the narrow gate. For the gate is wide and the way is easy that leads to destruction, and those who enter by it are many. For the gate is narrow and the way is hard that leads to life, and those who find it are few. (Matthew 7:13-14)

But a close examination of verse fourteen reveals that it says **nothing about eternal torment.** It is talking about destruction. This should give us a clue that Jesus is not speaking of our final judgment here. Now notice what he told him just after this:

> Beware of false prophets, who come to you in sheep's clothing, but inwardly are ravening wolves. By their fruits you will know them. Do you gather grapes from thorns, or figs from thistles? Even so, every good tree

produces good fruit; but the corrupt tree produces evil fruit. A good tree can't produce evil fruit, neither can a corrupt tree produce good fruit. Every tree that doesn't grow good fruit is cut down, and thrown into the fire. Therefore by their fruits you will know them. (Matthew 7:15-20 WEB)

Then he warns them again:

Not everyone who says to me, 'Lord, Lord,' will enter the kingdom of heaven, but the one who does the will of my Father who is in heaven. On that day many will say to me, 'Lord, Lord, did we not prophesy in your name, and cast out demons in your name, and do many mighty work in your name?' And then will I declare to them, 'I never knew you; depart from me, you workers of lawlessness. (Matthew 7:21-23)

Yes, this was part of the Sermon on the Mount recorded by Matthew. But when you put this in the context of what Jesus said throughout the course of his ministry, **this was merely a preview** of what Jesus would tell his disciples in **his greatest prophecy**, the Olivet Discourse (Matthew 24-25). The destruction of the great city of Jerusalem and of the magnificent temple that King Herod was refurbishing would occur in less than 40 years. The Israelite people were in grave danger. In a matter of 3 years or so, they would totally reject the Son of God, and declare; "His blood be on us and our children."(Matt. 27:25) Jesus was giving them a preview of the warning that would come later when he told those religious leaders in Matthew 23.

When we look at this account, we see that Jesus began by pronouncing a death sentence upon them. There was a garbage dump just outside the city which was formerly referred to as the Valley of Hinnom. It was now called Gehenna. This is the same place where the pagans sacrificed their children in the fire. This place was an abomination to God. Therefore, it was cursed and henceforth set out as garbage dump. Notice what Jesus told these lying hypocritical religious leaders:

> You serpents, you offspring of vipers, how will you escape the judgment of Gehenna? (Matthew 23:33 WEB)

Notice that I have also quoted the **World English Bible** for the passage above. You will not find the term **"Hell"** in this translation, and for a good reason. In fact, I would like to point up to you that **there is no Hebrew equivalent for the term "Hell."** If we look up the etymology of that word, we find that the original meaning of the word was "to cover up," thus we get our word "helmet." The root of this word can be easily traced, and it only extends back to the eighth century after Christ! This is a term that was **used during this period of time by non-Christians** denoting a place of punishment. Jesus **never** used this word. He used the Greek word γεεννη translated as **Gehenna.**

Jesus was speaking to a specific audience for a specific purpose. He was making the point that these ones were eventually going to be destroyed, and that would happen within the bounds of that generation as he expounded in Matthew chapter 24. **By using the term "Gehenna"** these ones would immediately get the point that he was giving them a death sentence because **this was the name of the garbage dump** outside the city of Jerusalem.

As Jesus continues excoriating them, he says:

Therefore I send you prophets and wise men and scribes, some of whom YOU will kill and crucify, and some YOU will flog in your synagogues and persecute from town to town, so that on YOU may come all the righteous blood shed on earth, from the blood of righteous Abel to the blood of Zechariah the son of Barachiah, whom you murdered between the sanctuary and the altar. Truly, I say to you, all these things will come upon this generation. O Jerusalem, Jerusalem, the city that kills the prophets and stones those who are sent to it! How often would I have gathered your children together as a hen gathers her brood under her wings, and you were not willing! See, YOUR house is left to YOU desolate. (Matthew 23:34-38)

Thus, in the passage of Matthew chapter 7 Jesus was giving them an earlier warning that they needed to listen to him, accept him, and be his followers. **There was a judgment coming.** As Jesus ministry progressed, this message became stronger and stronger. It climaxed in the above verse in Matthew chapter 23 as we see in the above passage.

Yes, this portion of the Sermon on the Mount was given specifically to those who would scoff at him, and reject him in front of Pilate, as well as those phony religious leaders, the members of the Sanhedrin who would eventually send our Lord to the cross. For they would utter the words: "His blood be on us and on our children!" (Matt. 7:25) By following these false teachers, they would be following the broad way that leads to destruction, and that destruction would come within that same generation in the year AD 70 when over one million Jews would be killed in the city of Jerusalem.

Now as we look at this last part of the Sermon on the Mount, we have to ask, why did Jesus give this warning to the people assembled there? It was because of God's love for his people. This was a preview. Jesus would expound upon these points in the remaining part of his ministry. But what Jesus said in this Sermon on the Mount **did not deal with some future eternal torment.** It was a warning which was very relevant and timely, one which would be expounded more fully at the proper time.

When speaking of the doctrine of eternal torment today, we find that among the churches, there is heavy reliance on the Creeds of Christendom for this view. For example, the Westminster Confession of Faith (AD 1646) states in Chapter 33:

> *The end of God's appointing this day is for the manifestation of the glory of His mercy, in the eternal salvation of the elect; and of His justice, in the damnation of the reprobate, who are wicked and disobedient. For then shall the righteous go into everlasting life, and receive that fullness of joy and refreshing, which shall come from the presence of the Lord; but the wicked who know not God, and obey not the Gospel of Jesus Christ, shall be cast into eternal torments, and be punished with everlasting destruction from the presence of the Lord, and from the glory of His power.*

The Augsburg Confession of 1530 adopted by the followers of Martin Luther and the Lutheran Church, in Article 17 states concerning the judgment to come by Christ:

*He will give to the godly and elect eternal life and everlasting joys, but ungodly men and the devils He will condemn to be **tormented without end.***

It seems clear that those who have put their faith in these creeds have been persuaded to believe that **the majority of the human race will have to endure eternal torment.** And if it is indeed true that only those who truly are converted, and have truly in their hearts professed complete faith in our Lord Jesus are exempt from this heinous torture, then we can see how this would seem to be true. After all, though those who are called **Christians** are the world's **largest religion**, this only accounts for about **one third** of the current population of the earth.

Thus, **if we believe this,** and using this as a basis of computation, it means that at least **two thirds** of the nearly eight billion people now alive are **destined for eternal torment** in Hell. But to add to this, it is often pointed out in our churches that only a small percentage of the ones who claim to be Christian are "truly believers." Even if as many as half of those who claim to be Christians are exempt, then that means that 5 out of every 6 people living in the world right now are going to have to endure a gruesome, horrendous eternal torment! But once again, we ask: How could this **possibly be** when God promised that through Jesus, **ALL families of the earth would be blessed?** Also, we **must** consider, does this sound like the God of whom Paul wrote when he said:

For while we were still weak, at the right time **Christ died for the ungodly.** (Romans 5:6)

but God shows his love for us in that while **we were still sinners, Christ died for us.** (Romans 5:8)

For to this end Christ died and lived again, **that he might be Lord both of the dead and of the living.** (Romans 14:9)

If we look at the fact that we have somewhere around 6000 years of recorded human history, can we even fathom the number of persons who would now be committed to such a destiny?

In his book, "Christ Triumphant" Thomas Allin calls attention to some of the writings that have shown the thinking of the preachers of this doctrine. Note his words:

Let me next show what this hell of the popular creed really means, so far as human words can dimly convey its horrors, and for this purpose I subjoin the following extracts-

> *"Little child, if you go to hell there will be a devil at your side to strike you. He will go on striking you every minute for ever and ever without stopping. The first stroke will make your body as bad as the body of Job, covered, from head to foot, with sores and ulcers. The second stroke will make your body twice as bad as the body of job. The third stroke will make your body three times as bad as the body of Job. The fourth stroke will make your body four times as bad as the body of Job. How, then, will your body be after the devil has been striking it every moment for a hundred million of years without stopping? Perhaps at this moment, seven o'clock in the evening, a child is just going into hell. Tomorrow evening, at seven o'clock, go and knock at the gates of hell and ask what the child is doing. The devils will go and look. They*

will come back again and say, the child is burning. Go in a week and ask what the child is doing; you will get the same answer, it is burning. Go in a year and ask, the same answer comes - it is burning. Go in a million of years and ask the same question, the answer is just the same - it is burning. So, if you go for ever and ever, you will always get the same answer - it is burning in the fire." The Sight of Hell. *** Rev. J. FURNISS, C.S.S.R.[1]

Additionally, we see the famous preacher Charles Spurgeon stated:

"When you die your soul will be tormented alone; that will be a hell for it: but at the day of judgment your body will join your soul, and then you wilt have twin hells, your soul sweating drops of blood, and your body suffused with agony. In fire, exactly like that we have on earth, your body will lie, asbestos like, forever unconsumed, all your veins roads for the feet of pain to travel on, every nerve a string, on which the devil shall for ever play his diabolical tune of hell's unutterable lament." Sermon on the Resurrection of the Dead. *** Rev. C. H. SPURGEON.[2]

Jonathan Edwards described God's view of you this way:

The God that holds you over the pit of hell, much as one holds a spider or some loathsome insect over the

---

[1] Allin, Thomas (2014-04-12). Christ Triumphant: Or Universalism Attested (Kindle Locations 73-117). . Kindle Edition.
[2] ibid

fire, abhors you, and is dreadfully provoked; his wrath towards you burns like fire; he looks upon you as worthy of nothing else, but to be cast into the fire; he is of purer eyes than to bear to have you in his sight; you are ten thousand times so abominable in his eyes, as the most hateful and venomous serpent is in ours. You have offended him infinitely more than ever a stubborn rebel did his prince: and yet it is nothing but his hand that holds you from falling into the fire every moment.[3]

Now these horrific statements above were made by those who have called themselves **preachers of the Gospel** of Jesus Christ! **The word Gospel means good news!** So **where** would these famous preachers get such a hideous picture as this? It certainly is not from the Bible! There are only two places in all of Scripture where God is reported to have hated anyone. And that was Esau, the brother of Jacob. But when you look at the meaning of the Greek word used here; it is very possible that what was meant was that he loved him less. Esau met Jacob upon his return to the land and it was apparent that he had not been cursed by God. Yes, he hates sinful deeds, but God does not hate people, even those who are evil.

While we are on the subject of torment, let's look at the meaning of that word in the Koine Greek, which is the original language of the New Testament. The Greek word here is βασανισμος which in the English spelling is **basanismos.** According to Thayer's Greek Lexicon, the

[3] Edwards, Jonathan (2011-03-30). Selected Sermons of Jonathan Edwards (p.50). . Kindle Edition

number one meaning of this is: a testing by the touchstone or by torture. Yes, the root word of this so called "torture" stems from the Greek word βασανος **(basanos)** which also, according to Thayer's Greek Lexicon, was "the touchstone, by which gold and other metals are tested." It further states that it was "the rack or instrument of torture by which one is forced to divulge the truth."

One of the most popular passages used to establish the idea of eternal torment is in the book of Revelation which states:

> and the devil who had deceived them was thrown into the lake of fire and sulfur where the beast and the false prophet were, and they will be tormented day and night forever and ever. (Revelation 20:10)

So now let's look more closely at this information for just a moment. What do we find spoken of here? While it is true that **we do not know** what this lake of fire is, because the Scriptures do not tell us, we do know that fire is often used to purify, such as is used in cauterization or for the purification of metals. Hence, from the meanings we have seen from these Greek words, **perhaps this "lake of fire" is symbolic of a place of testing.** This testing can definitely serve as torture to those disposed of evil and lying. This is a place where individuals are tested (i.e. tortured) until such a time as they tell the truth. For Satan this will be **the ultimate in torture** because we know from the Scriptures that he is a liar, and the father of lies (from John 8:44). Telling the truth has never been a part of his agenda.

But contrary to this, we are told in the Scriptures that God's steadfast love lasts forever. Note the words:

Oh, give thanks to the LORD, for **he is good**; for his steadfast love endures **forever!**" (1 Chronicles 16:34)

Yes! This term "steadfast love" is repeated **in 191 verses** in the Old Testament, and most of those are speaking of the steadfast **LOVE** God has for his obedient servants. So where would Jonathan Edwards get this idea of such a monstrous God! There is nowhere in Scripture that God has ever said that he abhors you, or any of the other things mentioned in that quote above.

With all of these macabre pictures these preachers have painted of hell, my question is this: Who could even conceive of the God of love doing such a thing?!! And when the Son of God came to the earth, did he not also say the following?

> You have heard that it was said, 'You shall love your neighbor and hate your enemy.' But I say to you, **Love your enemies** and pray for those who persecute you, (Matthew 5:43-44)

> But **love your enemies,** and do good, and lend, expecting nothing in return, and your reward will be great, and you will be sons of the Most High, **for he is kind to the ungrateful and the evil.** (Luke 6:35)

> A new commandment I give to you, that you love one another: just as I have loved you, you also are to love one another. By this all people will know that you are my disciples, **if you have love for one another."** (John 13:34 -35)

Would you notice particularly Luke 6:35 above? What does it say? Is there **any possible way** that the Lord Jesus would do the despicable things these preachers have visualized? What is kind about the torment of the ungrateful and the evil for eternity? Could it possibly be the same Lord who said: "But love your enemies, and do good, and lend, expecting nothing in return, and your reward will be great, and you will be sons of the Most High, **for he is kind to the ungrateful and the evil?"**

So what was the motivation of those who have purveyed such horror as Rev. J. Furniss, Charles Spurgeon, and Jonathan Edwards did many years ago? There are only two possible reasons. *or the Bible is ambiguous*

1. They believe that God is schizophrenic. This means that God is a God of love on one hand, and a God of hate on the other. *— Thats true*

2. They have done this in order to **manipulate people** – to scare them into believing, and acting on their beliefs, **and that includes giving their money** to the church. *how is that logical*

But we must ask the question in the light of the above facts from Scripture about the nature of God: Does this seem consistent with the nature of God? *YES*

Stepping back just a little bit, let's look again at what we noted earlier. Remember that Jesus said:

> You serpents, you offspring of vipers, how will you escape the judgment of Gehenna? (Matthew 23:33 WEB)

This garbage dump was precisely placed at the Valley of Hinnom in the Old Testament. The Valley of Hinnom is where the Israelites who had turned to the worship of Baal and Molech came to throw their living children into a fire as a sacrifice to this detestable god they formed. Of this horrific place the prophet Jeremiah recorded:

> For the sons of Judah have done **evil in my sight,** declares the LORD. They have set their detestable things in the house that is called by my name, to defile it. And they have built the high places of Topheth, which is in the Valley of the Son of Hinnom, to burn their sons and their daughters in the fire, **which I did not command, nor did it come into my mind.** (Jeremiah 7:30-31)

Following this God stated through the prophet:

> Therefore, behold, the days are coming, declares the LORD, when it will no more be called Topheth, or the Valley of the Son of Hinnom, but the Valley of Slaughter; for they will bury in Topheth, because there is no room elsewhere. **And the dead bodies of this people will be food** for the birds of the air, and for the beasts of the earth, and none will frighten them away. (Jeremiah 7:32-33)

This prophecy of judgment **was fulfilled**, and this place **became the place** that was called **Gehenna.**

The 12th-century Rashi, commenting on Jeremiah 7:31 stated:

> Tophet is Moloch, which was made of brass; and they heated him from his lower parts; and his hands being stretched out, and made hot, they put the child between his hands, and it was burnt; when it vehemently cried out; but the priests beat a drum,

that the father might not hear the voice of his son, and his heart might not be moved.[4]

Yes, it is true that this place was so very detestable to God that he made it a garbage dump. How could anyone think that this same God would send his children into the fire, not only to burn and scream until they expire, but even forever? Such a thing is totally inconsistent with the nature of God. This certainly is not the same God mentioned by the Apostle John in his epistle:

not true

> Anyone who does not love does not know God, because **God is love.** (1 John 4:8)

Additionally he stated:

> So we have come to know and to believe the love that God has for us. **God is love,** and whoever abides in love abides in God, and God abides in him. (1 John 4:16)

And the Apostle Paul said to the entire church at Rome:

> No, in all these things we are more than conquerors through him who loved us. For I am sure **that neither** death nor life, nor angels nor rulers, nor things present nor things to come, nor powers, nor height nor depth, nor anything else in all creation, will be able to separate us **from the love of God in Christ Jesus our Lord.** (Romans 8:37-39)

Could this God that has been conjured up by those purveyors of the doctrine of eternal torment in a fiery Hell actually exist? This is a question that must be answered.

---

[4] https://en.wikipedia.org/wiki/Moloch

Yes, and it is still true for those of us who believe. Nothing can separate us from the love of God.

But it is also true that God is one who demands justice. And as we have noted, this standard was given to man through Torah (the Old Covenant Law). **The punishment must fit the crime.**

From what we see in the majority of churches, we have to ask some pertinent questions about what they are preaching about God. If **God is love** as stated by the Apostle John in his epistle, then how could it possibly be that at least **5 out of every 6** people on the surface of the earth living right now will have to **face a destiny of eternal torment?**

This makes us ask concerning this type of preaching: **Which prevails, God's love or God's hate?**

Next, we will look at Scripture to examine **the grace of God.** Then these questions will become even larger!

Chapter Three

The Depth of God's Grace

Give ear, O LORD, to my prayer; listen to my plea for grace. (Psalm 86:6)

=============================

The Apostle John wrote regarding the Lord Jesus:

> And the Word became flesh and dwelt among us, and we beheld His glory, the glory as of the only begotten of the Father, full of grace and truth. John bore witness of Him and cried out, saying, "This was He of whom I said, 'He who comes after me is preferred before me, for He was before me.' " And of His fullness we have all received, and grace for grace. For the law was given through Moses, but grace and truth came through Jesus Christ. (John 1:14-17)

John made an important point in this passage. Grace and truth go hand in hand. Surprisingly, there is no record of our Lord ever uttering the word "grace." But this word is spoken of **concerning him over 100 times** in the New Testament.

Our Lord does, however, speak of truth many times as recorded by John. Truth is authenticity, sincerity, and honesty rolled up into one. These are indwelling qualities of God. In fact, we could say that **God IS truth.**

The song written by John Newton in the 1700s is right . . . the grace of God is amazing! Grace is the free and unmerited favor of God. There is no way we can achieve it. Its essence is in God's gift of salvation. God was under no obligation to provide a means of salvation, but because of his awesome love, he did. Salvation is indeed the most powerful expression of God's grace. The Apostle Paul told the Ephesian church:

> But God, being rich in mercy, because of the great love with which he loved us, even when we were dead in our trespasses, made us alive together with Christ—**by grace you HAVE BEEN saved**— and raised us up with him and seated us with him in the heavenly places in Christ Jesus, so that in the coming ages he might show the immeasurable riches of his grace in kindness toward us in Christ Jesus. For by grace **you HAVE BEEN saved** through faith. And this is not your own doing; **it is the gift of God**, not a result of works, so that no one may boast. (Ephesians 2:4-9)

Did you notice how this was worded? It said "by grace you **have been saved.** When speaking to these Ephesian Christians, Paul was saying that the act of being saved was **past tense** . . . it was **already** accomplished! The grace of God prevailed in this case and there is no way to attribute it to works, no way that it could have been earned.

The church at Ephesus was far from perfect. The city was famous for the magnificent temple of Diana; and the inhabitants of this city were very much given to superstition and idolatry, and even to what has been termed as "devilish arts." Diana was also named Artemis in some circles. In the realm of Classical Greek mythology, she was a Greek goddess, and had a twin brother, Apollo. She was also said to be the daughter of the Greek God Zeus.

As part of the worship of Diana, young girls were sent to the temple to serve for one year. Since she was the great Olympian goddess of hunting, wilderness and wild animals, these young girls would have to indulge in a silly routine called "playing the bear."

Diana was but one of many of the gods of the Greeks. The Apostle Paul sought to overcome this idea by playing on the thought that "the unknown God" was actually the Lord Jesus. But his attempt at this did not get much traction in Athens.

In order to accept Jesus Christ as their savior, these Ephesian Christians had to disown their heritage and cease to worship these "gods." There was great difficulty in this because the city of Ephesus derived much income from the magnificent temple of Diana. Thus, there became a hardship when the Christian population grew from Paul's work.

In the book of Revelation, Ephesus was the first of the seven churches that was addressed by John. By this time, Jesus tells them they had lost their love. Notice Jesus' words to this church:

But I have this against you that you have abandoned the love you had at first. Remember therefore from where you have fallen; repent, and do the works you did at first. If not, I will come to you and remove your lampstand from its place, unless you repent. Yet this you have: you hate the works of the Nicolaitans, which I also hate. (Revelation 2:4-6)

Now, after threatening to remove their lampstand, or in effect threatening to remove the church from existence, notice what else he says:

He who has an ear, let him hear what the Spirit says to the churches. **To the one who conquers** I will grant to eat of the tree of life, which is in the paradise of God.' (Revelation 2:7)

What did he mean by this last statement, "to the one who conquers?"

Here is what Adam Clarke said in his commentary:

To him who continues steadfast in the faith, and uncorrupt in his life; who faithfully confesses Jesus, and neither imbibes the doctrines nor is led away by the error of the wicked; will I give to eat of the tree of life. As he who conquered his enemies had, generally, not only great honor, but also a reward; so here a great reward is promised τω νικωντι, to the conqueror: and as in the Grecian games, to which there may be an allusion, the conqueror was crowned with the leaves of some tree; here it is promised that they should eat of the fruit of the tree of life, which is in the midst of the paradise of God; that is, that they should have a happy and glorious immortality.

There is also here an allusion to Gen_2:9, where it is said, God made the tree of life to grow out of the midst of the garden; and it is very likely that by eating the fruit of this tree the immortality of Adam was secured, and on this it was made dependent. When Adam transgressed, he was expelled from this garden, and no more permitted to eat of the tree of life; hence he became necessarily mortal. This tree, in all its sacramental effects, is secured and restored to man by the incarnation, death, and resurrection of Christ. The tree of life is frequently spoken of by the rabbins; and by it they generally mean the immortality of the soul, / and a final state of blessedness.[5]

Clarke seemed to indicate here that Jesus' comments meant that first they had to confess Jesus as Lord, and then they had to do a (certain process of works) to keep this in effect. But isn't this contrary to the above passage by Paul? Let's look again:

> For by grace you **HAVE BEEN** saved through faith. And this is not your own doing; **it is the gift of God,** not a result of works, so that no one may boast. (Ephesians 2:8-9)

Once again, we see that this is spoken of as having **already been accomplished!** The difference is that **God reads hearts**, and therefore **we cannot con God.**

Regarding the passage in Revelation 2:7 and **"the one who conquers,"** Albert Barnes had this to say:

> Greek, "To him that gains the victory, or is a conqueror" - τῳ νικωντι, (tō nikonti.) This may refer to any victory of a moral character, and the expression

[5] Adam Clarke's Commentary on the Bible (Taken from e-Sword version 10.2.1 Rick Meyers 2001-2013)

used would be applicable to one who should triumph in any of these respects:

(a) Over his own easily-besetting sins;

(b) Over the world and its temptations;

(c) Over prevalent error;

(d) Over the ills and trials of life, so as, in all these respects, to show that his Christian principles are firm and unshaken.

Life, and the Christian life especially, may be regarded as a warfare. Thousands fall in the conflict with evil; but they who maintain a steady warfare, and who achieve a victory, shall be received as conquerors in the end.[6]

It almost sounds as if he is saying the same thing – that there must be some works to go along with this gift to make it work. But could there be another meaning in the words of these two commentators?

The other possibility is that the works that occur are **the result** of the changed condition of the heart. So that when James, the overseer of the Jerusalem Church said: Jas 2:17 "So also faith by itself, if it does not have works, is dead," he was referring to the fact that faith is **shown by works,** and not a required act in order to achieve salvation. In other words, works will be the **result** of faith. Yes! **This is the result of great faith.** It will change how we act because our entire being is permeated with it!

---

[6] Albert Barnes' Notes on the Bible (Taken from e-Sword version 10.2.1 Rick Meyers 2001-2013)

But as regards God's grace, we are incapable of understanding this completely. Yes, although it is possible that we can understand that God loved us enough to save us by grace, but we cannot truly comprehend what it cost him to do this.

The amazing grace that is spoken of in that famous song is about **redemptive grace.** It is and has always been the way of mankind to disobey God. There is no denying this. When man chooses his own way and disobeys God, he chooses poorly. I am sure that you have examples in your own life of things that you have done which were against the ways of God that have caused you regrets. These may have even changed your life completely for the worse. In going down this path, we have caused ourselves immeasurable pain and suffering. But there comes a time, when we realize the error of our way. If we call out to God, this is where the amazing grace comes into effect. where is that found.

Jesus gave us the perfect parable concerning this. It is called the parable of the prodigal son.

We all know the story. But here it is again:

> And he said, "There was a man who had two sons. And the younger of them said to his father, 'Father, give me the share of property that is coming to me.' And he divided his property between them. Not many days later, the younger son gathered all he had and took a journey into a far country, and there he squandered his property in reckless living. And when he had spent everything, a severe famine arose in that country, and he began to be in need. So, he went and hired himself out to one of the citizens of that country, who sent him into his fields to feed pigs. And he was

longing to be fed with the pods that the pigs ate, and no one gave him anything. But when he came to himself, he said, 'How many of my father's hired servants have more than enough bread, but I perish here with hunger! I will arise and go to my father, and I will say to him, "Father, I have sinned against heaven and before you. I am no longer worthy to be called your son. Treat me as one of your hired servants."' (Luke 15:11-19)

Here is that "aha moment" that we all have had when we realize the foolishness of what we have done. His thought process was like this: **How stupid could I have been?** Look at where I started, and where I am now. This is the point when he decided that it was time to take action.

Perhaps this is how you decided to return to God. You know you deserve nothing. You know that there is no way that you can be forgiven. But notice how this parable continues:

And he arose and came to his father. But while he was still a long way off, his father saw him and felt compassion, and ran and embraced him and kissed him. And the son said to him, 'Father, I have sinned against heaven and before you. I am no longer worthy to be called your son.' But the father said to his servants, 'Bring quickly the best robe, and put it on him, and put a ring on his hand, and shoes on his feet. (Luke 15:20-22)

Wow! This is incredible, you think to yourself. There is no question that this father loved his son unconditionally. He didn't even wait for him to declare that he was sorry!

This wayward son realized his foolishness in squandering his inheritance and was finally able to see that. It is as if the light came on in his mind and in his heart. He realized that even if he had to be the lowliest one of his father's servants that would be better than the path that he had chosen.

So, from an application standpoint here we are looking at the grace of God. It is amazing. God will forgive us no matter what we do if we are willing to **honestly repent** and turn back to him. We can summarize this kind of grace as repentance and confession. **This will automatically produce a change in our actions.** We rely on grace to fulfill us personally and communally, over time.

Now this **does not mean** that we will not have to live with the consequences of our sin. For example, if we decide to rob a bank, **we will** have to live with the consequences. Even if we are not caught by the authorities, we will have to live with our conscience. But if we are caught, we will surely have to go to prison where a myriad of bad things can happen to us. We also realize that going back to Torah, **the punishment must fit the crime.** This we would most certainly see borne out in our life if we would sin in this manner.

Yes, God's grace can change us and make us realize that the essence of the good life is abiding in him and obeying him. This is the only place of true happiness. God is our creator. How could we possibly know what we need better than the one who created us?

Being inside of God's grace we realize that God has accepted us just as we are, **without condition, without having deserved it, and without any question.** This is exactly the way it came down in the parable that Jesus gave. The father showed the son grace for no other reason than that he loved him unconditionally. One of God's sons, David described it perfectly:

> Bless the LORD, O my soul, and all that is within me, bless his holy name! Bless the LORD, O my soul, and forget not all his benefits, (Psalm 103:1-2)

Now we see that David began this Psalm with praise and adoration for his loving God. Then he got very specific about the blessings. He says:

> Bless the LORD, O my soul, and forget not all his benefits, who **forgives** all your iniquity, who **heals** all your diseases, who **redeems** your life from the pit, who **crowns** you with steadfast love and mercy, who **satisfies** you with good so that your youth is **renewed** like the eagle's. The LORD works righteousness and justice **for all who are oppressed**. (Psalm 103:2-6)

Notice the highlighted words here. God **forgives,** God **heals,** God **redeems,** God **crowns** with steadfast love, God **satisfies,** and God **renews.** And notice what the next verse says: God works righteousness and justice for ALL who are oppressed. All of this is inside of God's grace, and more. We could actually read this entire Psalm, but notice what it says in verse 9 and 10.

> He will not always chide, **nor will he** keep his anger forever. (Psalm 103:9)

God will not always chastise, nor will he keep his anger forever! Let me repeat that last part. **He will not keep his anger forever.** That is great news! Remember what those famous preachers said about God in the last chapter. Does this statement written by David agree with them? We will talk more about that later.

> He does **NOT** deal with us according to our sins, nor repay us **according to our iniquities.** (Psalm 103:10)

Verse 10 is also good news, because if he dealt with those Israelite people according to what they deserved, they would have gotten nothing! It also applies to us today.

> For as high as the heavens are above the earth, so great is his steadfast love toward those who fear him; as far as the east is from the west, so far does he remove our transgressions from us. As a father shows compassion to his children, so the LORD shows compassion to those who fear him. (Psalm 103:11-13)

Pretty awesome isn't it? But that is **the nature of God**!

So now let's return to that parable of the prodigal son.

There is a very important point that shows the depth of God's grace. In her book, "Raising Hell," Julie Ferwerda states:

> I must have read the parable of the prodigal son in Luke chapter fifteen a hundred times, before I noticed the most important, defining detail . . . But while he was still a long way off, his father saw him and felt compassion for him, and ran and embraced him and kissed him. Did you see that? Before the young man could utter a word of remorse, before he had a chance to admit what a screw-up he'd been, the father had

been scanning the distant horizon for his son's form and ran to meet him with open arms. We can't help but feel a bit of the father's joy when he recounts to the older brother what this moment meant to him: . . . We had to celebrate and rejoice, for this brother of yours was dead and has begun to live, and was lost and has been found (Luke 15: 32).[7]

But let's step back for just a moment.

When we look at the background of this passage in Luke 15, we see that Jesus was spending lots of time with those who were labeled as "sinners" by the Scribes and the Pharisees. Now he was addressing these same Scribes and Pharisees who considered themselves to be righteous, in fact so righteous that they were offended that Jesus would spend time with these "sinners." But now Jesus tells them why. He had already given them two other parables. The first one was the parable of the lost sheep. Jesus told them how the shepherd would leave the 99 sheep and go search for the one lost sheep and would rejoice upon finding it. (Matthew 18:10-14; Luke 15: 4-7)

In the second parable, Jesus spoke of a woman who had lost a coin. She then looked over her entire house until she found it, and when she did she rejoiced in finding that which was lost. (Luke 15:8-9)

So then with this third parable, the message is the same, and that is the necessity of helping the lost. Jesus is here

---

[7] Ferwerda, Julie (2011-06-18). Raising Hell: Christianity's Most Controversial Doctrine Put Under Fire (Kindle Locations 313-328). Vagabond Group. Kindle Edition.

refuting these self-righteous hypocrites, and at the same time trying to convict them of their own sin. (Luke 15:11-32)

But the **really important thing** here and the thing which we are trying to emphasize is that **Jesus was speaking of the love of God!** It was a love strong enough for Jesus, the most righteous person ever to walk the face of the earth, to spend time with them in order to save their lost souls. The love and grace of the father is so great that he is not satisfied **if even one soul is lost.** This point cannot be emphasized enough. In the case of the prodigal son, the father loved that son so much that he ran to meet him! There were **NO CONDITIONS** set for the meeting with that son. This is the part of grace that we do not understand. It is indeed, a love that is **beyond the grasp of the human mind to comprehend!**

But this raises the question: What about those who have not come to that "aha moment?"

Should they be cast aside? Does that sound like something the father in this parable would do? This principle will be the topic of discussion in the chapters to come.

Chapter Four

Do you really want
to be the Judge?

True peace and joy. . . those are things that each of us strive
for in this life, but these are things that it seems few of us
completely have. When we start to look at such a thing, we
realize that the concept of peace is complex. It forces us to
first define peace. Peace is many different things to
different people. For those in war zones, it could be defined
as an end to the destruction and killing. To those who are
disturbed by their past, it could be described as an escape
from their past, perhaps with quieting thoughts, or some
kind of escape mechanism. Peace could refer to a time
when order is restored in the midst of chaos, such as a
declaration of martial law . . . Yes! The definition of peace is
very diverse. Each of these types of peace are at best
temporary. But the peace that most of us strive for is a
peace that is lasting, a peace that is truly rest for our soul.
But there are some who will likely never have such peace in
this life.

One such case is that of the family of Natalie Holloway. On
Thursday, May 26, 2005, a beautiful young woman named

Natalie Holloway and several of her classmates flew to Aruba for a five-day unofficial graduation trip. She had no idea that she would never return. After a few days of wild partying, her and her classmates were to go home on May 30, 2005, but Natalie did not show up for her flight. Unfortunately for her she befriended a man by the name of Joran van der Sloot, and was never seen again. Her disappearance to this day has never been resolved.

After a frustrating lack of information about this disappearance, two and one-half years later, Arubian prosecutors closed the case, but reopened it a few months later after receiving a video wherein Van der Sloot admitted to disposing of her body. For some reason Van der Sloot was never charged. But her father took up the cause and began searching in earnest for her remains, a search which went on for years, and lamentably yielded no results. But perhaps in a twist of fate, or by an act of God, in 2012, Van der Sloot was convicted of the murder of another young lady in Lima Peru.

Can you imagine the horror that Natalie Holloway must have endured? Can you imagine the torture that her parents must be going through even to this day, even though it appears obvious that their daughter was killed by this man and justice was eventually served? Who do they blame? Do they want Van der Sloot to be punished forever by God? Do they even **blame God** for this horrible event in the life and death of their precious daughter?

Each one of us carries some pain inside. For the parents of Natalie Holloway, there is the pain of great loss. Perhaps even the pain of guilt that they allowed their daughter to go on such a trip as the one that cost that precious girl her life.

For some of us it is pain that goes back to our childhood, perhaps being mistreated by a loved one. It could be a father who mistreated you, perhaps even mercilessly beating you. It could be a sibling who rejected you and made you feel inferior. It could be a relative or the friend of a relative who sexually abused you, or the immediate family that rejected you because of your beliefs. But the chances are almost 100% that whatever pain you are carrying around with you is the result of a relationship either gone bad, or lost.

The loss could include the loss of a beloved family member or a spouse by death. It could be the pain of injustice that has stolen your peace. Perhaps you have had a loved one killed as the result of an accident, a suicide, or worse yet, a murder similar to that which was just described. The result is that not only is there pain from this loss, but you have compounded the problem by blaming someone and holding hatred in your heart for that person, maybe even yourself. But what happens through this process of hatred is that **not only** do you not have peace, but **you have become a tormented soul!** In its most extreme form, the hatred and desire for getting even becomes the very essence of your being. If any of this that I have just described sounds familiar, and you hold hatred in your heart for someone in your life, then at this point, you have lost your soul to hate. You are no longer yourself, but a slave to this hatred. That is why we are urged to forgive one another. Remember the question that Peter asked Jesus? He asked:

> Lord, how often will my brother sin against me, and I forgive him? As many as seven times?" Jesus said to him: "I do not say to you seven times, but seventy-seven times" (Matt 18:21-22)

Following this, He told a story of how we become when we do not forgive. The account finishes the 18th chapter of Matthew. He said:

Therefore, the kingdom of heaven may be compared to a king who wished to settle accounts with his servants. When he began to settle, one was brought to him who owed him ten thousand talents. And since he could not pay, his master ordered him to be sold, with his wife and children and all that he had, and payment to be made. So, the servant fell on his knees, imploring him, 'Have patience with me, and I will pay you everything.' And out of pity for him, the master of that servant released him and forgave him the debt. But when that same servant went out, he found one of his fellow servants who owed him a hundred denarii, and seizing him, he began to choke him, saying, 'Pay what you owe.' So, his fellow servant fell down and pleaded with him, 'Have patience with me, and I will pay you.' He refused and went and put him in prison until he should pay the debt. When his fellow servants saw what had taken place, they were greatly distressed, and they went and reported to their master all that had taken place. Then his master summoned him and said to him, 'You wicked servant! I forgave you all that debt because you pleaded with me. And should not you have had mercy on your fellow servant, as I had mercy on you?' And in anger his master delivered him to the jailers, until he should pay all his debt. So also, my heavenly Father will do to every one of you, if you do not forgive your brother from your heart. (Matt. 18:23-35)

Do you see what happened to the man who refused to forgive? He became the judge! And as a result, **he once again became the very thing of which he asked to be forgiven.** And look at the price he paid for such a thing.

In a now famous and controversial book by William P. Young entitled "The Shack," the leading character, Mack has lost his daughter to a child molester who took her to a remote shack in the Oregon wilderness and brutally murdered her. In one of the chapters Mack is called by a character who is representative of God to come to judgment, but instead of being called **to be judged,** Mack is called **to be the judge.**[8]

It is with this thought that the author of the book, William P. Young, makes a profound point which we will now develop.

This eye-opening event caused Mack to see that he was judging the man who killed his daughter without even remotely knowing the full knowledge of the facts behind the details of the tortured life in which that man was forced to live, and which subsequently caused him to commit this heinous act. By a series of questions given to him, Mack eventually realized that **he was judging GOD** because of the death of his daughter.

Thus, it was brought to his attention, if Mack were God, **would he be willing** to send this man who brutally murdered his daughter to a place of **fiery eternal torment** to suffer for the endless eons of time, never to be

---

[8] Young, William P., The Shack, 2007; Windblown media. Newbury Park, CA 91320

released? **WOULD HE BE WILLING TO DO THAT?** What about the father of the man who **savagely tortured** his son while he was a child? **Should that man also** be sent to this burning place of torment forever? How far should Mack go back, sentencing people to this horrible place of fiery torment? **Then what about God?** Wasn't he ultimately responsible for the death of Mack's precious daughter?

Mack finally blurted out: **"YES! God is to blame!"**

In the next scenario of this story, Mack was asked to choose **only two** of his five daughters to spend eternity with God. The reasoning behind this was that since he believed that God sends most people to a place of eternal torment, and he is **JUDGING GOD, then it was only fair that he does the same.**

Mack then came to the shocking realization that **he could never** send any of his children to a place of **eternal torment**, no matter what they did. He screamed: "I can't, I can't, I won't!" But he was told: "YOU MUST!"

Finally, Mack pleaded with the question: **Could I go instead?** If you need someone to torture for eternity, I'll go in their place. Would that work? Could I do that" Then he fell down and cried out: "Please . . . I am begging you. Please . . . Please . . ."

Then Mack was told "Now you sound like Jesus. You have judged well"[9]

---

9 Ibid., pp158-163

Do you see the **profound significance** of this story? For God to torment someone forever is **totally outside of the boundaries of the love of God!**

Bringing this down to a personal level, we need to seriously ask ourselves:

> "Is this the position I really want to be in? Do I really want to become the judge of those who mistreat me or do wrong to those whom I love? What do I really know about the object of my hate? Do I really know what is behind their hatred? Can I see their past, and the deep suffering that they have felt? Perhaps they are tortured by the hatred that they were shown in their past, and merely lashed out at me or my loved one. Maybe they even took it to the next level and caused physical harm to me."

What has "I" got to do with it

Applying that to all those now reading, maybe that person was seeking peace through alcohol or drugs. Maybe he got behind the wheel of a car and killed your wife, or your child, or another loved one in an auto accident. Do you really want to **add to his torture and yours** by becoming the judge of him? Where does it end? Will you blame and judge his father for causing him to be such that he needed that alcohol fix which caused him to kill your son? That's right. . . now you have become not only his judge, but the judge of his father.

But what about God? Couldn't God have stopped all of this? Will you now judge God because your son is dead from this horrible accident, and all of these people have all of these problems?? Do you get the picture that is painted here? It just continues to escalate. So, as the result of all of this, if you are now in this position, **YOU have made yourself**

Really

THE JUDGE OF THE UNIVERSE! Is that really where you want to be?

If you start down this road, this is where you end up. You can never quit blaming someone for all that has happened. But now let me ask you this question? Somehow, do you think it's OK for God to send that person to a place of eternal torment, to burn forever for his crimes? Just stop for a moment and think about the intensity of such a sentence. **This is the moment of truth for YOU!** Would **YOU** take that individual that is so tormented by all that is in his past, and all that he has done and sentence him to a further, and even more extreme form of torture such as burning in a place of fiery torment? Would you even go so far as to say he must go there for eternity? **Think of that. . . eternity!** That means that after a thousand lifetimes of fiery torture, he still would be at the beginning of the time he must spend in agony! *God is not vs numbers*

Despite all of this above, there are a great number of people who believe that this is what God will do! Not only that, but they believe **that the vast majority** of the people on this planet will be consigned to this horrible place. But the truth is that this is due to a misunderstanding of a few passages of Scripture. Perhaps the biggest one of these is a passage that Jesus gave in the Sermon on the Mount. Here he said there were two gates, one leading to life, and the other leading to destruction – Matt 7:13-14. Let's look at this passage again. It says:

> Enter by the narrow gate; for wide is the gate and broad the road which leads to ruin, and many there are who enter by it; because narrow is the gate and

contracted the road which leads to Life, and few are those who find it. (Matthew 7:13-14 WNT)

But as previously stated, this greatly misunderstood passage **was NOT** a reference to the afterlife! When Jesus spoke these words, his specific audience was the Jews living in Judea. Jesus was **warning them** about **an event that would happen within that same generation.** Those who took the narrow way of following him, in essence, his followers would be spared in the destruction that would come, but those not following him would lose their human lives in the awful events preceding the destruction of Jerusalem and its temple which occurred in AD 70, where history recorded that **1.1 million Jews were killed, and only 97,000 were spared.**[10]

No matter what your perception of what the Bible says about this, if you believe that God wants to torture someone forever in the midst of a burning fire, you are wrong. Just as you would **NEVER** under any circumstances **burn your children in a fire** that lasts forever throughout the eons of the ages, the same is true of God! Remember that we were created in the image of God! God would never burn his disobedient children in a literal fire as you may have heard. We know from what God said in the Old Testament that this burning of children in a fire was **the major reason** God destroyed Jerusalem the first time. These unfaithful people were burning their children in sacrifice to the false God Molech. Let's look at what God said:

> For the children of Israel and the children of Judah have done nothing but evil in my sight from their youth. The children of Israel have done nothing but

---

[10] The Wars of the Jews, Josephus, Book 6, Chapter 9, Section 3

provoke me to anger by the work of their hands, declares the LORD. This city has aroused my anger and wrath, from the day it was built to this day, so that I will remove it from my sight because of all the evil of the children of Israel and the children of Judah that they did to provoke me to anger—their kings and their officials, their priests and their prophets, the men of Judah and the inhabitants of Jerusalem. They have turned to me their back and not their face. And though I have taught them persistently, they have not listened to receive instruction. They set up their abominations in the house that is called by my name, to defile it. (Jeremiah 32:30-34)

Now it is imperative that you notice the powerful impact of the last statement in this passage!

They built the high places of Baal in the Valley of the Son of Hinnom, to offer up their sons and daughters to Molech, though I did not command them, **NOR DID IT ENTER INTO MY MIND,** that they should do this abomination, to cause Judah to sin. (Jeremiah 32:30-35)

His chosen people were doing the unimaginable and worshipping gods made with hands. And what is even worse, if that is possible is that they were sacrificing their children by throwing them into the fire! Can you imagine that screaming child, suffering in pain? As God states, this is something that would **never even come into his mind to do!**

But there is still another point that is important here, and that is very important. Even these ones which were "destroyed," were not destroyed in the sense of how we normally think of destruction. They were sent to a place called Sheol, and were still conscious. In fact, even though Jerusalem was "destroyed," it was not gone forever. It returned under the love of God. And as for the people who went to the place called Sheol, they were not tormented!

In fact, if you will search the entire Old Testament Law covenant which is given in the first 5 chapters of the Bible known to the Jews as "The Torah" you will **NOT FIND A SINGLE REFERENCE TO ETERNAL TORMENT!** Wouldn't you think that if God was going to do such a thing to his chosen people when they were disobedient that he would make it **ABUNDANTLY** clear to them?

So now let's go back to our discussion of how we all want to be the judge of others. When you consider the fact that you do not know, nor will you ever know the details about why someone does the things that they do, do you really want to pronounce sentence upon them? The Bible tells us in 1 John that God is love. Do you know what that means? It means that love is the very essence of his being. Let's read the discourse that the Apostle John wrote on this:

> God is love, and anyone who doesn't love others has never known him. God showed his love for us when he sent his only Son into the world to give us life. Real love isn't our love for God, but his love for us. God sent his Son to be the sacrifice by which our sins are forgiven. Dear friends, since God loved us this much, we must love each other. No one has ever seen God. But if we love each other, God lives in us, and his love is truly in our hearts. God has given us his Spirit. That is how we know that we are one with him, just as he is one with us. God sent his Son to be the Savior of the

world. We saw his Son and are now telling others about him. (1 John 4:8-14 Contemporary English Version)

Then the Apostle finished his statement about God's love by stating:

God stays one with everyone who openly says that Jesus is the Son of God. That's how we stay one with God and are sure that God loves us. **God is love.** If we keep on loving others, we will stay one in our hearts with God, and he will stay one with us." - (1 John 4:14-16 Contemporary English Version)

Yes! God is love. He was willing to send His only begotten Son to this earth **to die for us.** It should be impossible for us to reasonably assert in our minds that God did this on behalf of mankind, yet on the other hand he would be willing to commit someone to a fiery torment for eternity! These two scenarios do not fit together. It is as the Apostle John wrote:

My little children, I am writing these things to you so that you may not sin. But if anyone does sin, we have an advocate with the Father, Jesus Christ the righteous. He is the propitiation for our sins, and not for ours only but also for the sins of the whole world. (I John 2:1-2)

Did you catch the awesome supremacy of this statement from a loving God? Let's look at that last statement again as stated in the Contemporary English version:

Christ is the sacrifice that **takes away our sins and the sins of all the world's people.** (I John 2:1-2)

Yes, it is a human tendency to continually judge people we come across in this life. But **we do not know the circumstances** of their background which led them to become what they are. If we were raised the same way, it is possible that we could be like them in every respect!

Since we now have become aware of this possibility, we must once again ask ourselves the question, "Do you really want to be the judge?"

Chapter Five

What about this place called Hell?

Since my goal in this book is to present the truth in scripture about what God's Word says, let us now look at what we find in the Bible about this place called "Hell."

The term "Hell" is found as translated below in some of our current translations. **Please take note** of the next chart which I have presented here. It shows the extent of the problem with our Bible Translations. The two columns represent the Old Testament, and the New Testament.

Translation	OT	NT
King James Version	31	23
New King James	19	13
New American Standard	0	13
English Standard Version	0	14
New International Version	0	15
New Living Translation	1	18
Contemporary English Version	0	20
Young's Literal Translation	0	0
World English Bible	0	0
Rotherham Emphasized Bible	0	0
1912 Weymouth NT	N/A	0
Tree of Life Version NT	N/A	0

As you can see from this chart, there are big differences in these Bible versions in the translation of this word. Why is this so? Probably the biggest reason is something you may not want to hear, but something which is real. It is called **translator bias**.

Is there a problem here? I have heard many people say, "You should read only the Bible. This is the only way you can get an unbiased look at what it REALLY says!"

If you are absolutely fluent in ancient Hebrew and Greek, and can depend 100% on the Hebrew and Greek texts available, **then I would say that this is possible,** but even then, it is not likely. Why? Since there are few people who fit in the first category, and no one who can assure you of the second item, **it will require much more diligence** than that in order to get to the truth. Very few people are willing to commit to such diligence.

Now having said all of this, I am one who believes **in the inerrancy of Scripture.** By now, you are probably really confused. How can I say that in the light of the evidence presented here? The answer is that **I did not say** that I believe in the inerrancy of **translation**. But before you get too upset, I would like to add something **very important**.

And that is this:

You can get the message of salvation from any of these Bible translations that are mentioned above.

Isaiah 55:11 still holds true:

"so shall my word be that goes out from my mouth; it shall not return to me empty, but it shall accomplish that which I purpose, and shall succeed in the thing for which I sent it."

Since the most popular Bible version is the King James Version, let's consider it first. The original instructions handed down to the translators contained the following item:

Richard Bancroft prepared the following instructions to the translators for King James:

> For the better ordering of the proceedings of the translators, his Majesty recommended the following rules to them, to be very carefully observed:

> 1. The ordinary Bible, read in the church, commonly called the **Bishop's Bible**, to be followed, and as little altered as the original will permit.[11]

Or previous authority

Here is what was said in an article from the Christian Courier regarding the King James Version.

> "In considering *any* version, however, it must be acknowledged that the translator **brings some of his theological background "to the table"** in producing his work. Such was no less true of the KJV scholars.[12]

So now the question arises, why is the *King James Version* and its modern language version the *New King*

---

[11] http://kjv.landmarkbiblebaptist.net/kjv-instructions.html

[12] https://www.christiancourier.com/articles/257-were-the-king-james-version-translators-biased-toward-the-faith-only-doctrine

James the only two translations to use the term **hell** in the Old Testament? The word from which this is translated in every instance is **sheol.** There is no basis for the *KJV* translating it as **hell** in every instance, all 31 of them. The Translators of the *NKJV* recognized this and that is why there are only 19 times the word was translated as **hell**. But the *NKJV* did continue to use the word in the following verses in the Old Testament. Here are three examples taken from the Psalms. I have paired them with the same verse as rendered in the *ESV*.

> Psalm 9:17 The wicked shall be turned into **hell,** *And* all the nations that forget God. **NKJV**
> Psalm 9:17 The wicked shall return to **Sheol**, all the nations that forget God. **ESV**
> Psalm 55:15 Let death seize them; Let them go down alive into **hell**, For wickedness *is* in their dwellings *and* among them. **NKJV**
> Psalm 55:15 Let death steal over them; let them go down to **Sheol** alive; for evil is in their dwelling place and in their heart. **ESV**
> Psalm 139:8 If I ascend into heaven, You *are* there; If I make my bed in **hell**, behold, You *are there.* **NKJV**
> Psalm 139:8 If I ascend to heaven, you are there! If I make my bed in **Sheol**, you are there! **ESV**

Although it was later changed, the Israelites during the time of David had a concept of the dead as shown by from this quote below.

According to Herbert C. Brichto, writing in *Hebrew Union College Annual,* the family tomb is the central concept in understanding biblical views of the afterlife. Brichto states that it is "not mere sentimental respect for the physical remains that is...the motivation for the practice, but rather an assumed connection between proper sepulture and the condition of happiness of the deceased in the afterlife." According to Brichto, the early Israelites apparently believed that the graves of family, or tribe, united into one, and that this unified collectivity is to what the Biblical Hebrew term Sheol refers, the common grave of humans. Although not well defined in the Tanakh, Sheol in this view was a subterranean underworld where the souls of the dead went after the body died.[13]

[handwritten: Brichto bulrsht]

This is confirmed by passages of Scripture such as this:

> Abraham breathed his last and died in a good old age, an old man and full of years, and **was gathered to his people.** (Genesis 25:8)

Later on, during the era of the second temple, the concept changed. Most of the modern translations recognized this as an important issue, and avoided it. Even Young's Literal Translation which was originally produced in 1862 and revised in 1888 avoided such bias.

For example, in Young's Literal Translation, *sheol* is found sixty-four times. In several other translations we may find it is translated "the pit" three times, "the grave" thirty-one times and "hell" thirty-one times. Also, in Young's Literal Translation we find *hades* is used eleven times, never being

---

[13] Herbert C. Brichto, writing in *Hebrew Union College Annual* From https://en.wikipedia.org/wiki/Sheol

What confusion?

translated as "hell. Adding to the confusion is that two other words are also translated hell in many translations of the New Testament. These are *Tartarus*, and *Gehenna*. In Young's Literal Translation we find *Tartarus* one time and *Gehenna* 12 times. In order to keep from being influenced by the bias of these translators, we need to be diligent, as per 1 Thess: 5:21 "Test all things; hold fast what is good."

Now let's look at the following translations. Here is a table which lists the number of times that the word "Hell" appears in each of the following:

Translation	Old Testament	New Testament
Young's Literal Translation	0	0
World English Bible	0	0
Rotherham Emphasized Bible	0	0
1912 Weymouth NT	N/A	0
Tree of Life Version NT	N/A	0

What these translations have decided to do is to **NOT** translate the word. That's right! Instead of translating the words **Sheol, Hades,** and **Gehenna** as **Hell,** these translations have done what is called a **transliteration.** In other words, they have taken the word and given it an English spelling. For example, in the case of the Greek name γεεννη, it was given the English spelling Gehenna, thus, no translation. This way it is left to the reader to make the connection. But why did they do this? In the New Testament, this is because the word Gehenna has its own definition and there is really no need to translate it. This avoids the controversy.

What controversy?

We described Gehenna earlier. It was a garbage dump outside of Jerusalem. It was named as such because of the heritage of the location. It was the same place in the Old Testament where the Israelite worshippers of the Baals and the god Molech sacrificed their children. This was detestable to Yahweh. It is described in the book of 2 Chronicles when speaking of the disobedient King Ahaz:

> Ahaz was twenty years old when he began to reign, and he reigned sixteen years in Jerusalem. And he did not do what was right in the eyes of the LORD, as his father David had done, but he walked in the ways of the kings of Israel. He even made metal images for the Baals, and he made offerings in the Valley of the Son of Hinnom and **burned his sons as an offering, according to the abominations of the nations** whom the LORD drove out before the people of Israel. (2 Chronicles 28:1-3)

As we described earlier in Chapter two, this was **one of the major factors** in the decision by God to destroy Jerusalem the first time. Let's look again at the proclamation of God concerning their future for these heinous acts.

> And the dead bodies of this people will be food for the birds of the air, and for the beasts of the earth, and none will frighten them away. (Jeremiah 7:33)

As always God kept his promise. The prophecy was fulfilled. Jerusalem was destroyed by the Babylonians, and the infamous Valley of Hinnom became a garbage dump just outside of the city after it was rebuilt. Why was this? Because this place was so detestable to God that it would **never come into his mind** to do such a heinous act as burning children in a fire. This is precisely what he said as we noted earlier in Jeremiah chapter 7. I want to quote this again just to show you **how** detestable it was to God:

> And they have built the high places of Topheth, which is in the Valley of the Son of Hinnom, to burn their sons and their daughters in the fire, **which I did not command, *nor did it come into my mind.*** Therefore, behold, the days are coming, declares the LORD, when it will no more be called Topheth, or the Valley of the Son of Hinnom, but the Valley of Slaughter; for they will bury in Topheth, because there is no room elsewhere. And the dead bodies of this people will be food for the birds of the air, and for the beasts of the earth, and none will frighten them away. And I will silence in the cities of Judah and in the streets of Jerusalem the voice of mirth and the voice of gladness, the voice of the bridegroom and the voice of the bride, for the land shall become a waste. (Jeremiah 7:31-33)

That's right! **God kept his promise**. He destroyed this place and made it a wasteland which was later known as **Gehenna**. In fact, this was the last straw for God. He did this because of this burning of children as a sacrifice to a false god, and many other detestable things that they were doing. This burning of children was truly detestable to God.

Despite the fact that most of our modern translations have translated the name Gehenna as Hell, we can find out what Jesus called it by looking at one of the Bible Translations that have transliterated this word into English.

Here are the occasions which use the word Gehenna in the *World English Bible:*

Matthew 5:22 But I tell you, that everyone who is angry with his brother without a cause will be in danger of the judgment; and whoever says to his brother, 'Raca!' will be in danger of the council; and whoever says, 'You fool!' will be in danger of the fire of **Gehenna.**

Matthew 5:29 If your right eye causes you to stumble, pluck it out and throw it away from you. For it is more profitable for you that one of your members should perish, than for your whole body to be cast into **Gehenna.**

Matthew 5:30 If your right hand causes you to stumble, cut it off, and throw it away from you. For it is more profitable for you that one of your members should perish, than for your whole body to be cast into **Gehenna.**

Matthew 10:28 Don't be afraid of those who kill the body, but are not able to kill the soul. Rather, fear him who is able to destroy both soul and body in **Gehenna.**

Matt 18:9 If your eye causes you to stumble, pluck it out, and cast it from you. It is better for you to enter into life with one eye, rather than having two eyes to be cast into the **Gehenna** of fire.

Matthew 23:15 Woe to you, scribes and Pharisees, hypocrites! For you travel around by sea and land to make one proselyte; and when he becomes one, you make him twice as much a son of **Gehenna** as yourselves.

Matthew 23:33 You serpents, you offspring of vipers, how will you escape the judgment of **Gehenna**?

Mark 9:43 If your hand causes you to stumble, cut it off. It is better for you to enter into life maimed, rather than having your two hands to go into **Gehenna**, into the unquenchable fire,

Mark 9:45 If your foot causes you to stumble, cut it off. It is better for you to enter into life lame, rather than having your two feet to be cast into **Gehenna**, into the fire that will never be quenched—

Mark 9:47 If your eye causes you to stumble, cast it out. It is better for you to enter into God's Kingdom with one eye, rather than having two eyes to be cast into the **Gehenna** of fire,

Luke 12:5 But I will warn you whom you should fear. Fear him, who after he has killed, has power to cast into **Gehenna.** Yes, I tell you, fear him.

James 3:6 And the tongue is a fire. The world of iniquity among our members is the tongue, which defiles the whole body, and sets on fire the course of nature, and is set on fire by **Gehenna**.

Yes, Jesus made reference to Gehenna as a place that was known by the audience, a place just outside of Jerusalem which was always burning. He was making reference to the garbage dump on the southeast side if the city, the same place where child sacrifices were made many centuries earlier by the faithless Israelites.

The big question is: Was there a deeper meaning to this reference to Gehenna? The answer to that question is **YES!** The problem we find in Christian circles is **just exactly**

what that meaning was when the word was spoken by Jesus.

Basically, there are Christians in three camps concerning the meaning of Gehenna. We will discuss these at length as this book unfolds. *NOT HEAVEN*

Is this place called Hell a place of Eternal Torment?

It is interesting to look at the etymology of the word "hell."

> The English word may be in part from Old Norse mythological *Hel* (from Proto-Germanic **halija* "one who covers up or hides something"), in Norse mythology the name of Loki's daughter who rules over the evil dead in *Niflheim*, the lowest of all worlds (*nifl* "mist"). **A pagan concept and word fitted to a Christian idiom.** In Middle English, also of the *Limbus Patrum*, place where the Patriarchs, Prophets, etc. awaited the Atonement. Used in the KJV for Old Testament Hebrew *Sheol* and New Testament Greek *Hades*, *Gehenna*. Used figuratively for "state of misery, any bad experience" since at least late 14c. As an expression of disgust, etc., first recorded 1670s.[14]

So, we must realize that this word actually means to hide or cover up something. It appears to have originated with the Norse Pagans in the middle ages. Therefore, this word did not exist until several centuries after the Bible was written. As I stated in the introduction, I am repulsed by the fact that we are stuck with the English translation of this name

---

[14] http://etymonline.com/index.php?allowed_in_frame=0&search=hell

as "Hell." It is a mistranslation from a pagan name and concept. It would have made much more sense for the original translators to have just transliterated the word Gehenna in all of our currently used translations as opposed to the use of an unrelated pagan word such as this. But unfortunately, after several centuries of using this word, we are stuck with the term "Hell" in place of Gehenna whether we like it or not.

In Chapter two, I made the argument that God having a place of **eternal torment** is contrary to his nature. To have such a place could indicate that his hate is stronger than his love. This statement was based on statistical evidence. The teaching by the majority of Christendom that since only 1/3 of the population of the earth is Christian, and since it teaches that even in the churches half or less of churchgoers are saved, then it follows that at least 5 out of every 6 people now living are bound for hell. Isn't this what we often hear in the churches today?

One of the most prominent books used in the Seminaries of Christendom is: *"**Systematic Theology**, An introduction to Biblical Doctrine"* by Wayne Grudem.

In this book we find the following words:

> It is appropriate to discuss the doctrine of hell in connection with the doctrine of final judgment. We may define hell as follows: *Hell is a place of **eternal conscious punishment** for the wicked.*[15]

---

[15] Systematic Theology, An introduction to Biblical Doctrine" by Wayne Grudem. (p. 1148)1994 Version

This is a very bold statement by Grudem, but is it true?

Grudem based his conclusion of this on an interpretation of the following:

1. Passages in the Olivet discourse of Matthew chapter 25,

2. The parable of Lazarus and the Rich Man and,

3. A few passages in the book of Revelation.

As I pointed out in my book *God's Promise of Redemption, a story of fulfilled prophecy,* the Olivet Discourse was given by Jesus to his disciples in answer to two questions. You cannot separate this passage from the audience relevance and from the audience timing. It is in all three Synoptic Gospels. The accounts are Matthew 24, Mark 13, and Luke 21. These are parallel accounts of the same event. This prophecy contains several very specific items which do not apply to any other time frame.

- He speaks of a time of big trouble in the future.
- A *definite, specific* period of time is stated: "**This** generation will not pass away"

Jesus **did not say that this would be something that would happen thousands of years later.** He was very specific when he said the events he was about to explain would happen within the time frame of **the generation being addressed.**

- The questions that are asked by the disciples are very direct, and Jesus answered them directly and explicitly.

- The audience to whom Jesus spoke is **distinctly** the generation Jesus said would see all of these things.
- _Detailed_ instructions are given by Jesus as to _what_ the disciples should do and _when_ they should do it. These instructions were so detailed, that they **would not fit any other time period** than that time period of the current generation.

Now returning to Grudem's argument in this section of **Systematic Theology**, he makes reference to the parable of the talents stating that the master said: _"Cast the worthless servant into the outer darkness; there men will weep and gnash their teeth."_ (Matthew 25:30) He also quotes Matthew 25:46 which says that the wicked _"will go away into eternal punishment, but the righteous into eternal life."_[16]

I am not sure which translation he used here in either case because it is not stated. Nonetheless, it is important to note that this is a **misapplication** of Scripture because Jesus was actually speaking (as he always did with crowds) in a parable (Matthew 13:34). This time it was directed at the wicked religious leaders of his day, and what would soon happen to them. We will unpack this passage (Matthew 25:46) in great detail in a later chapter.

Yes, in this parable we find the message of the stewardship of the treasure which all of God's servants have been given. The nation of Israel, and particularly the religious leaders stood before God as ones _**who hated the message of the Kingdom.**_ They disregarded the Kingdom of God as

---

[16] Ibid

spoken of by Jesus as nothing, and then later demonstrated this by putting to death the Son of God.

Because of this and other sins against God, Jesus was proclaiming that those religious leaders in particular, the nation in general, and specifically the city of Jerusalem with its temple would come under judgment and be destroyed. Matthew 25:46 speaks of age enduring (Greek – aionios) punishment, and does not mention eternal torment. And as we shall later examine, the word **ETERNAL has a deeper meaning** than what is obvious, and the word punishment is a word that speaks of **remedial** action. We shall examine these words and Matthew 25:46 again in a later chapter. Next Grudem goes to the parable of Lazarus and the rich man. It states the following:

> There was a rich man who was clothed in purple and fine linen and who feasted sumptuously every day. And at his gate was laid a poor man named Lazarus, covered with sores, who desired to be fed with what fell from the rich man's table. Moreover, even the dogs came and licked his sores. The poor man died and was carried by the angels to Abraham's side. The rich man also died and was buried, and in Hades, being in torment, he lifted up his eyes and saw Abraham far off and Lazarus at his side. And he called out, 'Father Abraham, have mercy on me, and send Lazarus to dip the end of his finger in water and cool my tongue, for I am in anguish in this flame.' (Luke 16:19-24)

Once again, I must repeat this, even at the risk of sounding too repetitious, in all cases, **the audience must be considered**. Jesus said that he always spoke to the people in parables.

Matt 13:34 All these things Jesus said to the crowds in parables; indeed, **he said nothing to them without a parable.**

Earlier, we noted that the Jewish people had an early concept of **Sheol,** that it was the dwelling place of the dead without regard to their choices in life. Sometime during the second temple period this view changed. This is noted in this Wikipedia article:

> While the Old Testament writings describe Sheol as the permanent place of the dead, in the Second Temple period (roughly 500 BC–70 AD) a more diverse set of ideas developed. In some texts, Sheol is considered to be **the home of both the righteous and the wicked, separated into respective compartments;** in others, it was considered a place of punishment, meant for the wicked dead alone.[4] When the Hebrew scriptures were translated into Greek in ancient Alexandria around 200 BC, the word "Hades" (the Greek underworld) was substituted for Sheol, and this is reflected in the New Testament where Hades is both the underworld of the dead and the personification of the evil it represents.[17]

Additionally, we have the document produced by **Jewish Historian Josephus** which outlines the thought of his day regarding **Hades.**

NOW as to Hades, wherein the souls of the good things they see, and rejoice in the righteous and

---

[17] https://en.wikipedia.org/wiki/Sheol

unrighteous are detained, it is necessary to speak of it. Hades is a place in the world not regularly finished; a *subterraneous* region, wherein the light of this world does not shine; from which circumstance, that in this region the light does not shine, it cannot be but there must be in it perpetual *darkness*. This region is allotted as a place of custody for souls, ill which angels are appointed as guardians to them, who distribute to them **temporary punishments**, agreeable to every one's behavior and manners.[18]

He also pointed out concerning this place that there was another compartment called the bosom of Abraham. He said concerning this that these ones:

but the just are guided to the *right hand,* and are led with hymns, sung by the *angels* appointed over that place, unto a region of *light,* in which the just have dwelt from the beginning of the world; not constrained by necessity, but ever enjoying the prospect of the good things they see, and rejoice in the expectation of those new enjoyments which will be peculiar to every one of them, and esteeming those things beyond what we have here; with whom there is no place of toil, no burning heat, no piercing cold, nor are any briers there; but the countenance of the just, which they see, always smiles them, while they wait for that rest and *eternal* new *life in heaven,* which is to succeed this region. This place we call *The Bosom of Abraham.*[19]

---

[18]The Works of Josephus, 1987 Hendrickson Publishers, p. 813
[19] Ibid.

Thus, from the comments of Josephus, we can understand that when Jesus spoke to these religious leaders about *Hades* having two compartments, they knew what he was speaking about. There is no place in this passage where they questioned him or refuted him on this concept. It was a concept with which they were familiar. So, what was Jesus talking about here?

This parable was specifically given with the idea of exposing the religious leaders of that day. These religious leaders were the rich man in this parable. Lazarus represents the spiritually starved people of Israel. The Scribes and Pharisees have **starved the people of spiritual truth** and elevated themselves as the only ones righteous.

This is also a prophecy of sorts in that the fortunes of these two classes were soon to be reversed. Those who followed Jesus were to be liberated prior to the siege of Jerusalem, and those who did not, as well as the religious leaders were about to endure enormous suffering at the hands of the Roman armies during the siege. The end of the matter, as shown by history, was the complete destruction of Jerusalem, the temple, and the end of the entire system of Levitical Sacrificial worship.

Notice what Josephus said concerning this place called Hades. He said it was a place of **temporary punishment.** This was the Jewish thinking at that time. Nowhere, in this parable does Jesus say that this was a place of **eternal** torment.

ELISHA & ENOCH

There is one more point that must be considered when we are considering the parable of Lazarus and the Rich man. That is the fact that there were no saints in heaven at that time. The door to heaven had not opened up yet. As Jesus told his disciples:

No one has ascended into heaven except he who descended from heaven, the Son of Man. (John 3:13)

Thus, heaven would not open until Jesus himself opened that door after he ascended. This even gives more credibility to the "two-compartment" system that existed in Hades.

Next, Grudem quotes from the Revelation to make his point.[20]

Here is the text:

And another angel, a third, followed them, saying with a loud voice, "If anyone worships the beast and its image and receives a mark on his forehead or on his hand, he also will drink the wine of God's wrath, poured full strength into the cup of his anger, and he will be tormented with fire and sulfur in the presence of the holy angels and in the presence of the Lamb. And the smoke of their torment goes up forever and ever, and they have no rest, day or night, these worshipers of the beast and its image, and whoever receives the mark of its name." (Revelation 14:9-11)

---

[20] Systematic Theology, An introduction to Biblical Doctrine" by Wayne Grudem. (p. 1149) 1994 Version

Now it is important to notice the (symbolic) language that is used here. Do you think that those who worshipped the beast received a **literal** mark on their foreheads? Do you think that they **literally** drank the wine of God's wrath? Do you think they were **literally** tormented with fire and sulfur **in the presence of the holy angels forever and ever?**

From Young's Literal Translation we see the following translation of verse 11.

> and the smoke of their torment doth go up to **ages of ages**; and they have no rest day and night, who are bowing before the beast and his image, also if any doth receive the mark of his name. (Revelation 14:11)

Young's literal translation **does not say** forever and ever because the Greek here in this verse is αιωνας αιωνων which literally translates as Young has done (up to **ages of ages**). We will discuss this concept later in great detail.

The point that Grudem is trying to make is the concept of **eternal torment**. But this is not what the text says. It says that *"**the smoke** of their torment goes up forever and ever."* This is the same (hyperbolic) language used by the prophet Isaiah. But you must see the **big truth here!** Do you see the difference? It does **NOT** say the **PEOPLE** will be tormented forever.

This entire chapter in the book of Revelation is about the city of Jerusalem which is Babylon the great. The end of this city was its destruction which occurred in the year AD70. The temple and the city were set on fire with a fire so intense that it melted the gold of the temple. The entire temple was turned to rubbish by those plunderers wanting to get the gold. This is a matter of historical fact. The idea of the smoke going up forever and ever **is a reference to the finality of the sacrificial, Levitical form of worship.** It was ended forever, and was no longer necessary because of the sacrifice of *the Lamb of God*.

How do we know it was speaking of Jerusalem? Note what verses 18 and 19 have to say concerning this:

> And another angel came out from the altar, the angel who has authority over the fire, and he called with a loud voice to the one who had the sharp sickle, "Put in your sickle and gather the clusters from the vine of the earth, for its grapes are ripe." So, the angel swung his sickle across the earth and gathered the grape harvest of the earth and threw it into the great winepress of the wrath of God. (Revelation 14:18-19)

Do you remember that God has always referred to his people as the vine? Here are a few of the references.

> Psalm 80:8 You brought a vine out of Egypt; you drove out the nations and planted it.
>
> Jeremiah 2:21 Yet I planted you a choice vine, wholly of pure seed. How then have you turned degenerate and become a wild vine?
>
> Hosea 10:1 Israel is a luxuriant vine that yields its fruit. The more his fruit increased, the more altars he built; as his country improved, he improved his pillars.

The vine was being gathered and put into the great winepress. God was **about to destroy the city of Jerusalem again.** This time it would mark an end to the Jewish system of worship that had prevailed for centuries.

This destruction coincides with **the same type of wrath** that God spoke of through the Prophet Isaiah. Notice that Isaiah used **the same hyperbolic language** when speaking of the destruction of Edom in his time:

> And the streams of Edom shall be turned into pitch, and her soil into sulfur; her land shall become burning pitch. Night and day it shall not be quenched; *its smoke shall go up forever*. From generation to generation it shall lay waste; none shall pass through it forever and ever. Isaiah 34:9-10)

Yes, the smoke went up in the same manner. The Levitical system of worship and the Old Covenant along with it were gone forever. The *Lamb of God* was now on the throne! Grudem's point about this place called hell **is not proven.** He has failed to show Gehenna as a place of eternal torment.

But there is no question that Gehenna (or Hell) **IS** a place to be greatly feared. Jesus made that clear in Luke 12:5 as noted earlier:

> Luke 12:5 But I will warn you whom you should fear. Fear him, who after he has killed, has power to cast into **Gehenna.** Yes, I tell you, fear him. (WEB)

It is clear that this is a **fearful place** for humans to have to go. So, what is it? We will address this subject in detail later. But for now, let's look at the concept of Annihilationism.

Chapter Six

Do the Wicked Perish?

"And they went and woke him, saying, 'Save us, Lord; we are **perishing**.' And he said to them, 'Why are you afraid, O you of little faith?' Then he rose and rebuked the winds and the sea, and there was a great calm." (Matthew 8:25-26)

Were they really perishing?

===============================

The story you are about to read **is an improvisation**, but it is based on a tragic incident that occurred on March 8, 2014.

Two men, Jason and Aaqil are sitting in an airport in Beijing China waiting for a flight to arrive. Jason is an American Christian and Aaqil is a Malaysian Muslim. They are both school teachers, teaching in the same school in Beijing. The American is teaching English and the Malaysian is teaching math. Both have been in China for the same amount of time, about a year, and both started at the school in Beijing the same day. Jason has volunteered to take Aaqil to the airport to meet his family. Aaqil is very anxious because he has been setting up the household and his family has finally been able to get the Visa they have been waiting for. At last, after a year, they will be together as a family again.

Jason knows that Aaqil is a Muslim because he has tried to witness to him about Jesus. Aaqil has never been verbal about his faith, and would change the subject every time it came up. Aaqil mentioned that he was a Muslim to Jason one day in a casual conversation in the break room at school. After that, Jason started trying to engage Aaqil in a conversation about Jesus. Aaqil told Jason that he and his family lived in an area of Malaysia where there were several Christian missionaries, and they had spoken to them before, but always rejected their message about Jesus. But as Jason continued to make comments to Aaqil, he made some inroads in Aaqil's thinking without knowing it. This went on for the last three months, but even though Aaqil was starting to think about what Jason said, he would not participate.

As they are sitting at the airport waiting for the flight to come in, Aaqil surprises Jason.

"This man Jesus who you worship," Aaqil said, "He is a strange guy, you know."

Jason is shocked that his friend would mention the name of Jesus, "Why is that?" Jason asked.

"He seems to be all about love." said Aaqil.

"What's strange about that?" answered Jason, still reeling with surprise.

"He said you should love your enemies. Whoever heard of such a thing? Why would he say such a ridiculous thing?"

Jason thought about it for a moment. Here was the opportunity he had been waiting for. Aaqil has obviously been looking at the New Testament that Jason gave him. Jason had quietly been passing those New Testaments out to several people in the school. Jason told him not to worry about reading all of it, but pointed out a few passages on the Sermon on the Mount, and told him to read the book of John.

"How do you know this?" Jason said.

"It was in that little brown book you gave me, I looked it over one evening after I got home from school."

"Good!" said Jason. "That was a New Testament Bible. How much did you read?"

"Oh, I read what you showed me to read . . . I think you called it the Sermon on the Mount, or something like that. I also read the entire book you called the book of John, you know...the one you showed me. It didn't take very long to read."

"At first, I laughed at some of the things in there, but the more I tried to put it out of my mind, the more I thought about it. It just kept coming back to my mind, the things that Jesus said about love. I have never heard such things in all of my readings in the Quran. It touched my heart."

Jason was inwardly leaping for joy, and asked him, "What else did you read that Jesus said about love?"

"Funny you should ask, because it bothered me so much for about a week after I read it that I went back and looked up everything Jesus said, and marked it in that little brown book with a highlighter."

"Wow, I am impressed." Jason proclaimed. "So, I know you are not sure about what Jesus said about loving your enemies, but what else stuck out in your mind about what Jesus said about love?"

"I thought you might ask, so I brought the book with me."

Jason noticed that the edges of the pages were darkened in the first part of that New Testament as Aaqil pulled it out of his pocket. It was obvious that he had been **looking at it a lot!**

"Here is something that really made me think." Aaqil started to read: "A new commandment I give to you, that you love one another: just as I have loved you, you also are to love one another."

"This Jesus guy, seems to be all about love . . . is that really true?"

Jason got a big smile on his face, and with more than a little enthusiasm he said, "Yes, it is true, Aaqil!"

Jason was now holding back the tears of joy. A Scripture flashed through his mind. It was Hebrews 4: 12, where it says:

> "For the word of God is living and active, sharper than any two-edged sword, piercing to the division of soul and of spirit, of joints and of marrow, and discerning the thoughts and intentions of the heart."

Jason continued as he said with a wobbly voice, "There is so much about his love in that little brown book you have. We need to discuss it more."

By now it was abundantly clear that the Holy Spirit was at work in the life of Aaqil. Jason knew that that little New Testament, all by itself had transformed the lives of thousands of people. Why, because of that scripture he just remembered, and now he could see it was happening right before his eyes.

"What do you think?"

"I think you are right" said Aaqil confidently.

But before he could say anything else, there was an announcement over the loudspeaker. Malaysia Airlines Flight 370 was officially missing! All communication stopped as the waiting families' joy turned to terror. For hours, Jason and Aaqil waited in the airport for some news. Their hearts were sinking more every hour as there failed to be any communication from the flight.

After several hours, the obvious outcome became real. Aaqil cleared his tears and looked right into Jason's eyes and cried out in agony, **"Please tell me that my precious wife and children are safe in the arms of a loving Jesus!!"**

Jason now has a serious dilemma. What should Jason tell Aaqil?

The majority of those in Christendom have been taught that if they had a chance, **even only once**, to accept the message of Christ **and rejected it**, that **they are bound for hell.** Yes, as we have previously discussed, the preachers of this say that God will deal with them justly, and maybe they will not have to suffer too bad, but the fact remains that you must come to terms with the fact that many of you are being told to believe that they are eternally separated from God, and must suffer at some level in hell.

But the purpose of this chapter is to consider if there is any truth to this. Will a loving God make people like this who have not accepted Jesus Christ as their Savior suffer again in what would perhaps even be a worse existence than what they experienced in their miserable lives on earth? We have been taught that God is love. This is the same God that King David, a Jew who lived centuries ago, described in this way:

> How precious is **your steadfast love**, O God! The children of mankind take refuge in the shadow of your wings. (Psalm 36:7)

> But as for me, my prayer is to you, O LORD. At an acceptable time, O God, in **the abundance of your steadfast love** answer me in your saving faithfulness. (Psalm 69:13)

> Who is a God like you, pardoning iniquity and passing over transgression for the remnant of his inheritance? He does not retain his anger forever, because he delights **in steadfast love.** (Micah 7:18)

The Apostle John, also a Jew, wrote this:

> Anyone who does not love does not know God, because **God is love**. (1 John 4:8)

In this is love, not that we have loved God but that **he loved us** and sent his Son to be the propitiation for our sins. (1 John 4:10)

Annihilationism

There is another group of Christians who believe that since **God is love**, he will not torment them forever, but that they will be **annihilated**. Where do they get this? Let's look at some of the Scriptures they use to support their argument. First, let's consider a few from the Old Testament:

He who sacrifices to any god, except to Yahweh only, **shall be utterly destroyed**. (Exodus 22:20)

The LORD will make the rain of your land powder. From heaven dust shall come down on you until **you are destroyed**. (Deuteronomy 28:24)

But the Hebrew word used here is *charam,* which more often means to **seclude, make accursed**, consecrate, or **forfeit!** They also use these passages:

But the wicked will **perish;** the enemies of the LORD are like the glory of the pastures; **they vanish**—like smoke they vanish away. (Psalm 37:20)

They are dead, they will not live; they are shades, they will not arise; to that end you have **visited them with destruction** and wiped out all remembrance of them. (Isaiah 26:14)

From the New Testament, we see:

As Moses lifted up the serpent in the wilderness, even so must the Son of Man be lifted up, that whoever believes in him **should not perish**, but have eternal life. For God so loved the world, that he gave his one and only Son, that whoever believes in him **should not perish**, but have eternal life. (John 3:14-16)

However, there is another passage which must be considered:

. . . he who is the blessed and only Sovereign, the King of kings and Lord of lords, **who alone has immortality**, who dwells in unapproachable light, whom no one has ever seen or can see. To him be honor and eternal dominion. Amen. (1 Tim 6:15-16 ESV)

William Fudge, who wrote the book: "The Fire that Consumes" wrote concerning Psalm 37:

In this psalm David defines die and destroy by a variety of figures from nature. The wicked will be like grass that withers or smoke that vanishes when they "die" and are "destroyed." These are not mere hollow hopes of Job's shallow and uninspired friends. They are the solemn promises of David as he speaks by the Holy Spirit (Matt 22:43; Acts 2:29–30). Those who trust in God might not see it happen now. But they are to wait patiently for the Lord's time, confident that he will bring his word to pass (vv. 7, 34). This psalm is surely instructive concerning the final fate of those who mock at God.[21]

But is Fudge correct in this? Is this instructive of the final fate of unbelievers? Now let's look at another passage:

> And do not fear those who **kill the body** but **cannot kill the soul**. Rather fear him who can **destroy both soul and body** in hell. (**Matthew 10:28 ESV**)

Once again, we see the indiscriminate use of a word which does **NOT** belong in our Bibles – **_hell._**

Notice the same passage from the **World English Bible.**

> Don't be afraid of those who kill the body, but are not able to kill the soul. Rather, fear him who is able to destroy both soul and body in **Gehenna.** (WEB)

Here we have a passage which I felt deserve special consideration especially considering that this is one of the most frequently used passages used by Annihilationists to prove that God does indeed destroy a person completely forever. William Fudge says of this passage:

> Our Lord's warning is plain. Man's power to kill stops with the body and the horizons of the present age. The death that humans inflict is not final, for God will **call forth the dead from the earth** and give the

---

[21] Fudge, Edward William. The Fire That Consumes: A Biblical and Historical Study of the Doctrine of Final Punishment, Third Edition (p. 55). Cascade Books, an imprint of Wipf and Stock Publishers. Kindle Edition.

righteous immortality. By contrast, God's ability to kill and destroy is limitless. It reaches deeper than the physical and extends beyond the present. God can kill both soul and body, both now and hereafter. We see that in Matthew's account, Jesus equates "kill" and "destroy," making them interchangeable. (emphasis mine)[22]

On the surface this sounds pretty good, but is this really consistent with the love of God? Is it possible that a God of love would actually call those judged adversely back to life after their "death" in order to kill them again? Does this make any sense?

In order to be specific and avoid confusion in this matter, we need to begin with a definition of the body, soul, and spirit as taken from Thayer's Greek Lexicon:

σῶμα
sōma (body)
Thayer Definition:
1) the body both of men or animals
    1a) a dead body or corpse
    1b) the living body
        1b1) of animals

ψυχή
psuchē (soul)
Thayer Definition:
1) breath
    1a) the breath of life
        1a1) the vital force which animates the body and shows itself in breathing

---

[22] Ibid p. 123

1a1a) of animals

1a1b) of men

1b) life

1c) that in which there is life

1c1) a living being, a living soul

2) the soul

2a)

2b) the (human) soul in so far as it is constituted that by the right use of the aids offered it by God it can attain its highest end and secure eternal blessedness, the soul regarded as a moral being designed for everlasting life

2c) the soul as an essence which differs from the body and is not dissolved by death (distinguished from other parts of the body)

πνεῦμα

pneuma

Thayer Definition:

2) the spirit, i.e. the vital principal by which the body is animated

2a) the rational spirit, the power by which the human being feels, thinks, decides

2b) the soul

3) a spirit, i.e. a simple essence, devoid of all or at least all grosser matter, and possessed of the power of knowing, desiring, deciding, and acting

3a) a life-giving spirit

3b) a human soul that has left the body

3c) a spirit higher than man but lower than God, i.e. an angel

3c1) used of demons, or evil spirits, who were conceived as inhabiting the bodies of men

3c2) the spiritual nature of Christ, higher than the highest angels and equal to God, the divine nature of Christ

Now what I think it is necessary to focus on here is the complexity of these words. It is important to realize that two of these three concepts are very much interrelated. In fact, the concept of spirit is so complex that Thayer devoted several columns of words to describe five definitions. I have not included the other three because they are irrelevant to this discussion.

But in Matthew 10:28, first we have the body. When you look at the definition here, we see that there is nothing special to report. We see that a body is just a body. It could be dead or alive.

But here is where it gets interesting. If we look at the last part of Matthew 10:28 it states:

". . . Rather fear him who can **destroy both soul and body** in hell (Gehenna).

Remember that earlier we noted that the Greek word for destroy is **apollumi.** As we stated, from Vine's expository dictionary: "The idea is not extinction, but ruin, loss, not of being, but of well-being."[23]

The context of this passage is important, and governs the reason for Jesus words here. Adam Clarke reports the context of this chapter very succinctly. Notice his words:

---

[23] Vines Expository Dictionary of New Testament Words, Fleming H. Revel Co. 1966 p. 302

Jesus calls, commissions, and names his twelve disciples, Mat 10:1-4. Gives them particular instructions relative to the objects of their ministry, Mat 10:5, Mat 10:6. Mode of preaching, etc., Mat 10:7-15. Foretells the afflictions and persecutions they would have to endure, and the support they should receive, Mat 10:16-25. **Cautions them against betraying his cause, in order to procure their personal safety, Mat 10:26-39.** And gives especial promises to those who should assist his faithful servants in the execution of their work, Mat 10:40-42.

In Matthew 10:28, Jesus was referencing the garbage dump outside of the city of Jerusalem. What Jesus was telling them was **not to worry about their personal safety** in all of the difficulties and persecutions they may face. God is all powerful and even though he is **capable** of destroying their body and soul in Gehenna, **he will not do so.** He goes on to show that **God will never forsake them.** He knows them so intimately that he knows the number of the hairs of their head. In the following verse, by use of an illustration he shows them how important they are.

Notice what follows:

Are not two sparrows sold for a penny? And not one of them will fall to the ground apart from your Father. But even the hairs of your head are all numbered. **Fear not,** therefore; you are of more value than many sparrows. **Matthew 10:29-30**

Therefore, any destruction of the souls on the part of anyone **is a reference to the ruination or loss of their well-being.** But such a loss is temporary.

No matter what, we must ask: How do we reconcile these passages? The Old Testament passages seem to state that the wicked would be destroyed. The first New Testament passage stated here says that by believing in Christ, we have "eternal" life. The second is saying that only God is immortal.

At first glance this argument that the wicked are permanently done away with seems very plausible. Let's look at some other passages about destruction and perishing.

Yahweh told Israel they would be destroyed and would perish. It is recorded by Moses:

"All these curses shall come upon you and pursue you and overtake you **till you are destroyed**, because you did not obey the voice of the LORD your God, to keep his commandments and his statutes that he commanded you. They shall be a sign and a wonder against you and your offspring forever. Because you did not serve the LORD your God with joyfulness and gladness of heart, because of the abundance of all things, therefore you shall serve your enemies whom the LORD will send against you, in hunger and thirst, in nakedness, and lacking everything. And he will put a yoke of iron on your neck **until he has destroyed you**. The LORD will bring a nation against you from far away, from the end of the earth, swooping down like the eagle, a nation whose language you do not understand, a hard-faced nation who shall not respect the old or show mercy to the young. It shall eat the offspring of your cattle and the fruit of your ground, **until you are destroyed**; it also shall not leave you grain, wine, or oil, the increase of your herds or the young of your flock, **until they have caused you to perish.** (Deuteronomy 28:45-51)

Yes, no question about it, Yahweh sent the Chaldeans into Judah to destroy it. Now let's look at a second example:

In his days, Nebuchadnezzar king of Babylon came up, and Jehoiakim became his servant for three years. Then he turned and rebelled against him. And the LORD sent against him bands of the Chaldeans and bands of the Syrians and bands of the Moabites and bands of the Ammonites, **and sent them against Judah to destroy it**, according to the word of the LORD that he spoke by his servants the prophets. (2 Kings 24:1-2)

These cases appear to be pretty clearly stated. However, we must ask: **In these cases, were they permanently destroyed, or were they temporarily destroyed?**

But the book of Isaiah also states:

The righteous perish, and no one lays it to heart. Merciful men are taken away, and no one considers that the righteous is taken away from the evil. (Isaiah 57:1)

The righteous perish? Really? Permanently? I don't think so!!

The Hebrew word for perish is *abad* which could mean to annililate, but certainly not in the above passage. More often it means to wander away, break, fail, lose, or be undone.

Does this evidence not indicate that **the meaning of perish in the above passages is temporary?** And Jesus himself proclaimed:

> Most certainly I tell you, unless a grain of wheat falls into the earth **and dies**, it remains by itself alone. **But if it dies, it bears much fruit.** (John 12:24)

Did the grain that died in this passage really die **a complete destruction?** If so, how could it bear "much fruit?"

But even in destruction there is always something that comes out of it. With fire it is ash and gas that remain. When a plant is killed by being pulled from the ground, its seeds are available to start new life.

One of the most fascinating cases of this is the story of the Redwood tree, the largest tree in the world. It is common for fire to break out in these forests. But when God created the Redwood tree, he did something fascinating. He gave these trees a very thick, fire-resistant bark. Their tiny cones, which lay on the forest floor, open only after a fire. Isn't that amazing? So, after every fire in the redwood forest, **new life came forth!** The natives of the area used to use this to their advantage and would purposely burn out the forest on occasion in order to keep it cleaned out and start more of these magnificent trees growing. It shows that even **after destruction** by one of the most complete entities of God, which is fire, **new life springs forth!**

The Greek word for destruction is απολλυμι. The English spelling is **apollumi.**

I will **emphasize again** the fact that in Vine's Expository Dictionary of Biblical Words we find: "The idea is not extinction but ruin, loss, not of being, but of well-being.[24]

This is clear from its use. . .

Vine gives several examples of this. Here are a few uses of **apollumi.**

> And no one puts new wine into old wineskins. If he does, the new wine will burst the skins and it will be spilled, and the skins will be **destroyed.** (Luke 5:37)

The wineskin was ruined, **not permanently destroyed.**

> What man of you, having a hundred sheep, if he has lost one of them, does not leave the ninety-nine in the open country, and go after the one that is **lost**, until he finds it? (Luke 15:4)

The sheep was lost, **not permanently destroyed**.

---

[24] Vines Expository Dictionary of New Testament Words, Fleming H. Revel Co. 1966 p. 302

For this my son was dead, and is alive again; he was **lost**, and is found.' And they began to celebrate. (Luke 15:24)

The son was **lost, but now was found**.

For God so loved the world, that he gave his only Son, that whoever believes in him should **not perish but have eternal life**. (John 3:16)

In other words, "should not be ruined, but have eternal life," or as Young's Literal Translation shows:

for God did so love the world, that His Son--the only begotten--He gave, that everyone who is believing in him **may not perish, but may have life age-during.** (John 3:16)

This indicates a slightly different meaning for eternal. We will have more on this later.

We see in the book of Hebrews that after we die, we perish from the earth, we go to the judgment.

And just as it is appointed for man to die **ONCE**, and after that comes judgment, (Hebrews 9:27)

If we look at this passage, it indicates that man only dies **ONCE.** Do you see **the power of this** statement? In effect man only perishes in human bodily form. He does NOT perish completely. If he were to be annihilated, **then he would die TWICE!** No! but after that death comes the judgment, and as Jesus stated, this judgment does not apply to those who believe, but becomes punishment for those who do not believe. Notice his words:

> For the Father judges no one, but he has given all judgment to the Son, that all may honor the Son, even as they honor the Father. He who doesn't honor the Son doesn't honor the Father who sent him. "Most certainly I tell you, he who hears my word, and believes him who sent me, has eternal life, and **doesn't come into judgment, but has passed out of death into life.** Most certainly, I tell you, the hour comes, and now is, when the dead will hear the Son of God's voice; and those who hear will live. For as the Father has life in himself, even so he gave to the Son also to have life in himself. He also gave him **authority to execute judgment,** because he is a son of man. (John 5:22-27 WEB)

Does this evidence we have just examined **debunk** the idea that God will annihilate the wicked? **It appears to do just that.** It also begs the question, is there really any sense of victory for our Lord if 2/3 or more of all those living will literally be annihilated? We will have more to say on this concept later?

Looking back, now we must consider the question: What about that passage in 1 Timothy 6:15-16? Doesn't this passage also indicate that there is no immortality beyond God? Let's look at it again:

> . . . he who is the blessed and only Sovereign, the King of kings and Lord of lords, **who alone has immortality**, who dwells in unapproachable light, whom no one has ever seen or can see. To him be

honor and eternal dominion. Amen. (1 Tim 6:15-16 ESV)

Regarding this passage, Commentator Albert Barnes said this:

Who only hath immortality *brilliant* - The word here - αθανασία athanasia - properly means "exemption from death," and seems to mean that God, **in his own nature, enjoys a perfect and certain exemption from death**. Creatures have immortality only as they derive it from him, and of course are dependent on him for it. He has it by his very nature, and it is in his case underived, and he cannot be deprived of it. It is one of the essential attributes of his being, that he will always exist, and that death cannot reach him; compare the expression in John 5:26, "The Father hath life in himself," and the notes on that passage. (emphasis mine)

Yes! God alone **by his nature** is immortal. But as the *thank you!* eternal omnipotent God, he has the power to give life to his creation as he desires. Unquestionably, concerning this matter, **it is up to God**. We will also address this in the next chapter.

But the Scriptures have more to say concerning this.

Now let's consider the following:

For the **grace of God** has appeared, **bringing salvation for ALL people,** training us to renounce ungodliness and worldly passions, and to live self-controlled, upright, and godly lives in the present age, waiting for our blessed hope, the appearing of the glory of our great God and Savior Jesus Christ, who gave himself for us to redeem us from all lawlessness and to purify for himself a people for his own possession who are zealous for good works. Declare these things; exhort and rebuke with all authority. Let no one disregard you. (Titus 2:11-15)

Therefore, as one trespass led to condemnation for **ALL** men, so one act of righteousness leads to justification and life **FOR ALL** men. (Romans 5:18)

Are there any conditions attached to Paul's statements here?

Some have answered that just because he does not say there are conditions does not mean that they do not exist. **But why would he say it?** Wouldn't he end this phrase by saying "so one act of righteousness leads to justification and life for **all men who put their trust in him in this life**?

Considering the terrible consequences of this by those who promulgate the doctrine of eternal torment or annihilation, I would think that Paul would want to be **crystal clear** on this point! But instead Paul stated:

For the gifts and the calling of God are irrevocable. For just as you were at one time disobedient to God but now have received mercy because of their disobedience, so they too have now been disobedient in order that by the mercy shown to you they also may now receive mercy. For God has consigned **ALL** to

disobedience, that he (may) have mercy on **ALL.**
(Romans 11:29-32)

Doesn't this passage make it clear that **ALL** are disobedient, but that God will nonetheless, also have mercy on **ALL**?

May

Some have reasoned this way concerning Paul's statement: "All" does not have a singular meaning in scripture or in common language. There is no reason to think that all should mean the same here in both instances. Are not those who belong to Christ God's purchased possession?

But if we look closely at this statement, **are we really** going to try to state that in Romans 11: 32 above that Paul is going to use the term "all" two times in the same sentence and the same context and **have a different meaning in each case?** If he did, he would surely explain it.

It is true that the church is Christ's purchased possession. (Acts 20:28) This is not being ignored by Paul.

But Paul **does mean** the same here in both cases. He puts together an entire discourse on the disobedience of man in Romans chapter 3, and shows how **ALL are worthless!**

> What then? Are we Jews any better off? No, not at all. For we have already charged **that all, both Jews and Greeks, are under sin,** as it is written: "**None is righteous, no, not one;** no one understands; no one seeks for God. **All have turned aside**; together they **have become worthless**; no one does good, not even one." (Romans 3:9-12)

Those who believe are justified, **YES!** But Paul is **NOT** declaring **ALL** to be righteous.

Notice his words:

> But now the righteousness of God has been manifested apart from the law, although the Law and the Prophets bear witness to it— the righteousness of God through faith in Jesus Christ **for all who believe.** For there is no distinction: for all have sinned and fall short of the glory of God, and are **justified by his grace as a gift, through the redemption that is in Christ Jesus,** (Romans 3:21-24)

The purpose of Paul's statement is **NOT** to deny the doctrine of justification here. **Those who believe have been saved, YES!** Praise God for this. But let us once again notice the words of Paul in the following verse. He said:

> For God has consigned **ALL** to disobedience, that he may have mercy on **ALL.** (Romans 11:32)

Must we say that because **ALL** are not saved, that God cannot show mercy to **ALL?** In Romans chapter 11, Paul is doing a discourse on his countrymen, the people of Israel. He is showing here that God **ABSOLUTELY WILL** show mercy on them. This is exactly what he has done throughout the entire Old Testament. After judgment **comes mercy.** We see it **over and over again.** Paul says almost the same thing to the Corinthian Church:

For as by a man came death, by a man has come also the resurrection of the dead. For as in Adam **ALL** die, so also in Christ shall **ALL** be made alive. But each in his own order: Christ the firstfruits, then at his coming those who belong to Christ.
(1 Corinthians 15: 21-23)

Is there something ambiguous about this? Read verse 22 again. What is it saying? Once again, I ask: Does "all" have **two different meanings within the same sentence?**

Some have objected by saying that "Romans 9 tells us that God will have mercy on the Jews first, then the Gentiles, but only if they accept Christ in this life. But that is **not** what he is saying. We know this for a fact, because the passage very clearly states that **ALL will** be made alive after death. *to be judged.*

Notice that in verse 22, Paul states that "as in Adam **ALL** die, so also in Christ shall **ALL** be made alive." Now just think about this statement for a moment. There is **no question** that **ALL** have died as a result of Adam's transgression. (This is a reference to spiritual death, but this is beyond the scope of this discussion. See Appendix II) Is this power **greater** than the power of Christ to make **ALL** alive? Paul did not make any conditions in his statement for a reason! The power of Christ is **absolutely supreme**. He is "our great God and Savior" as Paul told Titus (Titus 2:13).

In his book: ***The Inescapable Love of God,*** the author, Thomas Talbott makes an excellent point concerning two related passages: Romans 11:32 and 1 Corinthians 15:22. Note his words:

This is typically Pauline. In the eleventh chapter of Romans, he again wrote, "For God has imprisoned all in disobedience so that he may be merciful to all" (11: 32); and in the fifteenth chapter of 1 Corinthians, he also wrote, "for as all die in Adam, so all will be made alive in Christ" (15: 22). In each of these texts, we encounter a contrast between two universal statements, **and in each case the first "all" determines the scope of the second.** Accordingly, when Paul asserted in Romans 5: 18 that Christ's one "act of righteousness leads to justification and life for all," he evidently had in mind every descendant of Adam who stands under the judgment of condemnation; when he insisted in Romans 11: 32 that God is merciful to all, he had in mind every human whom God has "shut up to," or has "imprisoned in," disobedience; and when he asserted in 1 Corinthians 15: 22 that "all will be made alive in Christ," he had in mind everyone who dies in the first Adam. **The grammatical evidence here seems utterly decisive;** you can reject it only if you are prepared to reject what is right there before your eyes. And though there seems to be no shortage of those who are prepared to do just that, the arguments one actually encounters have every appearance, it seems to me, of a grasping at straws. (emphasis mine)[25]

Talbott's point is absolutely correct. Here we have evidence that is utterly decisive.

---

[25] Talbott, Thomas. The Inescapable Love of God (pp. 55-56). Cascade Books, an Imprint of Wipf and Stock Publishers. Kindle Edition.

Additionally, the passage we quoted earlier in Hebrews 9:27 makes it clear that every single one of us has to face judgment when we die. There is no question that **there will be a price to pay** according to the justice of a loving God. But the fact remains that God is love and he will be merciful to **ALL.** None will get fully what they deserve! Why? Because we deserve nothing. But praise God for the precious blood of Christ!

That **ALL** spoken of by Paul in Romans 11:32 does not mean that he will torment **SOME** or **MOST** for eternity. Note Paul's words to the church at Colossae.

> For in him all the fullness of God was pleased to dwell, and through him **to reconcile to himself ALL things,** whether on earth or in heaven, making peace by the blood of his cross. (Colossians 1:19-20)

How could Paul be clearer than he is in this passage? These words are given with the conviction of **the power of Christ's blood to redeem!**

Paul also told Timothy:

> This is good, and it is pleasing in the sight of God our Savior, **who desires all people** to be saved and to come to the knowledge of the truth. For there is one God, and there is one mediator between God and men, the man Christ Jesus, who gave himself **as a ransom for all**, which is the testimony given at the proper time. (1 Timothy 2:3-6 ESV)

Yet, as powerful as this statement is, the English Standard Version has actually **watered it down** from the original

Greek! Young's Literal Translation **shows the real power**
of this more clearly. *Then would will or will be*

> for this *is* right and acceptable before God our
> Saviour, **who doth WILL ALL men to be saved**,
> and to come to the full knowledge of the truth; for
> one *is* God, one also *is* mediator of God and of men,
> the man Christ Jesus, who did give himself a ransom
> **for all**--the testimony in its own times— (1 Timothy
> 2:3-6 YLT)

The Greek word translated above as "desires" and "wills" in
these two renderings is θελει pronounced *thaylay*. The
root word is θελω. According to Thayer's Greek Lexicon this
word means "to be resolved or determined, to purpose."[26]

So, the question here is this: If God is resolved to do
something, **is it possible to thwart that will?** If God is
determined that something will happen, **will it happen or
not?** I find it utterly amazing that so many people will state
that God is **absolutely sovereign**, and that he is
absolutely omnipotent, but at the same time will say
that he **does not get what he wants** in this case. Does
that make any sense?

Before we end this chapter, let's look at one more
passage written by Paul:

> Therefore God has highly exalted him and bestowed
> on him the name that is above every name, so that at

---

[26] Thayer's Greek-English, Lexicon Hendrickson Publishers, 2014
p.285

the name of Jesus **EVERY** knee should bow, **in heaven and on earth** and **UNDER** the earth, and **EVERY** tongue confess that Jesus Christ is Lord, to the glory of God the Father. (Philippians 2:9-11)

Paul got this from Isaiah 45.

By myself I have sworn; from my mouth has gone out in righteousness a word that shall not return: 'To me **EVERY** knee shall bow, **EVERY** tongue shall swear allegiance.' "Only in the LORD, it shall be said of me, are righteousness and strength; to him shall come and be ashamed all who were incensed against him. In the LORD **ALL** the offspring of Israel shall be justified and shall glory." (Isaiah 45:23-25)

The prophet Isaiah was the **secretary** here. **God was the author**. Paul reiterated this in Romans 11: 26, and 27 when he wrote:

And in this way **all Israel will be saved**, as it is written, "The Deliverer will come from Zion, he will banish ungodliness from Jacob"; "and this will be my covenant with them when I take away their sins." (Romans 11:26-27)

But now we see that the Apostle Paul has told the Philippian Christians this same thing. We will examine this passage in great detail in the next chapter.

Chapter Seven

What is that which is Truly Eternal?

I love the Toy Story series by Disney Pixar. I am not alone, as I am sure that other adults in the movie theater will watch the scenes with me and experience the full range of emotions from laughing out loud to weeping as the problems of the characters unfold. One of the fascinating characters in that series is the astronaut Buzz Lightyear. His favorite catchphrase was *"To Infinity and Beyond!"* Catchy, isn't it?

But in actuality, this phrase is a contradiction in terms because we define outer space as a place that is infinite, a place that has no end. Infinity already has the meaning of endlessness, so while that cute little catch phrase of Buzz Lightyear may sound good, it truly is meaningless. A similar case is the phrase "Eternity and Beyond." Whereas infinity carries with it the meaning of space, eternity carries with it the meaning of time. As we look around, we see that there have been many things named as such. It also sounds good, but the meaning is just not there.

But the question we need to ask now is **a very important one** to the subject at hand. When we read the words *eternal* or *everlasting* in the Bible, can we have confidence that the meaning is just that?

If you do a search of the word *eternal* in the **English Standard Bible**, you will find that it appears 73 times in the Bible. Add to that the word *everlasting*, we find that it appears 67 times. This totals 140 times.

What about the phrase, *"from everlasting to everlasting?"* Does that phrase make sense? Doesn't the word *everlasting* already carry with it the connotation of *eternal?* If we would want to say the exact same thing, in simpler terms, would we not just say it is *eternal?*

Yet you will find that exact phrase in the Old Testament of the **English Standard Bible** six times!

Here are the verses:

> Blessed be the LORD, the God of Israel, from **everlasting to everlasting**!" Then all the people said, "Amen!" and praised the LORD. (1 Chronicles 16:36)

> Then the Levites, Jeshua, Kadmiel, Bani, Hashab-neiah, Sherebiah, Hodiah, Shebaniah, and Pethahiah, said, "Stand up and bless the LORD your God from **everlasting to everlasting**. Blessed be your glorious name, which is exalted above all blessing and praise. (Nehemiah 9:5)

> Blessed be the LORD, the God of Israel, from **everlasting to everlasting**! Amen and Amen. (Psalm 41:13)

> Before the mountains were brought forth, or ever you had formed the earth and the world, from

everlasting to everlasting you are God. (Psalm 90:2)

But the steadfast love of the LORD is from *everlasting to everlasting* on those who fear him, and his righteousness to children's children, (Psalm 103:17)

Blessed be the LORD, the God of Israel, from *everlasting to everlasting*! And let all the people say, "Amen!" Praise the LORD! (Psalm 106:48)

But now that we think of it, we can look at one way that it does make sense. Why? Didn't God create the universe? So, it had a beginning, but we believe it to be **everlasting**. So, from that standpoint, that phrase could make sense. But the verses above are **NOT** speaking of the creation, **they are speaking about God.** In effect it is saying that God is from everlasting past to everlasting future. But if we say that God is eternal, that covers it.

So, since this phrase speaks of God, we need to look closer at this word **eternal.**

If we look up the word everlasting in the **Miriam Webster Dictionary,** we find it says:

1: lasting or enduring through all time: <u>eternal</u>

But wait a minute: If we look up eternal we find:

1 a: having infinite duration: everlasting

Then if we look up infinite we find:

1: extending indefinitely: <u>endless</u> <*infinite* space>
2: immeasurably or inconceivably great or extensive
: <u>inexhaustible</u> <*infinite* patience>

134

3: subject to no limitation or external determination

Interesting isn't it? From these definitions we can determine that eternal is a little different from everlasting, and infinite is more like eternal.

Now if we look up the word **eternal** in **Young's Literal Translation,** we find **only _two instances_** of the word:

> A habitation *is* the **eternal** God, And beneath *are* arms age-during. And He casteth out from thy presence the enemy, and saith, `Destroy!' (Deuteronomy 33:27)

> for the invisible things of Him from the creation of the world, by the things made being understood, are plainly seen, both His **eternal** power and Godhead-- to their being inexcusable; (Romans 1:20)

And if we look up **everlasting,** we find **_only one instance_** of the word:

> messengers also, those who did not keep their own principality, but did leave their proper dwelling, to a judgment of a great day, in bonds **everlasting**, under darkness He hath kept, (Jude 1:6)

Once again, we see a slight difference. These two English words have slightly different meanings. But there is also something more important. **The word eternal is only used in reference to God. He alone is eternal.**

We have a similar outcome if we check Rotherham's Emphasized Bible. Only *one instance of either word* is considered:

For, the unseen things of him, from a world's creation, by the things made, being perceived, are clearly seen, even his **eternal** power and divinity, — to the end they should be without excuse; (Romans 1:20)

Now let's look at Deuteronomy 33:27.

Rotherham's Emphasized Bible translates it as:

Above, is the God of aforetime, And, beneath, are the Arms of the ages, — So he driveth before thee the foe, And doth say—Destroy! (Deuteronomy 33:27)

So unquestionably, we see slight differences in these words. I would now like to explain why this fact is *one of great significance* to Christians.

When we consider the question of **eternal torment**, as expounded by most of Christendom, we need to know if it *really is eternal or not,* correct?

To get a correct understanding of these usages, we need to go back to the original languages in which the Bible was written. The Hebrew word translated as "eternal" in the Old Testament of our Bibles is "**olam**."

But the word used here in Young's Literal Translation **only one time describing the eternity of God** is the Hebrew word **qêdəmâh,** pronounced kayd'-maw; described in Strong's Hebrew dictionary as:

from 6923; the front, of place (absolutely, the fore part, relatively the East) or time (antiquity); often used adverbially (before, anciently, eastward):— aforetime, ancient (time), before, east (end, part, side,

-ward), eternal, [idiom] ever(-lasting), forward, old, past.[27]

But both of the above translations use the word *eternal* in Romans 1:20. We just looked at it above in the New Testament. It describes God's power and divinity as *eternal.*

Here in Romans 1:20, we observe something that is very important. We see a word that is *only used twice* in the New Testament. Since the New Testament was originally written in Greek, that word is αιδιος. pronounced *eye'deeows*.

Thayer's Greek Lexicon defines this word as eternal, everlasting.[28]

The other usage is in Jude 6:

> messengers also, those who did not keep their own principality, but did leave their proper dwelling, to a judgment of a great day, in bonds *everlasting,* under darkness He hath kept, (Jude 1:6)

But what about all of those other words that are translated as eternal and everlasting in the Bible?

Do they really mean eternal or not?

Do they really mean everlasting or not?

---

[27] Strong, James (2011-05-14). Strong's Hebrew Dictionary of the Bible (Strong's Dictionary) (Kindle Locations 26360-26362). Miklal Software Solutions, Inc.. Kindle Edition.

[28] Thayer's Greek-English Lexicon, p.14

These are important questions if we are to get to the truth of Scripture. So, let's look at some of these. First, we will look in the New Testament.

What about this passage which we hear often concerning eternal torment?

> I was a stranger and you did not welcome me, naked and you did not clothe me, sick and in prison and you did not visit me.' Then they also will answer, saying, 'Lord, when did we see you hungry or thirsty or a stranger or naked or sick or in prison, and did not minister to you?' Then he will answer them, saying, 'Truly, I say to you, as you did not do it to one of the least of these, you did not do it to me.' And these will go away into **eternal punishment**, but the righteous into **eternal life.** (Matthew 25:43-46)

In his book: "The Fire that Consumes: A Biblical and Historical Study of the Doctrine of Final Punishment, Third Edition," Edward William Fudge says this about this passage:

> Jesus concludes his Parable of the Sheep and Goats with the statement that the wicked "will go away to eternal punishment, but the righteous to eternal life." Jesus attaches the adjective "eternal" to the word "punishment" (kolasis), a noun of the class that names the result of an action. Both the life and the punishment pertain to the age to come, and are therefore "eternal" in the qualitative sense. This book attempts to show that both the life and the punishment are also unending, and are therefore "eternal" in the quantitative sense. This "punishment"

can encompass a broad spectrum of degrees of conscious suffering based on varying degrees of guilt, but the essence of this "punishment" is the total and everlasting dissolution and extinction of the person punished (Matt 10:28; 2 Thess 1:9).[29]

So, Fudge has made it clear that it is his aim to show in his book that the eternal punishment means that those so judged will suffer total destruction, never to be heard from again. But a closer examination reveals some **problems with this assessment.**

The question comes about in verse 46 where it says: "these will go away into **eternal punishment**, but the righteous into **eternal life."** The key to getting the correct understanding of this verse is to nail down the exact meaning of the original language words that are translated here with two words.

Those two most important words are *eternal,* and *punishment.* We need the exact meaning of *both of these words* to get the proper meaning of this passage.

The Greek word for eternal used here in this verse is αιωνιον, which has as its root word αιωνιος. **pronounced aionios.** This word is also defined in Thayer's Greek Lexicon as: "without beginning or end."[30] That sounds like

---

[29] Fudge, Edward William. The Fire That Consumes: A Biblical and Historical Study of the Doctrine of Final Punishment, Third Edition (p. 38-39). Cascade Books, an imprint of Wipf and Stock Publishers. Kindle Edition.

[30] Thayer's Greek-English Lexicon p. 20

a good definition doesn't it? But if that is true, then why have the writers of the New Testament chosen a different word to describe God who is the only one mentioned in the Bible as being "eternal?"

Good question! But if we look closer at this Greek word, we see some indications as to why. First of all, this Greek word αιωνιος **(aionios)** is derived from the Greek word αιων (aion) from which we see translated as *age* in the English Standard Bible, the NIV, and almost all of the newer Versions. Here is an example of the word αιων (aion).

> And he said to them, "Truly, I say to you, there is no one who has left house or wife or brothers or parents or children, for the sake of the kingdom of God, who will not receive many times more in this time, and in the **age** (αιωι) to come eternal (αιωνιον) life."(Luke 18:29-30)

Do you see the problem here? Luke is speaking of the age to come. If it is an age that is yet to come, then this word **cannot** mean eternal! Eternal is not something which is coming. Eternal means that *it is and always was* there. Yes, that is because the translated word here at the end of the verse has as its root word αιων which means "age."

It appears that there is a translation error here because knowing this, the verse **does not make sense!**

Let's look at some other renderings of this passage. These translations that I am using here are **over 100 years old**.

So, this is not something new. We are looking at **well-established scholarship** in translation!

First from **Young's Literal Translation**:

> he said to them, `Verily I say to you, that there is not one who left house, or parents, or brothers, or wife, or children, for the sake of the reign of God,   who may not receive back manifold more in this time, and in the coming age, life **age-during**.' (Luke 18:29-30)

Now from **Rotherham's Emphasized Bible:**

> And, he, said unto them—Verily, I say unto you—No one, is there, who hath left—house, or wife, or brethren, or parents, or children,—for the sake of the kingdom of God; who shall in anywise not receive manifold in this season, and, in the age that is coming, life **age-abiding**. (Luke 18:29-30)

Now let's look at one more, this time the **1912 Weymouth New Testament**:

> "I solemnly tell you," replied Jesus, "that there is no one who has left house or wife, or brothers or parents or children, for the sake of God's Kingdom, who shall not certainly receive many times as much in this life, and in the age that is coming the **Life of the Ages**." (Luke 18:29-30)

These translations **must be better on this verse** than the English Standard Version because they actually make sense!

In Thayer's Greek Lexicon we find that the meaning of the Greek word αιων as used by the Greek authors is:

1. Age, a human lifetime, life itself.
2. An unbroken age, perpetuity of time, eternity.
   Thus, we can see that this word is used in the New Testament in two ways. First, as an "age," that can be the length of "a human lifetime." Second, we see that it could be used as an "unbroken age" of an _**indefinite duration**_ of time, _**up to**_ perpetuity.[31]

But in order for us to really understand how this has been translated, we need to look at more examples.

The Hebrew word _**"olam"**_ has been translated in the Greek Septuagint as the Greek word _**"aionios"**_ in the Old Testament on a number of occasions. **The Greek Septuagint** was a Greek translation of the Hebrew Scriptures which was started almost **2300 years ago**, somewhere between 100-300 BC prior to the time of Christ and taking over 100 years to complete. In fact, it is often said that Christ quoted from the Septuagint. We see it today referred to as LXX to denote the seventy Jewish scholars who translated it from the Torah. It is still widely used today and often consulted to confirm word meanings from the Greek.

First let's look at how this word (_**aionios**_) is used in the New Testament by the translators. Here are four renderings of Matthew 25:41. First from the English Standard Version:

---

[31] Ibid. p. 19

"Then he will say to those on his left, 'Depart from me, you cursed, into the **eternal fire** prepared for the devil and his angels.

(Rotherham) Then, will he say unto those also, on his left hand: Depart ye from me, accursed ones! Into *the age-abiding fire*, which hath been prepared for the adversary and his messengers;

(WNT) "Then will He say to those at His left, '"Begone from me, with the curse resting upon you, into *the Fire of the Ages*, which has been prepared for the Devil and his angels.

(YLT) Then shall he say also to those on the left hand, Go ye from me, the cursed, to *the fire, the age-during*, that hath been prepared for the Devil and his messengers;

Do you notice that the meaning of this word translated as eternal in the ESV seems to be different in the other three translations? That is because these words *aionios* have the Greek word *aion* as the root word. And we know that the correct rendering of *aion* is "age."

Now we will look at four renderings of Luke 18:30.

(ESV) who will not receive many times more in this time, and *in the age to come eternal life."*

(Rotherham) who shall in anywise not receive manifold in this season, and*, in the age that is coming, life age-abiding.*

(Weymouth NT) who shall not certainly receive many times as much in this life, and *in the age that is coming the Life of the Ages*."

(YLT) who may not receive back manifold more in this time, and in the coming age, *life age-during*.'

Now let's look at an Old Testament passage that use the Greek *aionios* in the Greek Septuagint and *olam* in the Hebrew. Note these translations of Exodus 40:15.

(ESV) and anoint them, as you anointed their father, that they may serve me as priests. And their anointing shall admit them to a *perpetual priesthood throughout their generations*."

(KJV) And thou shalt anoint them, as thou didst anoint their father, that they may minister unto me in the priest's office: for their anointing shall surely be an *everlasting priesthood throughout their generations.*

(GNB) Then anoint them, just as you anointed their father, so that they can serve me as priests. This anointing will make them priests *for all time to come*."

(Rotherham) and shalt anoint them as thou didst anoint their father, and they shall minister as priests unto me,—so shall their anointing remain to them for an *age-abiding priesthood, to their generations.*

(YLT) and anointed them as thou hast anointed their father, and they have acted as priests to Me, and their anointing hath been to be to them for a priesthood *age-during, to their generations.'*

Which of these translations make the most sense? To say that the Jewish Priesthood is *perpetual or everlasting* does not mean the same as that it lasts *throughout their* generations (a shorter time). This is a contradiction in terms.

Let's look at one more set of comparisons. This will entail Daniel 12:2,3, which speaks of the resurrection. First notice how this passage is translated in the English Standard Version:

> And many of those who sleep in the dust of the earth shall awake, some to *everlasting life*, and some to shame and *everlasting contempt*. And those who are wise shall shine like the brightness of the sky above; and those who turn many to righteousness, like the stars *forever and ever*. (Daniel 12:2-3)

Now notice how it is translated in the Rotherham's Emphasized Bible:

> and, many of the sleepers in the dusty ground, shall awake,—these, shall be to *age-abiding life*, but, those, to reproach, and *age-abiding abhorrence*; and, they who make wise, shall shine like the shining of the expanse,—and, they who bring the many to righteousness, like the stars to times *age-abiding and beyond*. (Daniel 12:2-3)

Now notice Young's Literal Translation:

> `And the multitude of those sleeping in the dust of the ground do awake, some to life *age-during*, and some

to reproaches--to *abhorrence age-during*. And those teaching do shine as the brightness of the expanse, and those justifying the multitude as stars to *the age and forever*. (Daniel 12:2-3)

The difference becomes especially apparent in the Rotherham and Young's translations at the end of verse three. Notice the words:

like the stars to times *age-abiding and beyond*. (Rotherham)

the multitude as stars to *the age and forever*. (Young's)

Do you notice the difference between the words used? Rotherham's describes it as *age-abiding*, and then adds *and beyond*! This shows that age-abiding **does not** mean forever!

This passage shows the difference very plainly. The ESV simply says *forever and ever*. But since forever means never ending, we do not need the words *and ever* after forever. It really does not make sense. **Isn't this** sort of like Buzz Lightyear saying **"to infinity and beyond?"**

To further emphasize this point, notice how Jonah described his being in the belly of the great fish:

The waters closed in over me to take my life; the deep surrounded me; weeds were wrapped about my head at the roots of the mountains. I went down to the land whose bars *closed upon me forever*; yet you brought up my life from the pit, O LORD my God. (Jonah 2:5-6)

Here is a quote from John Wesley Hanson's book: *Aion-Aionios*:

If Jonah could say, "Out of the belly of hell cried I, earth with her bars was about me forever," – if he was, as he says he was, in "hell forever," when **only three days** in the fish, is it not evident that the word **does not of itself** signify an unlimited duration, and is it not further evident that when we see it applied to the consequences of sin we must give it a meaning that shall harmonize with the Divine character, and the nature of just punishment? Defining it thus, who can give one reason for understanding it as meaning endless? Considering who inflicts punishment, it is morally more absurd to give to everlasting the meaning of endless when applied to it, than it is mathematically absurd to say that Jonah's forever – 72 hours – was literally endless.

If Canaan was to pass from the possession of the Jews; if the hills were to be melted, and the priesthood of Aaron to end; the Jewish law to cease; the mountains to be destroyed; Gehazi's leprosy no longer to last; the bondmen's chains to be melted; Abraham to lose possession of his land; Jerusalem to be destroyed, and Jonah to remain in the fish **only three days when all were to be everlasting**, eternal, forever – what conceivable reason is there for supposing that punishment shall last forever, when only the same qualifying words are applied to it?[32]

what of *[handwritten note]*

[32] Hanson, John (2011-09-30). Aion-Aionios (Kindle Locations 1601-1606). Tentmaker Ministries & Publications, Inc.. Kindle Edition.

There are many more examples of how these words are misused by the translators. Hanson further expounds on this in the following excerpt:

Canon Farrar observes:143 "Thus in the Old Testament aion, aionios and many such varieties of expression (as eis aiona aionos) (apaiona kai eti, in saeculum et ultra, 'forever and beyond!') are in our version rendered 'forever,' or 'forever and ever'; but so far from necessarily implying endlessness, they are used of many Jewish ordinances **which ceased centuries ago,** such as the sprinkling of the lintel at the Passover (Exodus 12:24); the Aaronic priesthood and its institutions (Exodus 29:9, 40:15; Leviticus 3:17; Numbers 18:19); the inheritance given to Caleb (Joshua 14:9); Solomon's temple (1 Kings 8:13); the period of a slave's life (Deuteronomy 15:17; Job 41:4); the burning of the fire upon the altar ('The fire shall ever be burning upon the altar; it shall never go out,' Leviticus 6:13, etc.); and the leprosy of Gehazi (2 Kings 5:27). How purely figurative these phrases are, may be seen by such passages as the following: 'The land thereof shall become burning pitch; it shall not be quenched night or day; the smoke thereof shall go up forever' (Isaiah 34:10).

And so fully is this a recognized idiom that in Deuteronomy 23:3, 6, we find 'forever' put side by side with 'till the tenth generation'; and though it is added 'thou shalt not seek their peace and prosperity forever,' yet of the very Moabites and Ammonites, of whom this is spoken, we find a prophecy of peace and comfort in Jeremiah 48:47, 49:6. That the adjective aionios is applied to some things which are 'endless' does not, of course, for one moment prove that the word itself meant 'endless,' and to introduce this rendering into many passages would be utterly impossible and absurd. To translate it in a few passages by 'everlasting,' when in the large majority of passages it is rendered 'eternal,' is a purely wanton and arbitrary variation, which unhappily occurs in one and the same verse (Matthew 25:46)."[33]

Now as I stated earlier, In Thayer's Greek Lexicon we find that the meaning of the Greek word αιων as used by the Greek authors is:

Age, a human lifetime, life itself. An unbroken age, perpetuity of time, eternity.[20]

Thus, we can see that this word is used in the New Testament in two ways. First, as an "age," that can be the length of "a human lifetime." Second, we see that it could be used as an "unbroken age" *lasting for a long period of time, up to perpetuity.*

Here is a good illustration that shows the meaning of this word. If we look at Luke's Gospel account we find:

He will be great and will be called the Son of the Most High. And the Lord God will give to him the throne of his father David, and he will reign over the house of Jacob *forever* (αιων), and of his kingdom there will be no end." (Luke 1:32 -33)

---

[33] Ibid.(Locations 1607-1624)

But in Paul's writings we find that the forever of this verse is **_limited._** Notice the words:

> For "God has put all things in subjection under his feet." But when it says, "all things are put in subjection," it is plain that he is excepted who put all things in subjection under him. When all things are subjected to him, then the Son himself will also be subjected to him who put all things in subjection under him, that God may be all in all. (1 Corinthians 15:27-28)

So now let's look at this passage again:

> Matthew 25:46 And these will go away into **eternal punishment**, but the righteous into **eternal life.**

This passage was part of Jesus' most important prophecy given to his disciples on the Mount of Olives. Chapters 24 and 25 of Matthew are sometimes called the "Olivet Discourse." Here in chapter 25 Jesus was giving a parable. From the accounts of the Acts of the Apostles all the way through the epistles of John, we see that the persecution of the Church was not only undertaken by the religious leaders of the Jewish nation, it was started and led by them! This parable shows how the rejected King of the Jews was now judging the nation and was about to bring an end to the Jewish Age. Yes, those Jewish religious leaders were soon to be punished for their persecution of "the least of these." Hanson agrees with this analogy as he notes below:

> And what infallible token did he give that these events would occur "then"? Matthew 24:34: "Verily I say unto you, this generation shall not pass till all these

things be fulfilled." What things? The "son of man coming in his glory in the clouds", and the end of the existing *aion*, age, or economy, signalized by the destruction of Jerusalem and the establishment of the new *aion*, world, or age to come, that is, the Christian dispensation. Now on the authority of Jesus himself the *aion* then existing ended within a generation, namely, about AD 70. Hence, those who were sent away into *aionion* punishment, or the punishment of that *aion,* were sent into a condition corresponding in duration to the meaning of the word *aion*, i.e. age-lasting. A punishment cannot be endless, when defined by an adjective derived from a noun describing an event, the end of which is distinctly stated to have come.[34]

(For more information on the subject of Matt 24-25, see my book, *God's Promise of Redemption, a story of fulfilled prophecy,* 2015. (available at Amazon.com and other outlets))

From what we have just learned in this chapter, the word "eternal" here signifies that which is *lasting for a long period of time, UP TO perpetuity.*

Now let's look at three more Greek words before we end this chapter. Let's begin with one of the words for punishment which is κολασιν, the root word of which is κολασις. (kolasis).

---

[34] Hanson, John (2011-09-30). Aion-Aionios (Kindle Locations 2218-2219).

Notice what Thayer's Greek Lexicon says of this:

κολασις – correction, punishment, penalty[35]

So, the word used here, **kolasis**, means correction. Thus, we can derive from this that there is a **purpose** for the punishment mentioned in Matt. 25:46, and that is *for the purpose of correction*. In fact, in all of Greek literature you will not find this word used of anything other than corrective punishment. (See Barclay's comment p. 255)

But **what is just as important** to consider here are the words for punishment **which were not used by Jesus.** Jesus **did not use** either of these two Greek words (from Thayer's Greek Lexicon):

τιμωρεω – (English timoreo) – to be the guardian or avenger of honor; to take vengeance on one, to punish.[36]

In the case of the first (timoreo), the punishment is made for the sake of honor.

The Apostle Paul used this word in Acts 22:4-5 when speaking of a retributive punishment of those who were going against the Jewish law covenant. Note the usage below:

I persecuted this Way to the death, binding and delivering to prison both men and women, as the high priest and the whole council of elders can bear me

---

[35] Thayer's Greek-English Lexicon, Hendrickson Publishing, Eleventh Printing, 2014 p.353
[36] Ibid p. 624

witness. From them I received letters to the brothers, and I journeyed toward Damascus to take those also who were there and bring them in bonds to Jerusalem **to be punished.** (Acts 22:4-5)

Jesus also did not use the word timoria. From Thayer's Greek Lexicon we find:

τιμωρια - (English timoria) – vengeance, penalty, punishment[37]

In the sake of the second (timoria), the punishment is **purely for the purpose of retribution.**

The writer of Hebrews used this word when he noted that this would be used to punish the one who "has profaned the blood of the covenant by which he was sanctified, and has outraged the Spirit of grace?" (Hebrews 10:29) This would be the judgment of those ones that occurred at the destruction of Jerusalem which Jesus promised would occur within the same generation of his speaking. (Matthew 26:62-64)

But it is a fact that Jesus **did not use either one of these words.** Instead he used the word **kolasis** in Matthew 25:46 which is corrective punishment.

Now putting this all together, we can see that Matt. 25:46 speaks of a punishment that is **corrective** that can last **UP TO** perpetuity. It is up to God to determine the time frame.

Do you see the profound significance of this?

This begs the question for those of you who have children. Why do you punish your children? Is it because you hate

---

[37] Ibid p. 624

them and want to get even with them for what they have done? Of course not. It is because you love them and want to correct them.

This means there is a loving purpose to the correction of God! God is not throwing these ones into a state of eternal torture that goes on forever without purpose! God is giving them a type of correction that **WILL** be lasting.

Of course, any grace for us **at all** is only made possible by the sacrifice of our Lord and Savior, Jesus Christ.

Now these passages make sense:

> But love your enemies, and do good, and lend, expecting nothing in return, and your reward will be great, and you will be sons of the Most High, for **he is kind to the ungrateful and the evil.** (Luke 6:35)

Yes, he is kind to the ungrateful and evil, but to them there is PAIN to endure, but it is loving and kind corrective pain which will have an end at some point.

> Therefore, as one trespass led to condemnation for **ALL** men, so one act of righteousness leads to justification and life for **ALL** men. For as by the one man's disobedience **the many** were made sinners, so by the one man's obedience **the many** will be made righteous. (Romans 5:18-19 ESV)

> For as in Adam **ALL** die, so also in Christ shall **ALL** be made alive. But each in his own order: Christ the firstfruits, then at his coming those who belong to Christ. (1 Corinthians 15:22-23 ESV)

For this *is* good and acceptable in the sight of God our Savior; Who will have **ALL** men to be saved, and to come unto the knowledge of the truth. For *there is* one God, and one mediator between God and men, the man Christ Jesus; Who gave himself a ransom for **ALL**, to be testified **in due time.** (1 Timothy 2:3-6)

Notice this last phrase in the passage . . . to be testified *in due time.* Yes, there is *an end* to the corrective punishment of God, and the outcome is for the eventual good of those who suffer.

As I conclude this chapter, I would like to make the point very simply as this: The Greek word in question here is the noun αιον (aion). It simply means "age." *really*

Jesus used this noun at the beginning of the Olivet Discourse is in Matt 24:3 As he sat on the Mount of Olives, the disciples came to him privately, saying, "Tell us, when will these things be, and what will be the sign of your coming and of the end of the **age *(aion)*?**"

Now if you take this noun and make it an adjective as he did at the end of the Olivet Discourse in Matthew 24:46 when he said in the parable: Matt 25:46 "And these will go away into eternal *(aionian)* punishment, but the righteous into eternal *(aionian)* life." There is **no way** that this adjective can have a meaning greater than the noun. *why*

Thus, Rotherham has made a correct translation of this verse as follows:

Matthew 25:46 And, these, shall go away, into, *age-abiding*, correction, but, the righteous, into, *age-abiding,* life.

What is the length of age-abiding? We do not know. But we do know that it is **_not eternal_** as in the Greek word αιδιος (aidios) which is a word only found in the Scriptures when it speaks of the eternality of God. Aionian punishment only lasts for an age, and that age is determined by God and him alone. For when the corrective punishment has accomplished its purpose, it will be terminated by God.

Chapter Eight

Every Knee Shall Bow!

If we believe that the word of God is true, then we know that every person who has ever lived and is now dead has had to deal with this passage of Scripture:

> And just as it is appointed for man **to die ONCE,** and **after that comes judgment,** (Hebrews 9:27)

As we pointed out in the last chapter, those who believe in Annihilationism must (under that scenario) believe that those under adverse judgment from God will have to die **TWICE,** once in the body, then they will be resurrected again, and God will judge them adversely and they will have to die again. There is no way of getting around this passage for them, unless they state that this is only a reference to physical death. That, however, renders the necessity of that statement as void, for it is obvious that all people die physically only once. I would simply ask again: "Does it make any sense for the person being judged adversely to die, be raised up in the afterlife, be judged, and then killed again?" *not killed / tormented*

But now let's look at this from a different view. The writer of Hebrews is making this statement in a general context. Look at how this statement is worded. It is a reference to

MAN. This means **ALL** humans. So, **it is applicable to us** as well as those to whom he originally wrote. This tells us that physical death is not the end of our existence. But we also know that those of us **who believe _are promised_** that the Lord Jesus will be our advocate at the judgment. From the 1912 Weymouth New Testament we see:

> The Father indeed does not judge any one, but He has entrusted all judgement to the Son, that all may honour the Son even as they honour the Father. The man who withholds honour from the Son withholds honour from the Father who sent Him. "In most solemn truth I tell you that he who listens to my teaching and **believes** Him who sent me, has the Life of the Ages, and **does not come under judgement**, but **has passed** over out of death into Life. (John 5:22-24)

I referenced this translation of the Bible because it correctly renders the life given as "the Life of the Ages." This was discussed in the last chapter.

This means that if we are a believer, we do not have to worry, that **we have already passed** from death to life. Now I would like to state unequivocally that since Christ has now appeared in the heavens in the Most Holy to present his blood, the dead no longer go to a place called Hades which was described in Scripture as a two-compartment holding place for the dead. This place is no longer needed because of the atonement made by Christ using his own blood of redemption. Our Lord **has fulfilled his promise** to redeem mankind with his blood.

But when Christ appeared as a high priest of the good things that have come, then through the greater and more perfect tent (not made with hands, that is, not of this creation) **he entered once for all into the holy places**, not by means of the blood of goats and calves but **by means of his own blood, thus securing an eternal redemption.** (Hebrews 9:11-12)

The Apostle Paul reiterated that the doctrine of justification gives those of us who believe that most wonderful peace with regard to our destiny.

Therefore, since we have been justified by faith, we have peace with God through our Lord Jesus Christ. Through him we have also obtained access by faith into this grace in which we stand, and we rejoice in hope of the glory of God. (Romans 5:1-2)

And as he also pointed out:

Not only that, but we rejoice in our sufferings, knowing that suffering produces endurance, and endurance produces character, and character produces hope, and hope does not put us to shame, because God's love has been poured into our hearts through the Holy Spirit who has been given to us. (Romans 5:3-5)

Without a doubt, as we undergo sufferings as a result of our love for Christ, they become powerful reminders of the wonderful gift our Lord has given us. Why? Notice the words:

For while we were still weak, at the right time Christ died for the ungodly. For one will scarcely die for a righteous person—though perhaps for a good person one would dare even to die— but God shows his love for us in that while we were still sinners, Christ died for us.

Since, therefore, we have now been justified by his blood, much more shall we be saved by him from the wrath of God. (Romans 5:6-9)

Yes, **because of faith,** the Lord Jesus is standing in the gap for us. We do not have to experience the anger of God. This passage reminds us that Christ died **for the ungodly.** That included us! But now **only and simply because of our faith** in him, our Lord has seen fit to stand up for us. This would have been impossible had it not been for the immeasurable love he has shown for us. How much love? Notice as Paul continues to expound on this:

For if **while we were enemies** we were reconciled to God by the death of his Son, much more, now that we are reconciled, shall we be saved by his life. More than that, we also rejoice in God through our Lord Jesus Christ, through whom we have now received reconciliation. Therefore, just as sin came into the world through one man, and death through sin, and so death spread to all men because all sinned— (Romans 5:10-12)

The death that Paul is speaking about is not physical death. Just look at what he said! It is significant that **while we were enemies,** we were reconciled to God as he stated to the Ephesian Church:

And you were *dead in the trespasses and sins* But God, being rich in mercy, because of the great love with which he loved us, even when we were dead in our trespasses, made us alive together with Christ— *by grace you have been saved*—For by grace you have been saved *through faith*. And this is *not your own doing*; it is the gift of God, not a result of works, so that no one may boast. (Ephesians 2:1,4-5,8-9)

Paul also pleaded the same with the church in Corinth:

Therefore, we are ambassadors for Christ, God making his appeal through us. We implore you on behalf of Christ, **be reconciled to God.** For our sake he made him to be sin who knew no sin, so that in him we might become the righteousness of God. (2 Corinthians 5:20-21) *If so, we are all good*

This **IS the will of God** for all mankind. It is a wonderful gift that has been given to us for our faith in him. We cannot work hard enough to earn it. As Paul stated in verse 9, that is impossible.

Now as we return to Romans 5, we notice the following:

for sin indeed was in the world before the law was given, but sin is not counted where there is no law. Yet death reigned from Adam to Moses, even over those whose sinning was not like the transgression of Adam, who was a type of the one who was to come. (Romans 5:13-14)

What did Paul mean here?

From Adam until the time of Moses there was nothing that provided a sanctuary from sin. And even after the establishment of the law covenant with its sacrificial form of worship, the sacrifices did not provide a true escape from sin. But they were a constant reminder of sin and provided **a temporary covering** as they pointed to the time when the "greater Adam," the promised Messiah **would come** and would lay down his life for mankind.

As we continue to verses 15-17, we notice that Paul is making a parallel comparison:

> But the free gift is not like the trespass. For if **many** died through one man's trespass, much more have the grace of God and the free gift by the grace of that one man Jesus Christ abounded for **many**. And the free gift is not like the result of that one man's sin. For the judgment following one trespass brought condemnation, but the free gift following many trespasses brought justification. For if, because of one man's trespass, death reigned through that one man, much more will those who receive the abundance of grace and the free gift of righteousness reign in life through the one man Jesus Christ. (Romans 5:15-17)

Do you see the parallel here? Both groups have received the curse and **can receive** the blessings (**if they so choose**) due to the grace of God through Christ. This is why Paul used the word **many** in both cases. Both groups received spiritual death, but some received life, thus **"many" are still dead** in their sins. And as a result of the sacrifice of Christ, and their choice to accept it, **"many" have received spiritual life.**

1. Through his disobedience Adam brought spiritual death to many, but due to the free gift, the "greater Adam," Jesus gave the free gift of grace to that **same** group.
2. The gift given by Christ is much greater than Adam's sin because it only took one sin to bring condemnation to "the many" (in effect, everyone), but even after **many** trespasses, the free gift due to the single sacrifice of Christ brought justification.
3. The trespass of Adam brought spiritual death which resulted in the separation from God experienced by the unbeliever in this life, but **those who believe** will once again enjoy that spiritual fellowship with God **in this life**.

In essence **this is the doctrine of justification**. The gift is available to all, but it takes an exercise of faith to accept it. But now Paul goes on, by use of another parallel to say something that is absolutely astounding!

Therefore, as one trespass led to condemnation for **all men**, so one act of righteousness leads to justification and life for **all men**. (Romans 5:18)

Is this a contradictory statement that Paul made here? Did Paul just get sloppy with his words? **NO!** as we shall see:

For as by the one man's disobedience the many were made sinners, so by the one man's obedience the many will be made righteous. (Romans 5:19)

Some would say that Paul is qualifying "all" in verse 18 by the many in verse 19, **but this cannot be** because we know that Paul is once again creating a parallel. We know beyond a doubt that the term *"the many"* entails **everyone** in the first part of verse 19. Thus, the term *"the many"* must entail everyone in verse 19.

Paul later confirms this in his letter to the Corinthian church when he said:

> For as by a man came death, by a man has come also the resurrection of the dead. For as in Adam **ALL** die, so also in Christ shall **ALL** be made alive. (1 Corinthians 15:21-22)

Yes! These are indeed universal statements! In each of these statements, the first "all" determines the scope of the second. But the question is: How is this possible? Paul has just laid out before the Roman church the doctrine of **justification by faith**. Then he makes a statement *that appears to contradict* what he just said.

Let's notice what he said later when speaking of the unfaithful Jews:

> And in this way **all Israel will be saved,** as it is written, "The Deliverer will come from Zion, he will banish ungodliness from Jacob"; "and this will be **my covenant** with them when **I take away their sins.**" As regards the gospel, they are enemies for your sake. But as regards election, they are beloved for the sake of their forefathers. For the gifts and the calling of God are **irrevocable.** (Romans 11:26-29)

Yes! The gifts which God gave them, meaning their undeniable calling from the days of Abraham, and their indisputable calling as sons of God have been declared by God to be irrevocable!

> For just as you were at one time disobedient to God but now have received mercy because of their disobedience, so they too have now been disobedient in order that by the mercy shown to you they also may now receive mercy. For God has consigned **all to disobedience, that he may have mercy on all**. (Romans 11:30-31)

Yes, this passage that has been thought to be so difficult, and argued back and forth between those who differ concerning the fate of Israel, now becomes clear. God **has allowed** them to be disobedient so that he may **show them his grace.** As verse 32 states very clearly, **God is going to have mercy on them all!** Additionally, we can see now that Paul makes it clear that they have been elected by God, and **this election is irrevocable!**

Of course, they **will still** have to go through the judgment, and they will still **receive corrective punishment** for their sins, a punishment **that is just** according to the law covenant that they were living under. We know this is true because God does **NOT CHANGE!** That law covenant never spoke of eternal condemnation.

Yes, **God IS love**, and whom he loves, he disciplines. But on the other side of that discipline is God's awesome love and grace. Is it any wonder that after Paul proclaimed this, he breaks out in a powerful heartwarming praise of God, declaring that his grace is so powerful that there is **no way we can ever repay him?**

> Oh, the depth of the riches and wisdom and knowledge of God! How unsearchable are his judgments and how inscrutable his ways! "For who has known the mind of the Lord, or who has been his counselor?" "Or who has given a gift to him that he might be repaid?" For from him and through him and to him are all things. **To him be glory forever.** Amen. (Romans 11:33-36)

These last few verses expound of God's wisdom, and the designs of which are the result of infinite knowledge. As such, this action is above reproach. God is indeed the author of providence, and as such the Father of every good and perfect gift. There is no obligation here except by the choice of God, **and God has chosen love** despite the disobedience of this favored nation.

As we return to finish Romans chapter 5, we see:

> Now Law was brought in later on, so that transgression might increase. But where sin increased, grace has overflowed; in order that as sin has exercised kingly sway in inflicting death, so grace, too, may exercise kingly sway in bestowing a righteousness which results in the Life of the Ages through Jesus Christ our Lord. (Romans 5:20-21 WNT)

Do you see the **profound nature of this principle?** It is entirely consistent with the nature of God!

Is Paul stating then that it's OK to sin? Is he stating that there are no consequences for such action? Absolutely not! When we sin, there are **always** adverse consequences in our lives whether we want to admit it or not. For example, a man who is a thief may think he gets away with his stealing even if he does not get caught, but assuming he is subject to rational thinking, he has a moral compass that knows it is wrong and it will cause him to be miserable in that state. The more he steals, the more misery he heaps upon himself. In most cases, the person who has schemed successfully becomes so miserable that he will deliberately let down his defenses so that he will get caught in order to pay the consequences, thus relieving his misery but trading it for a more "justified" type of misery. Our bad choices absolutely never get us what we desire because of this. When we sin and make a mess of our lives that moral compass **exacerbates the misery we feel** and that **takes away** any prospective joy we may have perceived to have gotten when we committed the sin. It will eventually cause us to have regrets. In cases of egregious sin, our regrets will be deeply ingrained and may last a **lifetime.**

In matters that are ambiguous to his purposes God gives us some latitude as free moral agents, but that internal moral compass keeps wanting to bring us back to the center when we sin even if ignore it and keep on sinning. But finally, once again if one is a rational person and not a sociopath,[38]

so the punishment is regret

---

[38] Defined as a person having an egocentric and antisocial personality marked by a lack of remorse for one's actions, an absence of empathy for others, and often criminal tendencies.
www.merriam-webster.com/dictionary/psychopath

he must succumb to it. This is what God has ingrained in us whether we like it or not.

Thus, as Talbott proclaims in his book,[39] God is like a chess grandmaster, and we are like novices. When the Grandmaster plays against a novice, there is no question that he will win, not because he causally determines every move that the person makes, but because he is resourceful enough to counter any combination of moves that the novice freely decides to make. Similarly, with God who is all knowing and infinitely resourceful, he does not need to direct every single aspect of our lives in order to "checkmate" us in the end. His love is the determining factor. He may even protect us from some of the most adverse consequences along the way, but it is within us that he put that moral compass that guides us in the tiniest and most pervasive crevices of our hearts to know that our deepest desires can only be met when we are in harmony with his will in our lives. In the final analysis, all resistance to the overwhelming love and grace of God "will melt like wax before a flame."[40]

What about those who do not think rationally, such as the sociopath? God's love will once again prevail! Their thinking will lovingly be corrected, and when this happens, they will be subject to God's irresistible grace. There is no **forced subjection** or arm twisting in heaven.

---

[39] Talbott, Thomas. The Inescapable Love of God (pp. 194-195). Cascade Books, an Imprint of Wipf and Stock Publishers. Kindle Edition.

[40] Ibid, p195

Thus, we have harmony in all of what Paul has said. Yes, we see it again. **God IS Love**, and whom he loves, he disciplines. But **on the other side** of that discipline is **God's awesome love and grace.**

Now let's return to the passage we examined earlier:

And just as it is appointed for man **to die once**, and **after that comes judgment**, (Hebrews 9:27)

This passage was written to make the point that just as Christ died but once, so it is with man - that when we die, we are immediately ready for the judgment, and will soon be in the presence of God.

Then next, we must address the stunning words of the Apostle Paul:

The apostle Paul told the Philippian church:

Therefore, God has highly exalted him and bestowed on him the name that is above every name, so that **at the name of Jesus every knee should bow**, in heaven and on earth and under the earth, and **every tongue confess** that Jesus Christ is Lord, to the glory of God the Father. (Philippians 2:9-11)

Here Paul repeated the words of God recorded by the prophet Isaiah. As we look at these words as they were originally recorded, we see some eye-opening words . . . most likely words we have passed over lightly in the past. Notice what is recorded:

Declare and present your case; let them take counsel together! Who told this long ago? Who declared it of old? Was it not I, the LORD? And there is no other god besides me, a righteous God and a Savior; there is none besides me. Turn to me and be saved, all the ends of the earth! For I am God, and there is no other. By myself I have sworn; from my mouth has gone out in righteousness a word that shall not return: 'To me **every knee shall bow, every tongue shall swear allegiance.'** Only in the LORD, it shall be said of me, are righteousness and strength; to him shall come and be ashamed all who were incensed against him. In the LORD all the offspring of Israel shall be justified and shall glory." (Isaiah 45:21-25)

First of all, notice that God and his son are **one and the same**. Second, notice how he states that everyone in the earth needs to turn to him and be saved. This shows us that even though Israel was **chosen for a purpose**, they were **NOT** exclusively those allowed to receive salvation. Third, notice that God promises that **every knee shall bow, every tongue shall swear allegiance.** And finally, notice that he says plainly that **all the offspring of Israel shall be justified and shall glory.**

Do you catch the **extreme significance** of that last statement? Why would God state such a thing if it were not true? It cannot be hyperbole, because he plainly states *ALL* shall be justified. Note what Talbott proclaims in his book: "The Inescapable Love of God:"

In his letter to the Philippians, Paul again anticipated a time when "at the name of Jesus every knee should bend, in heaven and on earth and under the earth, and every tongue confess that Jesus Christ is Lord" (2: 10– 11); 85 and in his letter to the Colossians, he went so far as to declare that the very same "all things" created in Christ— including "all things in heaven and on earth .. . visible or invisible, whether thrones or dominions or powers" (1: 16)— would eventually be reconciled to God in Christ (1: 20). 86 One could hardly ask for a more specific statement; Paul here applied the concept of reconciliation, which is explicitly a redemptive concept, not only to all human beings, but to all the spiritual principalities and dominions as well. It is within this context, I believe, that Paul himself understood the nature of Christ's victory, the defeat of Christ's enemies, and the destruction of sin.[41]   *Yes, he wins completely*

Paul must have had that strongly on his mind all throughout his ministry, because he reiterates it to the Roman church also:

> For to this end Christ died and lived again, that he might be Lord both of the dead and of the living. Why do you pass judgment on your brother? Or you, why do you despise your brother? For we will all stand before the judgment seat of God; for it is written, "As I live, says the Lord, **every knee shall bow to me, and every tongue shall confess to God**." So, then each of us will give an account of himself to God. (Romans 14:9-11)

---

[41] Talbott, Thomas. The Inescapable Love of God (p. 63). Cascade Books, an Imprint of Wipf and Stock Publishers. Kindle Edition.

But once again, notice that Paul states some things that we sometimes pass over lightly and miss the power of the words.

Paul states here that Christ is the Lord of both the living and the dead. Then he goes on to show that in this judgment, *ALL will bow and confess* Jesus is Lord. So, is this a **heartfelt** confession that is made by everyone?

What about all of those who have **spit at God**, and shook their fist at God in anger. They may have even screamed "I hate you God," perhaps doing such a thing right before they die.

What about those who have **ruthlessly slaughtered** people in the masses, such as during the German holocaust?

What about those like Assyrian King Sennacherib who taunted the King of Judah stating that their God **could not** save them from his mighty power? And even after God had his angel slaughter all of his soldiers, he went back to his false God and worshipped him. God had him killed by the hands of his own sons. (See Isaiah 36 and 37)

However, we do have a model of how God turns people around so that they acknowledge and worship him even after extreme arrogance and disobedience. Nebuchadnezzar was the arrogant King of Babylon. God used him to destroy Jerusalem the first time. But God warned him of his arrogance by the mouth of the prophet Daniel who interpreted his dream. He told the king that if he did not repent of his evil, he would be driven to the fields to eat grass like a beast for a period of seven years. But

Nebuchadnezzar ignored Daniel's words and continued in his extreme arrogance. The entire account can be found in Daniel chapter four. But notice what happened to him as Daniel records:

> At the end of twelve months he was walking on the roof of the royal palace of Babylon, and the king answered and said, "Is not this great Babylon, which I have built by my mighty power as a royal residence and for the glory of my majesty?" While the words were still in the king's mouth, there fell a voice from heaven, "O King Nebuchadnezzar, to you it is spoken: The kingdom has departed from you, (Daniel 4:29-31)

Judgment was about to befall this king exactly as prophesied by Daniel:

> Daniel 4:33 Immediately the word was fulfilled against Nebuchadnezzar. He was driven from among men and ate grass like an ox, and his body was wet with the dew of heaven till his hair grew as long as eagles' feathers, and his nails were like birds' claws.

It came true *exactly as prophesied*. Nebuchadnezzar was a madman for seven years eating grass like a beast of the field. But what was the result of this judgment?

> At the end of the days **I, Nebuchadnezzar**, lifted my eyes to heaven, and my reason returned to me, and **I blessed the Most High,** and **praised and honored him** who lives forever, for his dominion is an everlasting dominion, and his kingdom endures from generation to generation; all the inhabitants of

the earth are accounted as nothing, and he does according to his will among the host of heaven and among the inhabitants of the earth; and none can stay his hand or say to him, "What have you done?" At the same time my reason returned to me, and for the glory of my kingdom, my majesty and splendor returned to me. My counselors and my lords sought me, and I was established in my kingdom, and still more greatness was added to me. Now I, Nebuchadnezzar, **praise and extol** and honor the King of heaven, for **all his works are right and his ways are just**; and those who walk in pride he is able to humble. (Daniel 4:34-37)

Now do you see the **powerful message** of this fulfilled prophecy? Here is an exact picture of what the prophet Isaiah proclaimed. **Did God have to twist Nebuchadnezzar's arm** to get him to bow to him and confess that he was Lord? **NO!**

The punishment **was corrective**. It worked exactly as it was intended. Yes, Nebuchadnezzar **went through hell** for a period of seven years and it changed him completely from an arrogant unbeliever to a humble believer, praising God to the fullest! What a beautiful picture of reconciliation on the part of a loving and just God!

So now, as we return to the verse in Philippians 2:9-11, we see once again:

Therefore, God has highly exalted him and bestowed on him the name that is above every name, so that at the name of Jesus every knee should bow, in heaven and on earth and under the earth, and every tongue confess that Jesus Christ is Lord, to the glory of God the Father. (Philippians 2:9-11) *There a mistake*

What I would like to do now is to ask you to put on your thinking cap. I have put together three scenarios for you to rationally consider, considering what we have discussed up to this point. I ask you to honestly use your reasoning to look at how this passage in Philippians 2:9-11 would be played out at the judgment according to the most prominent interpretations of what happens to the lost dead at the judgment. Although we know that "God's ways are higher than our ways," **we are created in the image of God;** we should be able to reasonably discern the following.

Scenario #1 deals with by far the most prominent view in the church today, perhaps because of a mistaken understanding of Matt. 25:41-46, as we discussed at great length in the last chapter. I will remind you that the punishment spoken of in this passage is (kolasis – Greek) which means corrective punishment. It is **NOT** (timoria – or timoreo Greek) meaning vengeance or retribution.

Scenario #1

The lost are condemned to eternal torment in Hell

The lost person immediately upon his physical death goes to the judgment. Since this personal eschatology teaches that the person **is tormented forever** at some level in Hell, that means there is no time **after this** that one can make this confession. Why? There is no afterwards. The torment goes on endlessly. Thus, we are limited in this scenario as to how it can be played out.

So, either our Lord tells them to confess, or, they quickly see the error of their way, and when told to confess, they comply.

Then after this confession is made, the Lord condemns them to **eternal** never ending torment which goes on endlessly throughout the eons of time, the level of torture depending upon the deeds they have done in their short life of 70 – 90 years or so.

Scenario #2

The lost are annihilated

Remember from Hebrews 9:27 that after we die, we perish from the earth, we go to the judgment. "And just as it is appointed for man to die ONCE, and after that comes judgment." So, as we learned earlier, man only perishes in human bodily form. He does NOT perish completely.

The lost person immediately upon his physical death goes to the judgment. Since this personal eschatology teaches that the person **is annihilated,** that means there is no time **after this** that one can make this confession . . . there is no afterwards. The lost person will cease to exist. Once again, we are limited in how this can be played out.

So, either our Lord tells them to confess, or, once again they quickly see the error of their way, and when told to confess, they comply. After the confession, the Lord condemns them to eternal destruction. They completely cease to exist. But then, this means **they would die twice,** thus completely **negating** the passage at Hebrews 9:27!

Scenario #3

The lost are punished with a view to reconciliation

The lost person immediately upon his physical death goes to the judgment. Since the person is punished according to their deeds, they have sentence pronounced and are immediately sent to their corrective (kolasis – Greek) punishment. The duration and intensity of the punishment will be dependent upon the sinful deeds they committed. Since this judgment is considered to be as **reconciliatory**, there **will be** an afterwards. The punishment will be like a refiner's fire, which burns off the impurities.

After the refiner's fire, which is most certainly not fire as we know it, the sinner is punished, and reconciled, but **only by the blood of Christ**. At that time, the sinner, now reconciled, and purged of his transgressions by fire, and the blood of Christ, willingly and **with heartfelt conviction, humbly bows** before the Lord and confesses Jesus as Lord and Savior.

There is **no forced confession**. There is no question that the now reconciled believer **honestly believes with total conviction that Jesus is Lord**. He also knows that because of his work at the cross, this will bring glory to God!

Once again, Talbott nails it when he points out a quote from J.B. Lightfoot:

> When Paul suggested that every tongue would come to confess that Jesus Christ is Lord, he chose a verb that throughout the Septuagint implies not only confession, but the offer of praise and thanksgiving as well; and furthermore, as J. B. Lightfoot once pointed out, such implications of praise exist "in the very passage of Isaiah [45: 23] which St. Paul adapts."

"Now a ruling monarch may indeed force a subject to bow against that subject's will, may even force the subject to utter certain words; but **praise and thanksgiving can come only from the heart,** as the Apostle was no doubt clear-headed enough to discern. In any case, those who bow before Jesus Christ and declare openly that he is Lord either do so sincerely and by their own choice or they do not. If they do so sincerely and by their own choice, then there can be but one reason— they too have been reconciled to God. And **if they do not do so sincerely** and by their own choice, if they are instead forced to make obeisance against their will, **then their actions are merely fraudulent and bring no glory to God.** A Hitler may take pleasure in forcing his defeated enemies to make obeisance against their will, but a God who honors the truth could not possibly participate in such a fraud." (emphasis mine)[42]

The prophet Isaiah long ago attested to the mercy of God. He is more merciful than we are, and always consistent with his love.

let the wicked forsake his way, and the unrighteous man his thoughts; let him return to the LORD, **that he may have compassion on him**, and to our God, for **he will abundantly pardon.** For my thoughts are not your thoughts, neither are your ways my ways, declares the LORD. For as the heavens are

[42] Talbott, Thomas. The Inescapable Love of God (pp. 65-66). Cascade Books, an Imprint of Wipf and Stock Publishers. Kindle Edition.

higher than the earth, so are my ways higher than your ways and my thoughts than your thoughts. (Isaiah 55:7-9)

[handwritten: Why wouldn't they & what why don't]

Do you see the significant power of this passage? Yes, God **will have compassion** on the wicked who return to him. But the point of this passage is often missed. When it says "my ways higher than your ways and my thoughts than your thoughts" it is saying that God has much more compassion than we inferior humans can conceive. Notice how this thought is finished as the prophet Isaiah writes under the inspiration of God:

> "For as the rain and the snow come down from heaven and do not return there but water the earth, making it bring forth and sprout, giving seed to the sower and bread to the eater, so shall my word be that goes out from my mouth; it shall not return to me empty, but **it shall accomplish that which I purpose, and shall succeed** in the thing for which I sent it. (Isaiah 55:10-11)

God is stating that without any question whatsoever, **what HE WILLS is going to be accomplished.** *[handwritten: this]*

So now, with all of this in mind, what do you think?

Which of these scenarios sounds more like the God of whom it is spoken?

> Anyone who does not love does not know God, because **God is love**. In this the love of God was made manifest among us, that God sent his only Son into the world, so that we might live through him. In

179

this is love, not that we have loved God **but that he loved us and sent his Son** to be the propitiation for our sins. (1 John 4:8-11)

Did not our Lord say:

But **love your enemies**, and do good, and lend, expecting nothing in return, and your reward will be great, and you will be sons of the Most High, for **he is kind to the ungrateful and the evil.** Be merciful, even as your Father is merciful. (Luke 6:35-36)

Under scenario #3 all of the qualities Jesus and the prophets spoke of are in complete harmony. What about Scenario#1, or Scenario#2. Can you **honestly say in your heart** that these scenarios conform to what is spoken of concerning our Lord above?

Do you have any regrets in this life? Does anything that you have done in your past seem to haunt you every day. . . perhaps a constant reminder to you of an irreversible sin you have committed? How many tears have you shed over this action?

But you know that you are powerless to change what has happened in your past. There is absolutely nothing you can do about it. But I believe that since someday, all things will be reconciled to God, you will be able to right that wrong that you have committed!

Women who have aborted babies, and have shed so many tears of anguish over that life that has been lost will once again see the child and rejoice. Those who are in prison for taking a life, whether by murder, manslaughter, or drunk driving will one day get to apologize to that person. Those who have had broken marriages due to their own shortcomings, will be restored into a loving relationship with that family they have forsaken. Those who have abused their children, creating a lifelong rift will one day be reconciled to them.

Perhaps this is the way it will be with those who have rejected Christ, and will have to suffer in Gehenna for a time as justified by our great Savior. Perhaps the purging fire, whatever form it may be will create a deep sense of sorrow in the hearts of those undergoing its cleansing effect so that in the end, they are crying out to God, praising him as the Lord and Savior of the universe! Oh, what a glorious time that will be!

Once again, we see why Paul broke out in praise to God at the end of Romans chapter 11:

> Oh, the depth of the riches and wisdom and knowledge of God! How unsearchable are his judgments and how inscrutable his ways! "For who has known the mind of the Lord, or who has been his counselor? Or who has given a gift to him that he might be repaid?" For from him and through him and to him are all things. To him be glory forever. Amen. (Romans 11:33-36)

Paul is praising God for a reason! It is because of **HIS LOVE,** because of **HIS JUSTICE**, because of **HIS WISDOM**. And we can likewise praise him!

Chapter Nine

The Potter and the Clay

I have wanted to see the Sistine Chapel for as long as I can remember. Why? It is one of the most amazing works of art on earth. In the year 1508 when Michelangelo was called by Pope Julius II to paint the ceiling of the Sistine chapel, he didn't want to do it. He knew that he would have to forego his first true love and that was sculpting. He also knew that this was a huge undertaking, for the Sistine Chapel is 130' long and 40' wide, and the ceiling is more than 60 feet above the floor. The ceiling covers an area of over 5000 square feet.

Once he decided to do it, he had major problems to overcome. How would he get up to the ceiling to paint it? Who would help him? How would he get the constant flow of materials up to that 60-foot level? Michelangelo overcame all of these problems, and instead of the 12 figures of the apostles the pope originally specified, Michelangelo painted over 3000 figures on that ceiling over the next four years. On October 31, 1512 when his work was unveiled the whole world came running to see the masterpiece that Michelangelo put on that ceiling.

Truly, history confirms that when God created this talented man Michelangelo, he created a man with extraordinary abilities. This is what God has done all throughout the course of human history. We are all nothing but a lump of clay in the hand of the Potter and Michelangelo was no different. Now, let me ask you a question. If Michelangelo can paint such a magnificent work of art, **what do you think the great Potter did in creating him?** Can all of those two-dimensional dead pictures compare with the 3-dimensional living ones God has made? Can you truly capture the **majesty of the Grand Canyon** on canvas? Can you truly capture the power of **Niagara Falls** in a painting? **God can!** God is sovereign, God is in control.

Now we go back in history to the time of the prophet Jeremiah. God wanted to give the prophet Jeremiah **a lesson on who is in control**. Note the following passage:

> The word that came to Jeremiah from the LORD: "Arise, and go down to the potter's house, and there I will let you hear my words." So I went down to the potter's house, and there he was working at his wheel. And the vessel he was making of clay **was spoiled** in the potter's hand, and **he reworked** it into another vessel, **as it seemed good to the potter to do**. Then the word of the LORD came to me: "O house of Israel, can I not do with you as this potter has done? declares the LORD. **Behold, like the clay in the potter's hand, so are you in my hand, O house of Israel**. (Jeremiah 18:1-6)

Jeremiah lived in the last days of a decaying nation. He was the last prophet to Judah, the southern kingdom. Judah continued on after the ten tribes of the north had been carried into captivity under Assyria. And Jeremiah comes in at the close of the reign of the last good king of Judah, the boy king Josiah, who led the last revival the nation experienced before it went into captivity.

The message here in chapter 18 was **uniquely given** to the prophet. It didn't come to him during a time of prayer or on a visit to the temple, but God chose to reveal his message to Jeremiah by showing him a simple ordinary occurrence in a common workshop. For just a moment, God shows us how he caused an important truth to be formed in the mind of the prophet. And **he understood exactly** what God was trying to tell him.

God was making sure that Jeremiah understood that as the God of the universe, **he has the power to do whatever he wants** with mankind. The illustration was clear. The potter took that piece that he was making and crushed it. Then he put that same piece of clay back on the wheel, and made it into another vessel, most likely one that was completely different than the one that was on the wheel previously.

This was a warning to that disobedient nation. They were **chosen by God**, chosen so that they could eventually fulfill God's promise to Abraham that we discussed in chapter 1, a promise given in Genesis chapter 12:

> And I will make of you a great nation, and I will bless you and make your name great, so that you will be a blessing. I will bless those who bless you, and him who dishonors you I will curse, and in you **all the families of the earth shall be blessed**." (Genesis 12:2-3)

So here we have Jeremiah telling his own people again by the use of a simple illustration that if they don't repent, they will be marred in the hand of the great potter and made into a different vessel. Did this wicked people listen to him? Did they repent? No. Even though he gave them 14 messages of judgment, they ignored them all, and their city of Jerusalem was eventually destroyed. In the aftermath, those who survived were exiled to Babylon.

But out of that destruction emerged a new generation of Israelite people, and the promise remained intact. But God used Nebuchadnezzar, the King of Babylon as his piece of clay to accomplish his purposes. In the last chapter we saw that God took that same piece of clay (King Nebuchadnezzar) and crushed it, "and **he reworked** it into another vessel, **as it seemed good to the potter to do.**"

The fact is, Yahweh God the **Great Potter**, has been in control since before the foundation of the world. How does this affect us who are believers? Paul told the Ephesian church in his letter to them:

> Blessed be the God and Father of our Lord Jesus Christ, who has blessed us in Christ with every spiritual blessing in the heavenly places, even as he **chose us in him before the foundation of the world**, that we should be holy and blameless before him. In love **he predestined us** for adoption as sons through Jesus to the praise of his glorious grace, with which he has blessed us in the Beloved. (Ephesians 1:3-6)

While it is true that this letter was written to the Church at Ephesus and not written directly to us, there is no prophecy here awaiting fulfillment, therefore there is no reason why it still does not apply to us. What a wonderful blessing has been bestowed upon us! This verse shows us who are believers, unequivocally that we have been predestined by God to be where we are in Christ. But if this is true, there are many questions which now arise. What about those who do not believe? What about those who die in their unbelief? Why were they not chosen?

Eighteenth Century commentator Adam Clarke provides one answer to this dilemma:

> The Jews **considered themselves** an elect or chosen people, and **wished to monopolize** the whole of the Divine love and beneficence. The apostle here shows that **God had the Gentiles as much in the contemplation of his mercy and goodness as he had the Jews**; and the blessings of the Gospel, now so freely dispensed to them, were the proof that God had thus chosen them, and that his end in giving them the Gospel was the same which he had in view by giving the law to the Jews, viz. that they might be holy and without blame before him.
>
> And as his object was the same in respect to them both, they should consider that, as he loved them, so they should love one another: God having provided for each the same blessings, they should therefore be άγιους, holy - fully separated from earth and sin, and consecrated to God and αμωμους, without blame - having no spot nor imperfection, their inward holiness agreeing with their outward consecration.

The words are a metaphor taken from the perfect and immaculate sacrifices which the law required the people to bring to the altar of God. **But as love is the fulfilling of the law,** and love the fountain whence their salvation flowed, therefore **love must fill their hearts towards God and each other**, and love must be the motive and end of all their words and works.[43]

Therefore, as Clark points out, the act of predestination was a loving act. In effect what Adam Clarke is saying is that **God has chosen all of us, and predestined all of us**, whether Jew or Gentile. Then he points out that the **fulfillment of the law is love**.

But this statement by Clarke is not one with which everyone agrees. For example, commentator Albert Barnes looks at it in a completely different light:

The word "us" here shows that the apostle **had reference to individuals**, and not to communities. It includes Paul himself as one of the "chosen," and those whom he addressed - the mingled Gentile and Jewish converts in Ephesus. That it must refer to individuals is clear. **Of no "community"** as such can it be said that it was "chosen in Christ before the foundation of the world to be holy." It is not true of the Gentile world as such, nor of anyone of the nations making up the Gentile world . . . it means to make a selection or choice with the idea of favor or love, and

---

[43] Adam Clarke's Commentary on the Bible (Commenting on Ephesians 1:4)

with a view to impart important benefits on those whom he chose. The idea of making **some "distinction" between them and others, is essential** to a correct understanding of the passage - since there can be no choice where no such distinction is made. He who chooses one out of many things makes a difference, or evinces a preference - no matter what the ground or reason of his doing it may be. Whether this refers to communities and nations, or to individuals, still it is true that a distinction is made or a preference given of one over another.[44]

Why is there such a profound disagreement on this subject by these two commentators? This is a perfect example of the **difference** between the **Arminian and the Calvinistic** view of the doctrine of election.

Who is right? Let's look a little deeper.

It is obvious that God has chosen certain individuals for certain roles throughout history. Using the analogy of the great Potter from Jeremiah 18, we will observe that some have been chosen as vessels of mercy. Here are some prominent examples:

> You are the LORD, the God who **chose Abram** and brought him out of Ur of the Chaldeans and gave him the name Abraham. (Nehemiah 9:7)

> Now the angel of the LORD came and sat under the terebinth at Ophrah, which belonged to Joash the Abiezrite, while his son **Gideon** was beating out wheat in the winepress to hide it from the Midianites.

---

[44] Albert Barnes' Notes on the Bible (further commenting on Ephesians 1:4)

And the angel of the LORD appeared to him and said to him, **"The LORD is with you,** O mighty man of valor."(Judges 6:11-12)

'Since the day that I brought my people Israel out of Egypt, I chose no city out of all the tribes of Israel in which to build a house, that my name might be there. But I **chose David** to be over my people Israel.' (1 Kings 8:16)

but he **chose the tribe of Judah**, Mount Zion, which he loves. (Psalm 78:68)

and say to them, Thus says the Lord GOD: On the day when **I chose Israel**, I swore to the offspring of the house of Jacob, making myself known to them in the land of Egypt; I swore to them, saying, I am the LORD your God. (Ezekiel 20:5)

If you were of the world, the world would love you as its own; but because you are not of the world, but **I chose you** out of the world, therefore the world hates you. (John 15:19)

From these few examples, God **chose** Abraham, Gideon, David, the tribe of Judah, Israel, and Jesus chose his apostles, all **as vessels of mercy.**

He **also chose** some as **vessels of wrath**. Here are some examples:

and Abel also brought of the firstborn of his flock and of their fat portions. And the LORD had regard for Abel and his offering, but for Cain and his offering he had **no regard**. So Cain was very angry, and his face fell. (Genesis 4:4-5)

And the LORD said to her, "Two nations are in your womb, and two peoples from within you shall be divided; the one shall be stronger than the other, **the older shall serve the younger."** (Genesis 25:23)

And the LORD said to Moses, "When you go back to Egypt, see that you do before Pharaoh all the miracles that I have put in your power. But I will **harden his heart**, so that he will not let the people go. (Exodus 4:21)

And I will **harden the hearts** of the Egyptians so that they shall go in after them, and I will get glory over Pharaoh and all his host, his chariots, and his horsemen. (Exodus 14:17)

And the LORD said to Satan, "Behold, **all that he has** is in your hand. Only against him do not stretch out your hand." So, Satan went out from the presence of the LORD. (Job 1:12)

God favored Abel, but had no regard for Cain. He favored Jacob over Esau, even though Esau was the firstborn. He favored Moses but hardened Pharaoh's heart. And even though Job was blameless and upright (Job 1:8), God allowed Satan to work evil upon him.

This raises the question, why have there been two groups of theologians fighting over the nature of these verses for centuries? **Here is why**.

It is said that if you believe in God's sovereignty alone, you will go overboard and claim that man has no responsibility.

If you go overboard and say that it is all up to the free will of man, you will be denying the sovereignty of God!

So, what is the solution to this dilemma? As I said previously, there is no question **that God is sovereign**. But **within the bounds** of God's sovereignty there **is a solution**. We have looked at this passage previously, but let's look at it again. This time we will check it from three different Bible Translations:

First, from the English Standard Version:

> This is good, and it is pleasing in the sight of God our Savior, who **desires all people to be saved** and to come to the knowledge of the truth. For there is one God, and there is one mediator between God and men, the man Christ Jesus, who gave himself as a ransom for all, **which is the testimony given at the proper time**. (1 Timothy 2:3-6)

Next from the King James Version:

> For this *is* good and acceptable in the sight of God our Saviour; Who **will have all men to be saved**, and to come unto the knowledge of the truth. For *there is* one God, and one mediator between God and men, the man Christ Jesus; Who gave himself a ransom for all, **to be testified in due time**. (1 Timothy 2:3-6)

Next from Rotherham's Emphasized Bible:

> This, is comely and acceptable before our Saviour God, Who **willeth, all men, to be saved**, and, unto a personal knowledge of truth, to come; For there is,

one, God, one, mediator also, between God and men,—a man—Christ Jesus: Who gave himself a ransom in behalf of all,—**the testimony, in its own fit times**: (1 Timothy 2:3-6)

So, which is it? Is this just a **passing desire** of God? Or is it his **sovereign will**? The Greek word for desires or wills is the word θελει (pronounced *thaylay*). Thayer's Greek Lexicon says of this word that it means **to be resolved or determined,** to purpose.

That means that God has **resolved it**. He has **determined it**. He has **purposed it**. YES! He **WILLS IT!** God's sovereignty **will not be denied.**

Do you see **the overwhelming significance of this passage?** It **IS** God's will for all men to be saved! This is an example of the **loving sovereignty** of God, but this is **NOT** to the exclusion of man's free will. How can I say that?

It is because man still has the choice of how God's will is to be accomplished. He can either take **the easier way**, and accept Jesus Christ as his Lord and Savior, or he can take **the hard way**, and "go through Hell" first. Believe me, this should not be a difficult decision. Jesus warned about the path through Gehenna when he said:

I will warn you whom to fear: fear him who after killing has power **to throw into Gehenna:** yes, I say to you, fear him. (Luke 12:5 WNT)

Make no mistake about it. Just because God wills all to be saved, if we are disobedient and reject him in this life, **we**

will suffer. BUT, there is an absolutely **loving purpose for Gehenna**. It is correctional. It is proportional. Remember, God **does not** change! They will be judged in a **proportional** manner just like the law covenant that God established back in the book of Leviticus. This law states:

"Whoever takes a human life shall surely be put to death. Whoever takes an animal's life shall make it good, life for life. If anyone injures his neighbor, as he has done it shall be done to him, fracture for fracture, eye for eye, tooth for tooth; whatever injury he has given a person shall be given to him. (Leviticus 24:17-20)

In fact, Mark recorded:

For everyone will be **salted with fire,** and every sacrifice will be seasoned with salt. (Mar 9:49 WEB)

Although this passage has been termed as "difficult" by some of the commentaries, Paul makes it clear when he writes:

each man's work will be revealed. For the Day will declare it, because it is revealed in fire; and the **fire itself will test what sort of work each man's work is.** If any man's work remains which he built on it, he will receive a reward. If any man's work is burned, he will suffer loss, but he himself will be saved, but as through fire. (1Co 3:13-15 WEB)

Notice that it specifically states, the fire **is not** for **torture,** but **for testing!** Thus, it is not a literal fire as we know it, although by its nature, it will be painful.

God is loving, God is just. But **beyond a doubt**, God **IS** sovereign. His sovereign will **IS** going to be accomplished. He will not torment his children for eternity any more than we would do such a thing to ours.

Vessels of Wrath

Now the question arises about those who were not chosen. The first one that comes to mind is the Pharaoh of Egypt during the time of the exodus by the nation of Israel. There is a very clear record of a previous Pharaoh who was a "vessel of mercy" to Joseph and his family. However, now we have a different Pharaoh who lived during the time of Moses. He had no regard for the promises made by the earlier Pharaoh. He decided to make slaves out of God's people. But despite this wickedness, there is no question that God hardened his heart. This cost him everything. Notice the following:

> But the LORD hardened Pharaoh's heart, and he did not let the people of Israel go. (Exodus 10:20)
> But the LORD hardened Pharaoh's heart, and he would not let them go. (Exodus 10:27)

God also did this to others:

> But Sihon the king of Heshbon would not let us pass by him, for the LORD your God hardened his spirit and made his heart obstinate, that he might give him into your hand, as he is this day. (Deuteronomy 2:30)

Jesus said that God hardened the hearts of many of his day:

Though he had done so many signs before them, they still did not believe in him, so that the word spoken by the prophet Isaiah might be fulfilled: "Lord, who has believed what he heard from us, and to whom has the arm of the Lord been revealed?" Therefore they could not believe. For again Isaiah said, "**He has blinded their eyes and hardened their heart**, lest they see with their eyes, and understand with their heart, and turn, and I would heal them." Isaiah said these things because he saw his glory and spoke of him. (John 12:37-41)

What about all of the large numbers of people in the Old Testament that God killed? Many (not all) of these seemingly did nothing to deserve death. Let me highlight to you just some of the many examples we find:

1. The entire population of the earth in the flood, except Noah and family. (Genesis 6)
2. The entire population of the city of Sodom and Gomorrah. (Genesis 19)
3. The firstborn of Egypt. This included many infants (Exodus 12)
4. The entire Egyptian Army. Isn't it true they were just following orders? To disobey meant death at the hands of Pharaoh. (Exodus 14)
5. An undetermined number of Israelites, some by fire, and some by plague. They were killed because of their complaints against God. (Numbers 11)
6. A large number of Israelites who rebelled against Moses, listed as over 14,700. (Numbers 16)

7. A large number of Israelites (70,000) because of the actions of their king in ordering a census. (2 Samuel 24)
8. 185,000 Assyrian Soldiers because of the arrogance of their king (Senacherib). (2 Kings 19)

In addition to these, we find that God killed the babies of Kings, not for the sins of the child, but for the sins of the King. These include:

1. Pharaoh's son due to the sin of his father. (Exodus 12) Remember that God hardened Pharaoh's heart. (Exodus 4:21)
2. David's firstborn of his adulterous union with Bathsheba. (2 Samuel 12)
3. Jeroboam's son for the sins of his father. (1 Kings 14)

Again, we see without question that God is in control. He is sovereign. **Did this mean that God was a bloodthirsty angry God,** killing people randomly with no care in his heart for them? Why did God kill all of these people? Was it because God hated them? **NO!** They were used by God **to serve the purpose of his will at that time.** But there was a glorious future hope for these people. The Sovereign God of the universe **had a plan.** It was God's promise of salvation, and it would show that he ultimately does **love and reconcile all people**, past and future, to himself!

John the Baptist, the forerunner chosen by God said of Jesus:

and **all flesh** shall see the salvation of God.'" (Luke 3:6)

The next day John saw Jesus coming toward him, and said, "Behold! The Lamb of God **who takes away the sin of the world!** (John 1:29)

But notice what Jesus said:

Matthew 11:28 Come to Me, **all** *you* who labor and are heavy laden, and I will give you rest.

Matthew 19:26 . . . with God **all things** are possible.

Matthew 28:18 **All authority** has been given to Me in heaven and on earth.

Luke 10:22 **All things** have been delivered to Me by My Father,

John 5:22 For the Father judges no one, but has committed **all judgment** to the Son,

John 6:39 This is the will of the Father who sent Me, that **of all He has given** Me I should **lose nothing,** but should raise it up at the last day.

John 12:32 And I, when I am lifted up from the earth, **will draw all people to myself.**"

John 17:2 as You have given Him authority **over all flesh**, that He should give eternal life to as many as You have given Him.

John 17:7 Now they have known that **all things** which You have given Me are from You.

John 17:10 And **all** Mine are Yours, and Yours are **Mine**, and I am glorified in them.

Yes! In Christ was the fulfillment of the promise given to Abraham. For indeed, **ALL** families of the earth have been and will be blessed. Do you see how knowing the loving purpose of God's judgment shows that there is no conflict between God's Sovereignty and man's free will? Do you see how it is not cruel for God to temporarily use certain people for vessels of wrath? You can be sure that those purposely used as vessels of wrath were justly dealt with in their judgment. God is sovereign, and that sovereignty does not include eternal torment, but to those deserving, it involves corrective punishment that is properly measured for the purpose of reconciliation to him.

As I conclude this chapter, I would like to relate one more parable that has been floating around on the internet at the time of this writing. I would **love to give credit** to the author, but despite my searching, **the author of this parable seems to be unknown.** However, it will perfectly portray the example that is needed to make my point. Here is one version of the parable:

In a mother's womb were two babies. One asked the other: "Do you believe in life after delivery?" The other replies, "why, of course, there has to be something after delivery. Maybe we are here to prepare ourselves for what we will be later. "Nonsense," says the other. "There is no life after delivery. What would that life be?" "I don't know, but there will be more light out there than in here. Maybe we will walk with our legs and eat from our mouths." The other says "This is absurd! Walking is impossible. And eat with our mouths? What a ridiculous concept. The umbilical cord supplies nutrition. Life after delivery is to be excluded. The umbilical cord is too short." "I think there is something and maybe it's different than it is here." the other replies, "No one has ever come back from there. Delivery is the end of life, and in the after-delivery it is nothing but darkness and anxiety and it takes us nowhere." "Well, I don't know," says the other, "but certainly we will see mother and she will take care of us." "Mother??" You believe in mother? Where is she now? "She is all around us. It is in her that we live. Without her there would not be this world." "I don't see her, so it's only logical that she doesn't exist." To which the other replied, "sometimes when you're in silence you can hear her, you can perceive her." I believe there is a reality after delivery and we are here to prepare ourselves for that reality. . .

This parable **perfectly** portrays **the foolishness of man** to question the existence of God. But now I would like to take it a step further.

Now let us just suppose that this scenario is real. The two babies are delivered. Now the mother speaks to the unbelieving baby:

"OK, I gave you nine months to believe that I existed, and you stubbornly refused to believe despite the fact that your twin had some really convincing and compelling evidence, and he continued to give that evidence to you over and over again for the entire period of time that you were in the womb! Your twin used every conceivable argument to try to convince you, but due to your stubborn pride, you refused to believe. I hate pride! I am a loving parent, but I am also a perfectly just one, so because of this, **I must now kill you.** And after your death, because of your stubborn disbelief, you will be eternally separated from me, and you will be relegated to a place called Hell **to be tormented with eternal fire forever**, and no possibility of escape. That means that after a thousand lifetimes, you will be no closer to the end of this torture than you were at the beginning."

Can you imagine a mother saying such a thing? Is this any different than believing that God would do such a thing to any of his children for ANY reason? But this is the exact scenario that most of the people in the churches today believe will happen to unbelievers after their death. Some of those in exclusivist cults even believe that unless everyone believes the way that they do they too will be relegated either to a burning hell, or will be annihilated. History shows that most people who are raised in a faith continue to believe the foundational principles of that faith throughout their lifetime in at least some measure. And even those who search diligently come up with varying beliefs in all areas of Theology. So, with this in mind, is it really possible that a God of love would annihilate **or send someone** to a place of **eternal torment** called Hell **because of an honest mistake** in theology? *or outright disobedience*

200

Chapter Ten

From Christ to Augustine

Concerning the events after the incarnation of Christ, we see that Scripture tells us:

And suddenly there came with the messenger a multitude of the heavenly host, praising God, and saying, 'Glory in the highest to God, and **upon earth peace, among men--good will.**' (Luke 2:13-14 YLT)

Then when the child Jesus was brought into the temple, as was the custom, we see:

Now there was a man in Jerusalem, whose name was Simeon, and this man was righteous and devout, waiting for the consolation of Israel, and the Holy Spirit was upon him. And it had been revealed to him by the Holy Spirit that he would not see death before he had seen the Lord's Christ. And he came in the Spirit into the temple, and when the parents brought in the child Jesus, to do for him according to the custom of the Law, he took him up in his arms and blessed God and said, "Lord, now you are letting your servant depart in peace, according to your word; for **my eyes have seen your salvation** that you have prepared **in the presence of all peoples,** a light for revelation to the Gentiles, and **for glory to your people Israel.**" And his father and his mother marveled at what was said about him. And Simeon blessed them and said to Mary his mother, "Behold, this child is appointed for the fall and rising of many in Israel, and for a sign that is opposed (and a sword will pierce through your own soul also), so that thoughts from many hearts may be revealed." (Luke 2:25-35)

So yes, **it was time for the promise** of God to be fulfilled that he would bring a savior. It was promised all the way back in the book of Genesis:

I will put enmity between you and the woman, and between your offspring and her offspring; he shall bruise your head, and you shall bruise his heel." (Genesis 3:15)

This was God's promise of salvation!

Since the founder of the Christian church was none other than the Lord Jesus, we must begin by asking some questions with regard to his teaching on the subject of eternal torment. I have heard preachers say that no one has taught more about hell than Jesus. While it is true that he mentioned the place called Gehenna several times in Scripture (which has been translated as hell by many translators) he does not say anything concerning the duration of the punishment. The closest thing we have is the following passage from the King James Version:

And if thy hand offend thee, cut it off: it is better for thee to enter into life maimed, than having two hands to go into hell, into the fire that never shall be quenched: Where their worm dieth not, and the fire is not quenched. And if thy foot offend thee, cut it off: it is better for thee to enter halt into life, than having two feet to be cast into hell, into the fire that never shall be quenched: Where their worm dieth not, and the fire is not quenched. And if thine eye offend thee, pluck it out: it is better for thee to enter into the kingdom of God with one eye, than having two eyes to be cast into hell fire: Where their worm dieth not, and the fire is not quenched. **For every one shall be salted with fire,** and every sacrifice shall be salted with salt. Salt *is* good: but if the salt have lost his saltiness, wherewith will ye season it? Have salt in yourselves, and have peace one with another. (Mark 9:43-50 KJV)

Commentator William Barclay explains the meaning of this passage.

The Jewish Rabbis had sayings based on the way in which some parts of the body can lend themselves to sin. "The eye and the heart are the two brokers of sin." "The eye and the heart are the two handmaids of sin." "Passions lodge only in him who sees." "Woe to him who goes after his eyes for the eyes are adulterous." There are certain instincts in man, and certain parts of man's physical constitution, which minister to sin. This saying of Jesus is **not to be taken literally**, but is a vivid eastern way of saying that there is a goal in life worth any sacrifice to attain it.[45]

Now concerning the KJV, remember that this translation's rendering of "hell" is the most liberal of all translations. Also, verses 44 and 46 are not found in the modern translations such as the NIV or the ESV. They are considered to be spurious due to the fact that they are not found in the older manuscripts. But there is one confirmed usage of this terminology in verse 46, so we will address it. This phrase used in the KJV was taken from the words of the prophet Isaiah:

> Isa 66:24 "Then they will go forth and look on the corpses of the men who have transgressed against Me. For their worm will not die And their fire will not be quenched; And they will be an abhorrence to all mankind."

This chapter of Isaiah, along with chapter 66 speaks of the rejection of the Jews to accept the gospel message of Christ. This would eventually result in the destruction along with over a million Jews. But regarding the nature of the "worm that dieth not" commentator Albert Barnes had this to say:

> This figure is taken from Isa 66:24. See the notes at that passage. In describing the great prosperity of the kingdom of the Messiah, Isaiah says that the people of God "shall go forth, and look upon the carcasses of the men who have transgressed against God." Their

[45] Daily Bible Study Series – William Barclay - http://www.studylight.org/commentaries/dsb/view.cgi?bk=40&ch=9

enemies would be overcome. They would be slain. The people of God would triumph. The figure is taken from heaps of the dead slain in battle; and the prophet says that **the number would be so great that their worm** - the worm feeding on the dead - **would not die**, would live long - **as long as there were carcasses to be devoured**; and that the fire which was used to burn the bodies of the dead would continue long to burn, and would not be extinguished until they were consumed. The figure, therefore, denotes great misery, and certain and **terrible destruction** (emphasis mine).[46]

This in fact is what occurred at the destruction of Jerusalem. Historian Josephus said that the bodies were piled so high in the city that people walked over them like they were nothing. However, the point that Jesus was making here is that we should avoid sin so that it does not overtake us causing us to discard our faith. But **nowhere in this passage** does he say that the time spent in Gehenna (or Hell) is eternal. In fact, if we look at the way Jesus ends this, we see that he says:

For every one shall be salted with fire, and every sacrifice shall be salted with salt. Salt *is* good: but if the salt have lost his saltness, wherewith will ye season it? Have salt in yourselves, and have peace one with another. (Mark 9:49-50 KJV)

As previously stated, Paul clarified this statement when he wrote:

---

[46] Albert Barnes' Notes on the Bible - Isa 66:24

each man's work will be revealed. For the Day will declare it, because it is revealed in fire; and the **fire itself will test what sort of work each man's work is.** If any man's work remains which he built on it, he will receive a reward. If any man's work is burned, he will suffer loss, but he himself will be saved, but as through fire. (1Co 3:13-15 WEB)

There is a **profound** principle here! It is that **the "fire" tests and purifies,** signifying it is **not fire as we know it,** but nonetheless, by its very nature, it will be painful.

Now I want to call attention to some comforting words that were originally prophesied by Isaiah:

Comfort, comfort my people, says your God. Speak tenderly to Jerusalem, and cry to her that her warfare is ended, that **her iniquity is pardoned,** that she has received from the LORD's hand double for all her sins. A voice cries: "In the wilderness prepare the way of the LORD; make straight in the desert a highway for our God. Every valley shall be lifted up, and every mountain and hill be made low; the uneven ground shall become level, and the rough places a plain. And **the glory of the LORD shall be revealed, and all flesh shall see it together**, for the mouth of the LORD has spoken." (Isaiah 40:1-5)

This prophecy was partially fulfilled by the appearance of John the Baptist as he paved the way for the Lord. Notice how this is brought out in Luke's Gospel:

during the high priesthood of Annas and Caiaphas, the word of God came to John the son of Zechariah in the wilderness. And he went into the entire region around the Jordan, proclaiming a baptism of repentance for the forgiveness of sins. As it is written in the book of the words of Isaiah the prophet, "The voice of one crying in the wilderness: 'Prepare the way of the Lord, make his paths straight. Every valley shall be filled, and every mountain and hill shall be made low, and the crooked shall become straight, and the rough places shall become level ways, and **all flesh shall see the salvation of God.**'" (Luke 3:2-6)

The language is almost identical to what was prophesied by Isaiah! John the Baptist **was** that voice crying in the wilderness. He **was** the one who cried out "**all flesh shall see the salvation of God.**"

In John's Gospel, we see Jesus speaking to Nicodemus.

If I have told you earthly things and you do not believe, how can you believe if I tell you heavenly things? No one has ascended into heaven except he who descended from heaven, the Son of Man. And as Moses lifted up the serpent in the wilderness, so must the Son of Man be lifted up, that whoever believes in him may have eternal life. "For God so loved the world, that he gave his only Son, that whoever believes in him should not perish but have eternal life. For God did not send his Son into the world to condemn the world, **but in order that the world might be saved through him.** (John 3:12-17)

Jesus told Nicodemus that he would be **lifted up**. This was to be similar to the pole that Moses put the serpent on in Numbers 21:8,9. In that case, after the curse of the serpents when many people were bitten, Moses got a pole and put a fiery serpent on it. Everyone who looked at that serpent on that pole lived. Jesus was making the point that those who look to him in belief would live. He reiterated that point in verses 15 and 16.

But now we must consider a point that is often overlooked and **is of profound significance!**

Next, Jesus told Nicodemus that God sent him into the world that the **entire world (κοσμος) would be saved**. This is an eventuality that would only occur to some after a time of testing and purification. Note how the Good News Bible renders Mark 9:49:

> Everyone will be purified by fire as a sacrifice is purified by salt. (Mark 9:49)

Then later he said:

> And this is the will of him who sent me, **that I should lose nothing** of all that he has given me, but raise it up on the last day. For this is the will of my Father, that everyone who looks on the Son and believes in him **should have eternal life,** (life age-abiding, Rotherham) and I will raise him up on the last day." (John 6:39-40)

Then as the prophecy completely unfolds, we see Jesus praying in John chapter 17 just prior to his crucifixion:

> When Jesus had spoken these words, he lifted up his eyes to heaven, and said, "Father, the hour has come; glorify your Son that the Son may glorify you, since

you have given him **authority over all flesh**, to give **eternal life to all whom you have given him.** (John 17:1-2)

Next, we see the Apostle Paul making similar statements, many of which we have already seen in earlier chapters. When you look at these in their entirety, they make a **powerful case for the love of Christ** to eventually reconcile all to himself.

Therefore, as one trespass led to condemnation for **ALL** men, so one act of righteousness leads to justification and life **FOR ALL** men. (Romans 5:18)

For God has consigned **ALL** to disobedience, that he may have mercy on **ALL**. (Romans 11:32)

For from him and through him and to him are **ALL** things. To him be glory forever. (Romans 11:36)

For as in Adam **ALL** die, so also in Christ shall **ALL** be made alive. (1 Corinthians 15:22)

so that at the name of Jesus **EVERY** knee should bow, in heaven and on earth and **UNDER** the earth, and **EVERY** tongue confess that Jesus Christ is Lord, to the glory of God the Father. (Philippians 2:10-11)

For by him all things were created, in heaven and on earth, visible and invisible, whether thrones or dominions or rulers or authorities—**all things** were created through him and for him. (Colossians 1:16)

and through him to reconcile to himself **ALL** things, whether on earth or in heaven, **making peace by the blood of his cross**. (Colossians 1:20)

This, is comely and acceptable before our Saviour God, Who **willeth, all men**, to be saved, and, unto a personal knowledge of truth, to come;
(1 Timothy 2:3-4 Rotherham)

That last verse plainly states that **it is the will of God** that all men will be saved. Yes, it may require some to go through **a long purifying period** in order to reach that point, but my question is this. Is God the Sovereign God of the universe or not? **If he wills something, will it happen or not?** And as we have examined the writings of the Apostle Paul on the subject of salvation, I would like to give you one more item as food for thought.

Please consider this point which is profoundly important!

How many times do we see in the 13 epistles that Paul wrote **any mention of Hell, Gehenna, or Hades**?

Even if you search in the King James Translation, which is the most liberal of all translations of the use of the word "hell," **you will not find a single incidence** of Paul using any of these words!

If most of mankind is indeed bound for hell as many of the preachers of this day continue to preach, with fists pounding and feet stomping, **wouldn't you think** that God's apostle to the nations **would have had his writings full of warnings** about such a detestable and horrid place as a pit of eternal fire and damnation?

Other Writings

I have in my Kindle library a book called "Forbidden books of the original New Testament" by William Wake. The title is obviously a bad one because there is really no such thing as "the original New Testament." The Bible canon was developed over a period of the first 250- 300 years or so of Christian history. Those who were writers of the Bible canon were mostly apostolic in nature. Even though there are writings that were excellent during this period of time from the church fathers, they are not included in the Bible canon because they are not of the apostles or those alive at the time of Christ such as Luke, and James, the brother of Jesus.

There is also no record of any church council having a purpose to make a Bible canon. I have also found no evidence of these books being "forbidden" by anyone during this time frame. Even as late as the sixteenth century, during the time of Martin Luther, we see there was controversy over the books to be included in the Bible canon. Luther was adamant that the books of Hebrews, James, Jude and Revelation be removed from the canon. Commentator William Barclay is reported to have determined that the book of 2 Peter was not actually written by Peter and therefore should be removed.[47]

According to the editor who put this volume of "Forbidden books" together, some of these books are thought to possibly be forgeries being put forth by those who had an agenda to fulfill. Whether this is true or not will probably always be unknown.

But even though this may be a bad title, these books are important. They do give insight as to the thinking of the

---

[47] Taken from the e-sword module Daily Study bible by William Barclay (Look at "The Objections)

believers of the early church. One of the books that I found fascinating was "The Gospel of Nicodemus" which the editor says was originally called "The Acts of Pontius Pilate." It gives a lot of detail that is missing around the crucifixion of our Lord. It also gives an extraordinary account of two people who were said to be the sons of Simeon who held Jesus in the temple as a baby. In this Gospel account these two sons had passed away and were resurrected right after Jesus' death. I assume this is based on the passage of Matthew 27 where we see:

> The tombs also were opened. And many bodies of the saints who had fallen asleep were raised, and coming out of the tombs after his resurrection they went into the holy city and appeared to many.
> (Matthew 27:52-53)

According to "The Gospel of Nicodemus," these two sons of Simeon each wrote down things they saw before their resurrection. If you want to see the details of what was written, I would encourage you to read it. It says that each of the sons separately wrote down what they saw and their records matched precisely. In chapter 27 concerning the account of Jesus descending into Hades it is recorded:

> 1 Death and the devils in great horror at Christ's coming . . . 3 Who art thou, who has no signs of corruption, but that bright appearance which is a full proof of thy greatness, of which yet thou seemest to take no notice? . . . 12 Perhaps thou art that Jesus, of whom Satan just now spoke to our prince, that by the death of the cross thou wert about to receive the power of death. 13 Then the King of Glory trampling upon death, seized the prince of hell, deprived him of

all his power, and **took our earthly father Adam with him to his glory.**[48]

Now you may be asking yourself: Why would you put this questionable account of a book which is possibly a forgery under consideration here?

There is a very good reason for the inclusion of this.

There are only **two possible scenarios** that come to bear on this passage in *The Gospel of Nicodemus*:

1. The account is true as recorded. If it is true, then it is clear beyond any doubt whatsoever that the aionian (age enduring) punishment is **not eternal**, but is temporary and reconciliatory.

2. Even if this account is **a forgery**, and made up by some well-meaning person, then **it clearly shows** that there was a common belief regarding eternal punishment, and that whoever wrote this **did not** believe in such a horrific future for certain people.

or what

Clement of Alexandria

Clement of Alexandria was born around 150 AD, and lived until about 211 AD. Many have proclaimed that he was the first Christian Philosopher. The Christian apology to which much acclaim has been set is entitled *The Stromata*. It begins by showing how God loves the man he created and

---

[48] Wake, William (2012-05-17). Forbidden books of the original New Testament (p. 134-135). Kindle Edition. ("The Gospel of Nicodemus")

continues to show that through the blood of Christ there is a path to the **reconciliation of all men.**[49]

Here are some quotes from this work that show the will of God with respect to man. First, we see the belief that Clement had concerning the reconciliation of man to God:

> But it is the highest and most perfect good, when one is able **to lead back any one from the practice of evil** to virtue and well-doing, which is the very function of the law. So that, when one falls into any incurable evil, -- when taken possession of, for example, by wrong or covetousness, -- **it will be for his good if he is put to death.** For the law is beneficent, being able to make some righteous from unrighteous, if they will only give ear to it, and by releasing others from present evils; for those who have chosen to live temperately and justly, it conducts to immortality.[50]

Why would Clement say that if one falls into incurable evil, it would be preferable that he be put to death? For from our **traditional belief in eternal torment**, this would be the **most horrible outcome imaginable**. From the following quotations we see why he would say that.

> Would, then, that these heretics would learn and be set right by these notes, and turn to the sovereign

---

[49] http://www.earlychristianwritings.com/clement.html

[50] http://www.earlychristianwritings.com/clement.html (Taken from The Stromata, Book i, chapter xxvii)

God! But if, like the deaf serpents, they listen not to the song called new, though very old, may they be chastised by God, and undergo paternal admonitions previous to the Judgment, till they become ashamed and repent, but not rush through headlong unbelief, and precipitate themselves into judgment. For there are partial corrections, which are called chastisements, which many of us who have been in transgression incur, by falling away from the Lord's people. But as children are chastised by their teacher, or their father, so are we by Providence. But **God does not punish**, for punishment is **retaliation** for evil. **He chastises, however, for good to those who are chastised,** collectively and individually.[51]

Yes, as Clement points out in this excerpt above, *Really* **there is no purpose in punishment if it does not have a view to reconciliation.** But there is a definite purpose in the chastisement of God, and that is for their good, that they may be reconciled **through the blood of Christ** back to God. This is the triumph of the blood of Christ!

But other things are desirable for other considerations, such as faith, for escape from punishment, and the advantage arising from reward, which accrue from it. For, in the case of many, fear is the cause of their not sinning; and the promise is the means of pursuing obedience, by which comes salvation. Knowledge, then, desirable as it is for its own sake, is the most perfect good; and consequently,

---

[51] Ibid. The Stromata, Book vii, chapter xvi

the things which follow by means of it are good. **And punishment is the cause of correction to him who is punished**; and to those who are able to see before them he becomes an example, to prevent them failing into the like.[52]

Clement wrote two epistles to the Corinthian Church. Notice the way he words this passage in the opening of Chapter 6 of his first epistle.

1. Redemption for such as have been eminent for their faith, kindness, and charity to their neighbours. By hospitality and goodliness was Lot saved out of Sodom, when all the country round about was destroyed by fire and brimstone.

2. The Lord thereby making it manifest, that he will not forsake those that trust in him; but will bring the disobedient to **punishment and correction.**[53]

Yes, according to Clement, one of the most respected Church Fathers, **there is corrective punishment** after death. This confirms what Scripture tells us, from the writings of the apostle Paul, that God will reconcile ALL things to himself.

In him **we have redemption through his blood**, the forgiveness of our trespasses, according to the

---

[52]Ibid. The Stromata, Book vi, chapter xii

[53] Wake, William (2012-05-17). Forbidden books of the original New Testament (p. 193) Kindle Edition.

riches of his grace, which he lavished upon us, in all wisdom and insight making known to us the mystery of his will, according to his purpose, which he set forth in Christ as a plan for the fullness of time, **to unite all things in him, things in heaven and things on earth.** (Ephesians 1:7-10)

Origen of Alexandria (AD 185—254)

Origen of Alexandria was a pupil of Clement. He lived from about AD 185 to about AD 254. He is considered to be one of the greatest of the Christian theologians.

He was foremost in the refutation of the mystic Gnosticism of his day. He was also a polished Christian philosopher who was **fluent in Greek** and the Greek philosophical traditions. Throughout his life, he composed a great many documentaries and commentaries. His most famous work was ***DePrincipiis*** (On First Principles), but he also composed several other works such as ***Origen Against Celsus***, a ***Commentary on John***, and among other things, several letters. His work ***Origen against Celsus,*** was a response to the Pagan philosopher Celsus, who vociferously attacked Christianity.

Origen was famous for his teaching of the **restoration of all things.** This was based on a passage in 1 Corinthians chapter 15:

For as in Adam **all die**, so also in Christ shall **all be made alive**. But each in his own order: Christ the firstfruits, then at his coming those who belong to Christ. Then comes the end, when he delivers the kingdom to God the Father after destroying every rule and every authority and power. For he must reign until he has put **all his enemies under his feet**. The last enemy to be destroyed is death. For "God has put all things in subjection under his feet." But when it says, "all things are put in subjection," it is plain that he is excepted who put all things in subjection under him. When all things are subjected to him, then the Son himself will also be subjected to him who put all things in subjection under him, that God may be all in all. (1 Corinthians 15:22-28)

The subjection of all things "under his feet" is a reference to the **restoration of all things to God.** It could be said that this was one of the **most important concepts** in the philosophy of Origen. He probably learned much of this as a pupil of Clement whose view of man's destiny was called restorationism.

As a student of Clement, it is reasonable to assume that his philosophical views originated from this training.

Regarding the restoration of man to God, notice the words of Origen:

Now I am of opinion that **another species of punishment may be understood to exist**; because, as we feel that when the limbs of the body are loosened and torn away from their mutual supports, there is produced pain of a most excruciating kind, so, when the soul shall be found to be beyond the order, and connection, and harmony in which it was created by God for the purposes of good and useful action and observation, and not to harmonize with itself in the connection of its rational movements, it must be deemed to bear the **chastisement** and torture of its own dissension, and to feel the punishments of its own disordered condition. And when this dissolution and rending asunder of soul shall have been **tested by the application of fire**, a solidification undoubtedly into a firmer structure will take place, and **a restoration be effected.**[54]

Notice that Origen's belief was that the pain of this punishment would be for the purpose of **chastisement**, and the **ultimate restoration** of the individual.

As one of the most highly regarded theologians of his day, Origen believed that **God is in control and is absolutely sovereign.** As such he believed that God's will would be fully accomplished in the redemption.

William Barclay said of him:

Origen believed that after death there were many who would need prolonged instruction, the sternest discipline, even the severest punishment before they were fit for the presence of God. Origen **did not eliminate hell;** he believed **that some people would have to go to heaven via hell.** He believed

---

[54] Origen (2011-10-27). The Works of Origen: De Principiis, Letters of Origen, Origen Against Celsus (3 Books With Active Table of Contents) (Kindle Locations 3373-3380). . Kindle Edition.

that even at the end of the day there would be some on whom the scars remained.

He **did not** believe in eternal *punishment*, but he did see the possibility of **eternal *penalty***. And so the choice is whether we accept God's offer and invitation willingly, or take **the long and terrible** way round through ages of purification.

There are many others, in fact, most of the church fathers up to the time of Augustine who believed in the ultimate reconciliation of man to God. In his book, ***Christ Triumphant, or Universalism Attested***, Thomas Allin shows that the following individuals also believed in this concept. These include Ambrose, the Bishop of Milan, Basil of Caesarea, Gregory, Bishop of Nyssa, and the great theologian Jerome, the son of Christian historian Eusebius.

Regarding Gregory, the Bishop of Nyssa, Barclay also commented:

Gregory of Nyssa offered three reasons why he believed in universalism. First, he believed in it because of the *character of God*. "Being good, God entertains pity for fallen man; being wise, he is not ignorant of the means for his recovery." Second, he believed in it because of *the nature of evil*. Evil must in the end be moved out of existence, "so that the absolutely non-existent should cease to be at all." Evil is essentially negative and doomed to non-existence. Third, he believed in it because of *the purpose of punishment*. **The purpose of punishment is always remedial.** Its aim is "to get the good separated from the evil and to attract it into the communion of blessedness." **Punishment will hurt**, but it is **like the fire** which separates the alloy from the gold; it is **like the surgery** which removes the diseased thing; it is like the **cautery which burns out** that which cannot be removed any other way."[55]

Augustine of Hippo

While most of the early church fathers mentioned above were from the east, there arose from the west one **who would become a dominating force in the early Christian church**. His name was Augustine of Hippo. He was raised by his mother in an upper-class Roman environment. Thus, it appears that his native language was Latin. Although his mother was a devout Christian, his father was a Pagan who was converted shortly before his death. His mother was determined that he would be raised as a Christian. However, it is reported that at the age of 11, during his early schooling Augustine became familiar **with Latin literature that highlighted pagan beliefs and practices**. This led him to leave Christianity for a time and follow the Manichaean religion **from which he developed his doctrine of eternal torment.**

It is **very important** for all to see **the background** upon which the revered "Church Father" Augustine studied. It was **a pagan religion!** Here is what we find about the Manichean religion:

---

[55] http://www.auburn.edu/~allenkc/barclay1.html

Manichaeism is a religion founded by Iranian prophet Mani during the 3rd century CE. It mainly talks about the struggle between good and evil and the light and the darkness, therefore considered as a form of religious Dualism. It is classified as a religion that is a combination of Christianity, **Zoroastrianism, Buddhism** and Judaism.[56]

He also became quite a problem for the authorities because of his mischievous behavior. But later on, by the time he had grown to maturity and become a man, he returned to the Christian upbringing that his mother taught him and decided to become a Priest.

Although he was a brilliant student, **he was never able to master the Greek language** due to a heavy disdain for his Greek teacher. By the time he realized the importance of it, it was too late. This created problems for him as a theologian. **He was**, however, **a master of the Latin language.**

Since all of the early writings of the early church were in Greek, and Augustine was unable to master it, he was improperly influenced by some of his predecessors. So, as Augustine continued to rise in the ranks of the Western Church, so did his theology. His promotion of **eternal torment** became the **dominant** position in the church from about the fifth century onward. In other words, the doctrine of **eternal torment was NOT TAUGHT** in the church for **the first four hundred years!**

Even though he was **surrounded by those who believed in the ultimate reconciliation** of the lost, **he**

---

[56] (Taken from Manichaeism – Home: anichaeismreligion.weebly.com/

continued to promulgate the horrendous Pagan doctrine of eternal punishment.

Here is a quote which explains his reasoning:

> **It is quite in vain,** then, that some–indeed very many–yield to merely human feelings and deplore the notion of the eternal punishment of the damned and their interminable and perpetual misery. They do not believe that such things will be. Not that they would go counter to divine Scripture–but, yielding to their own human feelings, they soften what seems harsh and give a milder emphasis to statements they believe are meant more to terrify than to express the literal truth. " 'God will not forget,' " they say, " 'to show mercy, nor in his anger will he shut up his mercy.' " This is, in fact, the text of a holy psalm. But there is no doubt that it is to be interpreted to refer to those who are called "vessels of mercy," those who are freed from misery not by their own merits but through God's mercy. Even so, if they suppose that the text applies to all men, there is no ground for them further to suppose that there can be an end for those of whom it is said, " 'Thus these shall go into **everlasting punishment**.' " Otherwise, it can as well be thought that there will also be an end to the happiness of those of whom the antithesis was said: " 'But the righteous into life eternal.'[57]

If we trace the reason for this mistaken notion of eternal punishment, we can trace it back to Augustine's **lack of**

---

[57]http://www.saviourofall.org/2003Newsletters/42003Augustine.html

training in the original language of the New Testament which was Greek. The words "everlasting punishment" from the gospel of Matthew 25:46 are the Greek words κολασιν αιωνιον which when most properly translated means **age-enduring correction**. The Greek words, αιδιος τιμορια (aidios timoria) **were not used!** These were the words from the Greek that would truly mean eternal punishment. Yes, it is true that this age-enduring correction could go on for a very long period of time, depending on the nature of the punishment, but at some point, **it will end in that person seeing the love of Christ** in the light of the blood of the cross. Then he will be praising God for the rest of eternity.

And as we discussed in the previous chapter, God does have both those who have been designated as vessels of mercy, and vessels of wrath. But does that mean that God is cruel to some and kind to others? How is it that we could be convinced that a God of love would act in such a manner? Isn't it obvious that this is totally counter to the nature of God? John Wesley Hanson shows the contrast between Origen and Augustine as follows:

> The contrast between Origen's system and Augustine's is as that of light and darkness; with the first, Fatherhood, Love, Hope, Joy, Salvation; with the other, Vengeance, Punishment, Sin, Eternal Despair. **With Origen God triumphs in final unity; with Augustine man continues in endless rebellion**, and **God is defeated**, and an eternal dualism prevails. And the effect on the believer was in the one case a pitying love and charity that gave the melting heart that could not bear to think of even the devil unsaved, and that antedated the poet's prayer,— "Oh,

wad ye take a thought and mend," and that believed the prayer would be answered; and in the other a stony-hearted indifference to the misery of mankind, which he called "one damned batch and mass of perdition."[58]

So how was it that Augustine erred in this matter? Hanson describes it this way:

Augustine assumed and insisted that the words defining the duration of punishment, in the New Testament, teach its endlessness, and the claim set up by Augustine is the one still held by the advocates of "the dying belief," that *aeternus* in the Latin, and *aionios* in the original Greek, mean interminable duration. It seems that a Spanish presbyter, Orosius, visited Augustine in the year 413, and besought him for arguments to meet the position that punishment is not to be without end, because *aionios* does not denote eternal, but limited duration. Augustine replied that though *aion* signifies limited as well as endless duration, the Greeks only used *aionios* for endless, and he originated the argument so much resorted to even yet, based in the fact that in Matt. xxv: 46, the same word is applied to "life," and to "punishment." The student of Greek need not be told that Augustine's argument is incorrect, and he scarcely needs to be assured that Augustine did not

---

[58] Hanson, J.W. (2014-09-16). Universalism: The Prevailing Doctrine of the Christian Church During Its First 500 Years (Kindle Locations 3213-3220). . Kindle Edition.

know Greek. This he confesses. He says he "hates Greek," and the "grammar learning of the Greeks." it is anomalous in the history of criticism that generations of scholars should take their cue in a matter of Greek definition from one who admits that he had "learned almost nothing of Greek," and was "not competent to read and understand" the language, and reject the position held by those who were born Greeks! That such a man should contradict and subvert the teachings of such men as Clement, Origen, the Gregories and others whose mother-tongue was Greek, is passing strange. But his powerful influence, aided by civil arm, established his doctrine till it came to rule the centuries.[59]

The purpose of this chapter is to show what happened in the history of the early Church to show how the doctrine of the reconciliation of all mankind got suppressed and how the doctrine of eternal torment came into being. Had Augustine been more diligent in his study of the Greek language, his error most likely would not have happened. It is truly amazing that Augustine was able to wrongfully contradict the teachings of these well learned Church Fathers even though their "mother tongue" was Greek. And now because of this deception derived from Pagan religions, the majority of Christendom has accepted the atrocious belief of eternal torment.

---

[59] Ibid. (Kindle Locations 3238-3246)

Chapter 11

Rewards!
God's Promise for the Believer

"Surely there is a reward for the righteous; surely there is a God who judges on earth." Psalm 68:11

■■

I can't imagine what it must be like to be an atheist. First of all, what great faith it must take to believe that everything around us happened by accident. But Oh! What sadness must grip the heart of that one when he is facing death!

The scenario for that individual must be as follows: You go out of existence, just like a plant that has died. No future, no warmth, nothing but the coldness of eternity while your formerly spirit filled body rots in the grave, or in the extreme heat of a cremation fire.

However, the believer knows that God has stated in his word that He put eternity in the heart of man. "He has made everything beautiful in its time. Also, He has put eternity in their hearts, except that no one can find out the work that God does from beginning to end." (Ecclesiastes 3:11)

Therein lies the problem. We can only find out what God has in store for man **from knowing God and His son**, and **by putting our trust in Him**. This is based on faith – yes, but it is also based on knowledge which can only be obtained by looking into His word.

On the other side of the coin we find people who state: "Well if God's grace is so great, then why shouldn't I just go ahead and sin as much as I want and live a life of pure selfishness? After all, I will be reconciled, right?

Well there are two problems with this. First of all, all of this sin **will not make you happy**. The truth is that **you will be miserable** in your sin. Secondly, if you spend your life living in such a manner, you will **spend eternity missing out** on some really **wonderful rewards and that** includes the peace of God you will experience **NOW!**

At this point, we must face a passage of Scripture which is startling when we first see it. The apostle Paul wrote the following under inspiration:

Now he who plants and he who waters are one; but each will receive his own reward according to his own labor. (1 Corinthians 3:8 NASB)

And also,

"For we must all appear before the judgment seat of Christ, so that each one may receive what is due for what he has done in the body, whether good or evil." (2 Corinthians 5:10 NKJV)

With this in mind, I would like to focus on the positive aspects of this judgment. Later on, in the same chapter:

"Anyone who belongs to Christ is a new person. The past is forgotten, and everything is new. God has done it all! He sent Christ to make peace between himself and us, and he has given us the work of making peace between himself and others. What we mean is that God was in Christ, **offering peace and forgiveness to the people of this world.** And he has given us the work of sharing his message about peace." (2 Corinthians 5:17-19 CEV)

Jesus reiterated this in the last chapter of the Bible when he imparted it to the apostle John who wrote:

"And behold, I am coming **quickly, and My reward is with Me**, to give to every one according to his work." (Revelation 22:12)

Although the focus of this passage was to those suffering under the intense persecution of the Jewish Sanhedrin and the Roman Empire, the principle still stands today. That principle is: **God loves us and wants to reward us for the good works we do!** Yes, the unchangeable God is still exercising the same principle that he stated in the Old Testament thousands of years ago:

"For the eyes of the LORD run to and fro throughout the whole earth, to show Himself strong on behalf of *those* whose heart *is* loyal to Him." (2 Chronicles 16:9 NKJV)

For those of us who have a heart that is loyal to him, **we want him to see our deeds**! It will be the basis of our rewards! If we are going to stand before God in such a manner, we are assured that our deeds will be the evidence we bring to Christ's courtroom to demonstrate that our faith is real. They will show God the measure of our faith. The Apostle Paul noted:

> For by the grace given to me I say to everyone among you not to think of himself more highly than he ought to think, but to think with sober judgment, each according to the measure of faith that God has assigned. (Romans 12:3)

In fact, Paul stated that he was praying for the saints, that they may fulfill the complete measure of their faith:

> To this end we always pray for you, that our God may **make you worthy of his calling** and may fulfill every resolve for good and every work of faith by his power, **so that the name of our Lord Jesus may be glorified in you**, and you in him, according to the grace of our God and the Lord Jesus Christ. (2 Thessalonians 1:11-12)

This is the love of God! It is love in its purest and most unselfish form imaginable. With this in mind, let's look at what else God's word has to say about the rewards that God gives those whose heart is loyal to him.

The Old Testament book of Ruth is perhaps the most unique book in the Bible. It outlines a severe tragedy which happened to a Jewish family of four who tried to flee from the famine in the land of Israel to the land of Moab. During this stay, the mother Naomi lost her husband and both of her sons. Her two daughters-in-law survived and were taking care of Naomi. But Naomi realized she needed to return to the land of Israel. One of her Moabite daughters-in-law, Ruth, shows her loyalty to Naomi by returning with her to Israel.

Since Naomi and Ruth were destitute, the only thing open for Ruth was to glean the fields during the harvest. The field she was directed to was that of a wealthy relative of Naomi named Boaz. As a result of this loyalty Ruth was **rewarded** by Boaz, who became the kinsman redeemer to her.

So, she fell on her face, bowed down to the ground, and said to him, "Why have I found favor in your eyes, that you should take notice of me, since I *am* a foreigner?" And Boaz answered and said to her, "It has been fully reported to me, all that you have done for your mother-in-law since the death of your husband, and *how* you have left your father and your mother and the land of your birth, and have come to a people whom you did not know before. The LORD repay your work, and a **full reward be given you by the LORD** God of Israel, under whose wings you have come for refuge." (Ruth 2:10-12)

Ruth **was indeed fully rewarded**, and the result was that she married Boaz. This God sent union led to the births of David the King of Israel, and eventually through that line of descent, led to the birth of Christ. But this was part of God's plan all along. Boaz was a descendant of Abraham to whom God made the original promise.

Abraham was promised he would be repaid for his faithfulness. God told him:

After these things the word of the LORD came to Abram in a vision, saying, "Do not be afraid, Abram. I *am* your shield, **your exceedingly great reward**." (Genesis 15:1)

The union of Ruth and Boaz played a crucial role in that reward, because this union led to Christ through whom the original promise to Abraham could be fulfilled. But the point of telling this wonderful story is to reiterate the fact that **God looks for opportunities to reward** those who are his servants. This is part of our blessing as a believer!

When Jesus gave the Sermon on the Mount, he had rewards on his mind. Notice what he said as he spoke before the crowds:

> "Blessed are you when others revile you and persecute you and utter all kinds of evil against you falsely on my account. Rejoice and be glad, **for your reward is great in heaven**, for so they persecuted the prophets who were before you. (Matthew 5:11-12)

> For if you love those who love you, **what reward** do you have? Do not even the tax collectors do the same? (Matthew 5:46)

> "**Beware** of practicing your righteousness before other people in order to be seen by them, for then you will have **no reward** from your Father who is in heaven. Thus, when you give to the needy, sound no trumpet before you, as **the hypocrites** do in the synagogues and in the streets, that they may be praised by others. Truly, I say to you, they **have received their reward**. so that your giving may be in secret. And **your Father who sees in secret will reward you.** And when you pray, **you must**

not be like the hypocrites. For they love to stand and pray in the synagogues and at the street corners, that they may be seen by others. Truly, I say to you, **they have received their reward**. But when you pray, go into your room and shut the door and pray to your Father who is in secret. And **your Father who sees in secret will reward you**." (Matthew 6:1-2, 4-6)

"And when you fast, do not look gloomy like the hypocrites, for they disfigure their faces that their fasting may be seen by others. Truly, I say to you, they have received their reward. But when you fast, anoint your head and wash your face, that your fasting may not be seen by others but by your Father who is in secret. And **your Father who sees in secret will reward you**."(Matthew 6:16-18)

Did you count those passages as you read them? Eight times in the Sermon on the Mount as recorded in the sixth chapter of Matthew he mentions rewards! Some of these that he mentioned were negative because the hypocritical Pharisees would parade **their** presence, **their** giving, and **their** prayers so that people **would see them** and **praise them** for their righteousness. What Jesus was saying here was that because they were doing it **for their recognition**, and **their praise**, this recognition would be their only reward. You see, **God reads hearts!** What was their motivation for their deeds? Was it for God to receive praise and honor? Or was it done in order that **they** would receive it?

The God who reads men's hearts **wants to reward** those who do things for the right motivation. Notice what is said above in his Word: "Rejoice and be glad, **for your reward is great in heaven.**" These are the rewards that are important because they last forever. But this was not Jesus last word on this. In Luke 14 we have another account that shows the importance of rewards. As the chapter begins, we see that Jesus was invited to dinner at the home of the leader of the Pharisees. On the surface this sounds like a good thing. But actually, there was a hidden agenda. The verse states it this way:

> One Sabbath, when he went to dine at the house of a ruler of the Pharisees, they were watching him carefully. (Luke 14:1)

Why were they watching him carefully? There was no pure motive here. They hated Jesus. It was because they wanted to accuse him of breaking the Sabbath. How was this so? It was because they had invited a man with an incurable disease, and they wanted to see if Jesus would heal him. This alone shows the condition of their hearts. Instead of being happy if Jesus healed the man, they were going to accuse him of breaking the laws of God. But this is not the point I want to make regarding this passage.

Let's move to a little later in the passage. As we watch what Jesus said in verse 12, I am sure he did not endear himself to the one who invited him. He said:

> "When you give a dinner or a banquet, do not invite your friends or your brothers or your relatives or rich neighbors, lest they also invite you in return and you be repaid. But when you give a feast, invite the poor, the crippled, the lame, the blind, and you will be

blessed, because they **cannot repay** you. **For you will be repaid at the resurrection of the just.**" (Luke 14:12-14)

Did you notice the profound nature of that last statement? Jesus was telling them that **by doing good works** toward others with no possibility of being paid back for their deeds, they would be **repaid by God AFTER THEIR DEATH!**

Yes! This is the true nature of a loving God. Just as you would be looking for any opportunity to praise or reward your own children for their good works, so our loving God does for us! It is exactly as stated by the writer of 2 Chronicles in the Old Testament when he said under the inspiration of the Holy Spirit:

For the eyes of the LORD run to and fro throughout the whole earth, to give strong support **to those whose heart is blameless toward him**. (2 Chronicles 16:9)

Yes! He is continually searching hearts to find those who love him enough to obey him and seek him. The Greek word for rewards is μισθος, (pronounced misthos). This word means "dues paid for work; wages, hire" (From Thayer's Greek Lexicon). That means that when we do good deeds here on earth for others, or for the work of Christ, **he will pay us wages**! But these wages will not be given to us at this time, for as he said:

"Do not lay up for yourselves treasures on earth, where moth and rust destroy and where thieves break in and steal, but lay up for yourselves **treasures in heaven**, where neither moth nor rust destroys and where thieves do not break in and steal. For where your treasure is, there your heart will be also. (Matt 6:19-21)

The Scriptures are completely accurate in assessing that **God is love.** Less than three centuries after the death of Christ, Origen made showed that God's justice and goodness are such that he wants to **pay us wages** for the good things that we do. Origen said that in his day, there were certain ones who sought to say that God's justice is different that his goodness. But Origen went on to show from a verse in Psalm 78:34 that that is not true.

So, he made their days vanish like a breath, and their years in terror. **When he killed them, they sought him**; they repented and sought God earnestly. They remembered that God was their rock, the Most High God their redeemer. (Psalm 78:33-35)

Contrary to most commentators, notice how Origen interprets this verse:

And of those also who fell in the desert, let them hear what is related in the seventy-eighth Psalm, which bears the superscription of Asaph; for he says, "When He slew them, then they sought Him." He does not say that some sought Him after others had been slain, but he says that the destruction of those who were killed was of such a nature that, **when put to death, they sought God.** By all which it is established, that the God of the law and the Gospels is one and the same, a just and good God, and that **He confers benefits justly, and punishes with kindness;** since neither goodness without justice, nor justice without goodness, can display the (real) dignity of the divine nature.[60]

Yes, Origen believed that God was so good that **even after these men died, they repented**. Could this be proof from the Old Testament of the truth of Isaiah's words?

By myself I have sworn; from my mouth has gone out in righteousness a word that shall not return: **'To me every knee shall bow, every tongue shall swear allegiance.'** (Isaiah 45:23)

Origen continues to explain regarding the love, justice, and rewards of God:

And this is a point which I wish impressed upon those who peruse these pages, that with respect to topics of such difficulty and obscurity we use our utmost endeavour, not so much to ascertain clearly the solutions of the questions (for every one will do this as the Spirit gives him utterance), as to maintain the rule of faith in the most unmistakeable manner, by striving to show that **the providence of God**, which equitably administers all things, governs also immortal souls on the justest principles, (**conferring rewards) according to the merits and motives of each individual**; the present economy of things **not being confined within the life of this world,** but the pre-existing state of merit always furnishing the ground for the state that is to

---

[60] Origen (2011-10-27). The Works of Origen: De Principiis, (Kindle Locations 2470-2476).

follow, and thus by an eternal and immutable law of equity, and by the controlling influence of Divine Providence, the immortal soul is brought to the summit of perfection.[61]

Origin, who lived less than three hundred years after Christ, clearly believed that God so loved that he would eventually **bring all souls** to the summit of perfection in the life to come. But the Scriptures explain clearly that there will be suffering for those who reject him in this life. But knowing this, it should not surprise us that God **not only** wants to reward us; he is **continually looking** for ways to reward us believers as his children.

David was on the run from King Saul who was seeking to kill him. Saul wanted to find David so bad that he led a group of three thousand men to try and find him. What should David do? Should he retaliate and try to kill Saul before Saul killed him? NO! Instead, David went into the camp while Saul was sleeping and took Saul's spear. Then after removing himself to a safe place, he called out to Saul to show him that he could have killed him. But he would not do it! Why? Because **he respected God's appointment** of Saul as King. Notice what he does:

> And David answered and said, "Here is the spear, O king! Let one of the young men come over and take it. **The LORD rewards every man for his righteousness and his faithfulness**, for the

[61] Origen (2011-10-27). The Works of Origen: De Principiis, Letters of Origen, Origen Against Celsus (3 Books With Active Table of Contents) (Kindle Locations 4118-4126). . Kindle Edition.

LORD gave you into my hand today, and I would not put out my hand against the LORD's anointed. Behold, as your life was precious this day in my sight, so may my life be precious in the sight of the LORD, and may he deliver me out of all tribulation." Then Saul said to David, "Blessed be you, my son David! You will do many things and will succeed in them." So David went his way, and Saul returned to his place. (1 Samuel 26:22-25)

David knew this principle. He was aware that he had favor with God, and that to do such a thing as kill the anointed one of God **would lead to disapproval** from him. Instead, he preserved Saul's life, **waiting on God's timing**, and he knew that for this he would receive a reward. Of course, we know that **he DID receive that reward** later on when God made him King over all of Israel.

We cannot work our way to heaven. The apostle Paul wrote to the church in Ephesus:

For by grace you have been saved through faith. And this is not your own doing; it is the gift of God, not a result of works, so that no one may boast. (Ephesians 2:8-9)

The important principle here that we must realize is that even though our works will not get us to heaven on their own merits, **they are important**. Even though David did receive a reward in this life, God has much **bigger rewards** available for us if we will do good works for the Kingdom of God while here on this earth. This is the benefit of the believer! But just exactly how much does this count for us in heaven? Notice the words:

> And everyone who has left houses or brothers or sisters or father or mother or children or lands, for my name's sake, **will receive a hundredfold** and will inherit eternal life. (Matthew 19:29)

Wow! See how much God wants to reward us! We all have issues that keep us from doing much more for Christ. But God will reward us for what we do for the sake of the kingdom. In closing this chapter, I would like to share a story which I have found in my old Sunday school library which seems appropriate here:

> A Water Bearer in India had two large pots; each hung on each end of a pole, which he carried across his neck. One of the pots had a crack in it, and while the other pot was perfect and always delivered a full portion of water at the end of the long walk from the stream to the master's house, the cracked pot arrived only half full.

> For a full two years this went on daily, with the bearer delivering only one and a half pots full of water to his master's house. Of course, the perfect pot was proud of its accomplishments, perfect to the end for which it was made. But the poor cracked pot was ashamed of its own imperfection, and miserable that it was able to accomplish only half of what it had been made to do. After two years of what perceived to be a bitter failure, it spoke to the Water Bearer one day by the stream.

"I am ashamed of myself, and I want to apologize to you."

"Why?" asked the bearer. " What are you ashamed of?" "I have been able, for these past two years, to deliver only half my load because this crack in my side causes water to leak out all the way back to your master's house. Because of my flaws, you have to do all of this work, and you don't get full value from your efforts," the pot said.

The Water Bearer felt sorry for the old cracked pot, and in his compassion he said, "As we return to the master's house, I want you to notice the beautiful flowers along the path."

Indeed, as they went up the hill, the old cracked pot took notice of the sun warming the beautiful wild flowers on the side of the path, and this cheered it some. But at the end of the trail, it still felt bad because it had leaked out half its load, and so again it apologized to the bearer for its failure.

The bearer said to the pot, "Did you notice that there were flowers only on your side of your path, but not on the other pot's side? That's because I have always known about your flaw, and I took advantage of it. I planted flower seeds on your side of the path, and every day while we walk back from the stream, you've watered them. For two years I have been able to pick these beautiful flowers to decorate my master's table. Without you being just the way you are, he would not have this beauty to grace his house."

So, what is the moral of this story? Each of us **has our own unique flaws; we're all cracked pots.** But we know that we as believers are saved, and if we will do good works for the sake of the Kingdom of God, he will not only use us to create something beautiful, but God will use those flaws in such a way that it will bring glory to him.

This is the blessing of the believer, knowing that in **OUR** weakness we find **HIS** strength.

> But he said to me, "My grace is sufficient for you, for my power is made perfect in weakness." Therefore I will boast all the more gladly of my weaknesses, so that the power of Christ may rest upon me. (2 Corinthians 12:9)

This is the promise to the believer. Let us take hold of it and prosper!

Epilogue

As I conclude the writing of this book, I do so **full well knowing** that someone will pick up this book and after looking at a few pages **will declare that I am guilty of heresy!** Yes, this, **even though** it is a fact that the doctrine of eternal torment **was not taught** for the **first four hundred years** of the early church until the time of Augustine! As former President John F. Kennedy used to say: "Well, let me say this about that." Looking at the definition of this dreaded term, we find from the Oxford Dictionary that heresy is "belief or opinion contrary to orthodox religious (especially Christian) doctrine."

So, who can be classified as a heretic? Well in the days of church fathers Origen and Clement, Augustine would have been a heretic. The opposite would have been true by the time Augustine climbed to the top of the theological ladder with his pagan underpinnings of eternal torment. When we look at those throughout the course of history who have been called "heretic," we find perhaps the most famous of all is Protestant reformer Martin Luther.

As my research for this book progressed, I was swayed in different directions. Prior to my research, I would have to say that I was bewildered concerning this topic. Even though my theological training in seminary outlined the position of eternal torment for the lost, this position was difficult for me to advocate or support. I basically ignored my thoughts about this for years. As I started to examine the subject again, it soon became apparent to me that the doctrine of eternal torment seemed to be contrary to the love of God. Finally, I decided to take on the study in earnest.

First of all, I decided that as a basic foundation for my study, I must look at the **attributes of God**, since these will be the basis for the **actions of God.** The primary relative attributes of the infinite God of the Universe as related to the creation are as follows:

Immutability – This means that the nature, attributes, and will of God are all exempt from change. God is always the same! (Malachi 3:6; James 1:17)

Omnipresence – God, in the totality of his essence, penetrates and fills the entire universe. He is everywhere, all the time. (Psalm 139:7-10; Jeremiah 23:23-24)

Omniscience – He has perfect knowledge of all things, past, present, and future. (1 Samuel 23:10-13; Job 23:10; 37:16; Psalm 139:1-4)

Omnipotence – He is all powerful, able to do all things which are the object of his power. (Exodus 15:6; Deuteronomy 9:29; 1 Chronicles 29:11; Psalm 147:5)

With this as a baseline, I decided that I should go back to the beginning in Genesis and look at the promises of God and build upon them with a look at how the rest of the Scriptures lined up with these promises. Since God is omniscient, and omnipresent, the fact that Adam and Eve sinned was **not a surprise.** In fact, he made provision for this event before the foundation of the world, just as he knew us then also. (Jeremiah 1:5; John 17:24; Ephesians 1:4; 1 Peter 1:20)

Thus, the promise in Genesis 3:14-15 began the process of redemption. Here God told the serpent (Satan) that the offspring of the woman (Eve) would eventually "bruise his head." The beginning of this promise was carried out through Abraham. God promised Abraham that "in you **all the families of the earth shall be blessed.**" (Genesis 12:3) Notice that God **did not ask** Abraham if he was willing to participate. It is was **the determined will of God** that this was going to happen! This is a perfect reflection of his omnipotence! God is in complete control. Additionally, there were **no conditional requirements** imposed upon Abraham. **It was going to happen no matter what!**

This theme was carried all the way through the Old Testament, and just before Jesus came upon the scene, his forerunner, John the Baptist stated: "**all flesh** shall see the salvation of God!" This was in perfect harmony with what the immutable (unchangeable) God said to Abraham. It was now about to come to pass. Yes – the Lord Jesus, the Christ, "the Lamb of God who takes away the sin of the world" (John 1:29) was now walking the earth! This is the one of whom the Apostle Paul stated "at the right time, Christ died for the ungodly" and "while we were still sinners, Christ died for us," (Romans 5:6-8) and also: "For to this end Christ died and lived again, that he might be Lord both of the dead and the living." (Romans 14:9)

When God's chosen people, the descendants of Abraham, committed the detestable act of sacrificing their children by throwing them into the fire of the false god Molech, he told them that they had done a detestable evil in his sight "to burn their sons and daughters in the fire, which I did not command, **nor did it come into my mind.**" (Jeremiah 7:30-31) As a result of this, and other atrocities, he **destroyed the city** and made the area next to Jerusalem a garbage dump which eventually came to be known as Gehenna. But even though their bodies were dead, their spirits were gathered in Sheol, awaiting the judgment which would come after the resurrection of Christ.

This brings me to the claim by some that those who do not accept Christ **in this life** will be **annihilated** in the judgment. Those who lay claim to this idea use such Old testament passages as:

He who sacrifices to any god, except to Yahweh only, **shall be utterly destroyed**. (Exodus 22:20)

The LORD will make the rain of your land powder. From heaven dust shall come down on you until **you are destroyed**. (Deuteronomy 28:24)

But the Hebrew word used here is **charam,** which more often means to **seclude, make accursed, consecrate,** or **forfeit!** All of these are **temporary conditions.** They also use passages such as this one:

But the wicked will **perish;** the enemies of the LORD are like the glory of the pastures; **they vanish**—like smoke they vanish away. (Psalm 37:20)

But in Isaiah 57:1 we see that it says the **righteous perish**. The Hebrew word for perish is **abad** which could mean to annililate, but **certainly not in the above passage**. More often it means to wander away, break, fail, lose, or be undone.

They also use such New Testament passages as:

Don't be afraid of those who kill the body, but are not able to kill the soul. Rather, fear him who is able to **destroy** both soul and body in **Gehenna.** (**Matthew 10:28 WEB**)

However, we find that the Greek word for destroy is απολλυμι. The English spelling is **apollumi.** I will **emphasize again** the fact that in Vine's Expository Dictionary of Biblical Words we find: "The idea is **NOT** extinction but **ruin, loss, not of being, but of well-being**.[62] Thus, this Greek word does **NOT** support annihilationism.

Then there is the passage of Scripture that the annihilationists must try to get around which is Hebrews 9:27 which states:

And just as it is appointed for man to die **ONCE**, and after that comes judgment, (Hebrews 9:27)

If we look at this passage, it indicates that man only dies **ONCE**. Do you see **the power of this** statement? In effect man only perishes in human bodily form. He does **NOT** perish completely. If he were to be annihilated after the judgment, **then he would die TWICE!**

But contrary to the concept of annihilation, during all of the pages of the Old Testament, we see the principle that **the punishment must fit the crime.** This was a basic principle of the Old Covenant. The punishment was **for the purpose of correction.** It was not because God wanted

---

[62] Vines Expository Dictionary of New Testament Words, Fleming H. Revel Co. 1966 p. 302

vengeance upon them. It was a corrective discipline much the same as you would give your children. How do I know this? This is where it got really interesting!

As I studied the passage most commonly used "And these will go away into eternal punishment" (Matthew 25:46) to show that God sends people to a place of eternal torment forever, I was determined to **thoroughly dissect this argument.** Through my research I found out that the words Jesus used were **very specifically crafted** in this verse to display precisely that this punishment was **NOT** for the sake of vengeance (Greek – **timoria**) but for the sake of correction (Greek – **kolasis**). I also discovered that the time frame was not "eternal" as we know it (Greek – **aidios**), but it was for an age (**aion** – Greek). Knowing that the Old Covenant law showed that "the punishment **must** fit the crime" and knowing the fact that God does **NOT** change, this absolutely **slammed the door** on the idea that God would torment **anyone forever** in a burning fire.

I am now persuaded strongly that this position is correct. Since I consider myself a "Berean Christian" (Acts 17:10-11), I must say that this position is subject to continual evaluation, as should be the case with all of us.

We as believers can praise God that our Lord loved us enough to fulfill his promise, and to come to the earth as promised through the seed of Abraham to die for us. It is clear that if you are Christian, **you must believe** that people are only **saved by grace through faith in Jesus Christ.** You also must believe that it is the **blood of Christ** that allows for the redemption of mankind. That is the difference between salvation and redemption. Salvation is the "what," and redemption is the "how" of the work of Christ on the cross.

Through the pages of this book, we have been on a journey to look at what the Bible says about the love of God and his mercy. The Scriptures assure us that "God is love." This is not just a quality of God's personality; **it is the essence of his being!** Do you get the full impact of that statement? If God **IS** love, then it is **not possible** to act in a manner that is outside of this quality. The Scriptures **affirm** this, for Paul wrote:

> And we know that for those who love God **all things work together for good**, for those who are called according to his purpose. (Romans 8:28)

Paul wrote this to encourage the church in Rome, for they were undergoing severe persecution from the Jews and from the Roman authorities. Nero was the maniacal Emperor of Rome at the time, and in his madness, he liked to make shirts of candle wax and put them on Christians and light them for his entertainment.

In Romans 8:28, Paul was not implying that God does not love all people. As we pointed out earlier, Jesus said:

> But **love your enemies**, and do good, and lend, expecting nothing in return, and your reward will be great, and you will be sons of the Most High, **for he is kind to the ungrateful and the evil.** (Luke 6:35)

You who are parents, can you imagine setting fire to your child? No matter what bad thing that they may do, can you imagine burning them, even for a moment? Is it possible for a God who **IS** love to have a desire to inflict more pain than a human parent? This principle tells us that the fire of purification that is spoken of in Scripture **is different** than what we know in the physical realm; but the Scriptures indicate that it has the same effect on a person that literal fire has on precious metals. It allows the dross to be removed. It purifies; but make no mistake, **it is painful.**

Just exactly what is the difference between this belief and that of those who would espouse the traditional view of punishment? It is very simply that instead of believing that God sends people to a burning hell where they are tormented forever, without any hope, and without any purpose other than the anger of God, the believer in **Christian reconciliation believes that since God is a God of love, he corrects** those who are deserving of punishment in a manner **consistent** with the way he has dealt with mankind in the entirety of the Scriptures. Concerning the traditional view of eternal punishment, we have to ask the question, does it not in **effect chop off** the effect of the atonement of our Lord at the knees? Does it not **limit the power** of the cross? If the Coast Guard were sent to a sinking cruise ship where thousands of people were floating in the water as the ship went down to the depths of the ocean, and they were only able to rescue 33 percent of the people, **is there any possibility** that it could be considered a success?

Therefore, it is perfectly logical to reason that the idea that most of the world will not only be lost, but must essentially suffer in eternal torment forever is a **gross**

contradiction of the love of God? We have been created in God's image. As such, we have been given a moral sense. How many people seeing the hopelessness and lack of consistency of this contradiction within the person of God have abandoned all hope and relegated themselves to agnosticism. Has this view that God would torment the masses for an infinite period of time made those agnostics believe that the moral convictions they were born with are without value? Has the teaching of this doctrine in the churches caused them to lose the meaning of hope?

We often sing a hymn in our churches named Victory in Jesus. Does it not contain these words?

> He loved me ere I knew him
> And all my love is due him
> He plunged me to victory
> Beneath the cleansing flood

As a believer, do you really think he loved us before we knew him? Or do you espouse that God has two aspects to his personality, **one of love**, and **another of hate** who oppose one another, and that we are just chessboard tokens which are easily manipulated and discarded without thought.

Earlier we highlighted the story of the potter and the clay from Jeremiah chapter 18. In this illustration God gave to Jeremiah, the potter took a piece of clay and put it on the wheel for the purpose of forming it as he saw fit.

I once heard a story that went something like this:

> Imagine yourself as that piece of clay. You are comfortable in your state – just a lump of red clay,

nothing else. You have some flaws, but you are content as you are. Then all of a sudden God picks you up and puts you in his hands and starts picking pieces of debris out of your body. "Quit that" you say. "It hurts." Then when he is finished, he thinks you are ready for the potter's wheel.

Next, he puts you on the potter's wheel. You start spinning. "Hey stop this," you yell, "get me off of this wheel, I'm getting dizzy." But to make matters worse, God puts water all over you, and then puts his hands on you and starts changing your shape. It's painful! You continue to yell, "Ouch, what are you doing?!! You're hurting me." But instead of quitting, God intensifies the pressure as you scream in pain. He doesn't like what he sees, and takes you off of the wheel. Just as you are feeling relief, he crushes you as you scream again. He puts you back on the wheel and forms you into a beautiful piece of pottery. As he takes you off of the wheel and you say, "It's about time, do you realize how much pain you put me through!"

What you have gone through is nothing compared to what is yet to come. Once God inspects you and sees you are ready, he fires up the oven and puts you in. You scream in agonizing pain as the fire of that oven transforms your body to a permanent shape. "Please take me out of here!" you say, but God ignores you. When he finally completes the process of baking you, he takes you out and lets you cool off. You feel relief, until he picks you up again, and starts painting you. Then you go back in the oven again! After more screaming in agonizing pain, he takes you out and sets you in front of a mirror. After you cool off, you look at the beautiful work that God has done in changing you from a plain old lump of clay into a beautiful piece of pottery. At last you see that **it was all for your good**, and with tears in your eyes, **you bow in humble adoration** to the God of love **who turned YOU** into that beautiful work of art!

Author Unknown

I believe that this is the finality of the story of what God wanted Jeremiah to see as he took him to the potter's house. And it is true of every single one of us living today. We will be shaped and molded into a beautiful work of art. But during this process, God uses us for whatever he wants. It may be a vessel of mercy, or a vessel of wrath; (Romans 9:21-23) but this is not our permanent state. Since **God is love,** he will eventually put us on that wheel and make something beautiful out of all of us!

The difference is that for those who believe, the process will be less painful. In fact, we will be blessed so greatly as to experience God's love throughout the entire process. **If we reject the Lord** in this life, we will have to **endure the painful, but purifying fire of Gehenna**, perhaps even for a **very long time.** Even if this is the case, the eventual end will be beautiful.

I would like to say that **I do NOT embrace the term "Universalist or Universalism."** The reason is that when most people hear this term, **it leaves Christ out of the equation.** Additionally, you usually hear the following questions: "If everybody will be saved, then why did Jesus need to go to the cross? Why do we need to evangelize? Why would Jesus give the great commission? When people ask questions like this **it shows their ignorance** of just exactly what is entailed in the process God uses. That is, it seems more accurate to me to call it **"Christian Reconciliation"** which I believe is more precise. For it is **ONLY** by the **shed blood of our Savior,** and his **resurrection** that salvation is **possible.** And Yes, **a visit to Gehenna will be painful!** Remember that Jesus said:

> Don't be afraid of those who kill the body, but are not able to kill the soul. Rather, fear him who is able to **destroy** (Greek apollumi – perish, to be lost, ruin) both soul and body in Gehenna. (Matthew 10:28 WEB)

Yes, destruction is a **temporary condition.** Many times, God destroyed things only to bring them back. The Apostle Paul stated:

> For in him all the fullness of God was pleased to dwell, and through him **to reconcile** to himself **all things,** whether on earth or in heaven, making peace by the blood of his cross. (Colossians 1:19-20).

This should be our message to others!

God's will in this matter was accomplished **at great cost to him!** It is profoundly true those who stubbornly refuse to accept him in this life will have a painful price to pay. But the difference is that we who believe that God's sovereignty reigns supreme espouse a God of love who will put someone through the fire of purification (which is not fire as we know it, but God's purification fire) for their own good, and with an outcome which benefits them and pleases him.

As I searched for a quote to sum up my feelings, none was said more succinctly than Commentator William Barclay who put it this way:

But I want to set down not the arguments of others but the thoughts which have persuaded me personally of universal salvation.

First, there is the fact that there are things in the New Testament which more than justify this belief. Jesus said: "I, when I am lifted up from the earth, will draw *all* men to myself" (John 12:32). Paul writes to the Romans: "God has consigned *all* men to disobedience that he may have mercy on *all*" (Rom. 11:32). He writes to the Corinthians: "As in Adam *all* die, so also in Christ shall *all* be made alive" (1 Cor. 15:22); and he looks to the final total triumph when God will be everything to everyone (1 Cor. 15:28). In the First Letter to Timothy we read of God "who desires *all* men to be saved and to come to the knowledge of the truth," and of Christ Jesus "who gave himself as a ransom for *all*" (1 Tim 2:4-6). *The New Testament itself is not in the least afraid of the word all.*

Second, one of the key passages is Matthew 25:46 where it is said that the rejected go away to *eternal punishment*, and the righteous to eternal life. The Greek word for punishment is *kolasis,* which was not originally an ethical word at all. It originally meant the pruning of trees to make them grow better. I think it is true to say that in all Greek secular literature *kolasis* **is never used of anything but remedial punishment.** The word for eternal is *aionios.* It means more than everlasting, for Plato - who may have invented the word - plainly says that a thing may be everlasting and still not be *aionios*. The simplest way to out it is that *aionios* cannot be used properly of anyone but God; it is the word uniquely, as Plato saw it, of God. Eternal punishment is then literally that kind of remedial punishment which it befits God to give and which only God can give.

Third, I believe that it is impossible to set limits to the grace of God. I believe that not only in this world, but in any other world there may be, the grace of God is still effective, still operative, still at work. I do not believe that the operation of the grace of God is limited to this world. I believe that the grace of God is as wide as the universe.

Fourth, I believe implicitly in the ultimate and complete triumph of God, the time when all things will be subject to him, and when God will be everything to everyone (1 Cor. 15:24-28). For me this has certain consequences. If one man remains outside the love of God at the end of time, it means that that one man has defeated the love of God - and that is impossible. Further, there is only one way in which we can think of the triumph of God. If God was no more than a King or Judge, then it would be possible to speak of his triumph, if his enemies were agonizing in hell or were totally and completely obliterated and wiped out. But God is not only King and Judge, God is *Father* - he is indeed Father more than anything else. No father could be happy while there were members of his family forever in agony. No father would count it a triumph to obliterate the disobedient members of his family. The only triumph a father can know is to have all his family back home. The only victory love can enjoy is the day when its offer of love is answered by the return of love. The only possible **final** triumph is a universe loved by and in love with God.[63]

Conclusion

As I bring this volume to a conclusion, once again I would like to ask: **Why is there nothing**, not a single word, annotation, or inclination in the Old Testament about eternal torment? Why is it true that Paul **never mentions eternal torment** anywhere in his writings? Wouldn't you think the **entire Scriptural record** would be **overflowing with warnings** from God concerning this **overwhelmingly horrendous destiny** for the lost? I **ask you to think carefully about this.** It is not an accident that the Scriptures are so composed.

Through the pages of this book, you have seen that my research has led me to the sincere conclusion that God's judgment **IS** purposeful, **NOT** just a release of his vengeance. It is my sincere hope that this thesis has been helpful to you in seeing the true love and grace of God. Jesus spoke of a place that he called Gehenna. The translators have wrongly rendered it as "Hell." But there is also joy in knowing that even though Gehenna is most likely **an eternal PLACE for the lost** to bend a knee, repent, and ultimately confess Jesus as Lord and Savior, **the time the lost will spend there is NOT eternal.** However, the unrepentant may be there for an extensive period of time up to the point of eternity until they willingly understand their need of the Lord Jesus.

---

[63] https://www.tentmaker.org/biographies/barclay.htm

Only because of the blood of Jesus, those who leave will be completely repentant and absolutely ready to bend their knee and acknowledge Jesus as Lord. They will be praising him throughout the ages of ages. The life of King Nebuchadnezzar (Dan 4: 24 – 37) is a foundational Old Testament example of our graceful God through Jesus providing his mercy. Yes . . . even for the formerly wicked King Nebuchadnezzar.

In his book "Christianity without insanity, For Optimal Mental/Emotional Health," Dr. Boyd Purcell relates a story that is very appropriate here.

> I heard the pastor of a large Evangelical Church preaching on the radio several months ago that he does not want to be guilty of anything, but if he is guilty of something, he wants to be guilty of trusting God for too much rather than too little. I immediately thought, wow, what a great statement, ditto that for me! This was said in the context of the beginning of a building program to better minister to the church members and to reach out and win more lost souls to Christ before it is eternally too late . . .[64]

Dr. Purcell got the interview and asked the Pastor several questions to draw him out including the passage speaking of being " salted with fire" (Mark 9:49) Finally the Pastor pointed out his belief that sinners have no chance to be saved after death and that the church has always believed in the doctrine of eternal punishment in hell. He then asked

---

[64] Purcell, Boyd. Christianity Without Insanity: For Optimal Mental/Emotional/Physical Health (p. 193-195). CreateSpace Independent Publishing Platform. Kindle Edition.

Dr. Purcell what he would so when he faced God in the final judgment and found out that he was wrong about his view. Dr. Purcell very succinctly stated:

"That is a very good question." I will say, "God, I am sorry, **I trusted you for too much** rather than too little." **I then asked him** what he will say at The Final Judgment when he finds that he has been wrong concerning the doctrine of eternal damnation, "God, I am sorry, **I trusted you for too little . . .** ?"[65]

In the Prologue, I proposed a scenario about Eli and Sarah, a couple who endured the heinous treatment of the Nazi regime in World War II. My question to you was, considering what these two went through, and the limited exposure they had to the Gospel, what is to happen to Eli and Sarah, in the afterlife?

In chapter 5, I proposed another scenario wherein Jason, a Christian had been talking to Aaqil, a Muslim, and was obviously making some progress, but Aaqil's wife and children were killed in an airline crash. Aaqil pleaded with Jason, "Please tell me that my precious wife and children are safe in the arms of a loving Jesus."

In both cases, we can lovingly and truthfully say that Eli, Sarah, Aaqil's wife and children **are indeed safe** in the arms of a loving Jesus according to his will, according to his time and according to his word. For God **IS** Love (1 John 4:8). His mercy and justice **ARE** perfect (Isa 30:18). He **IS KIND** to the ungrateful and the evil (Luke 6:35). His

---

[65] Ibid. (Emphasis Mine)

steadfast love **endures** forever (Lam 3:22). The apostle Paul was right to break out in praise to him when he said:

> For God has **consigned all to disobedience**, that he may have **mercy on all.** Oh, the depth of the riches and wisdom and knowledge of God! How unsearchable are his judgments and how inscrutable his ways! For who has known the mind of the Lord, or who has been his counselor? Or who has given a gift to him that he might be repaid? For from him and through him and to him are all things. To him be glory forever. Amen. (Rom 11:32-36)

Appendix I

Objections Considered

Author's note: Much of the information in this appendix is a repeat of what has already been stated. It has been added as a convenience for those who would like to search using the scripture index for certain passages that they feel may need to be brought to bear on this subject, and find answers regarding them. Many of these objections and passages have been presented to me by others, and has served for the basis for my research on this subject. The questions are in no particular order. If you have a question on a certain passage you would like to find, it is suggested that you use this appendix in conjunction with the Scripture index.

Objection: It is ridiculous to believe that everyone is saved by God. But these "all" statements need to be qualified by other passages of Scripture. It is the whole of scripture that must be considered.
Some hold this idea based on such scriptures as:

Romans 5:18 Therefore, as one trespass led to condemnation for **all men**, so one act of righteousness leads to justification and life for **all men.**

Romans 11:32 For God has consigned **all** to disobedience, that he may have mercy on **all**.

Answer: I agree that these statements need to be qualified by other passages, and in this case, there are many other "all" statements which support this. But in this case, the term "all" most certainly **could not** mean two different things **when used in the same sentence**.

There is a **total misunderstanding** of the term "Universal Reconciliation." It **still is dependent** on the person **surrendering themselves to Christ**. To say otherwise, is to falsify the truth contained in the doctrine. In effect with their generalized words they have COMPLETELY oversimplified the DOCTRINE. There are **no free passes** with God!

What we are putting under consideration here is what Paul wrote to the Church at Colossae.

> and through him to reconcile to himself all things, whether on earth or in heaven, making peace by the blood of his cross. (Colossians 1:20)

For some this will mean they will have to endure painful **age long correction** according to the justice of God. This means that the time spent in Gehenna is up to God, and depends on when the individual is willing to humble themselves and surrender to the love of Christ. But this does **NOT** mean endless torment.

This concept in no way goes against the doctrine of justification. One must have faith to be justified by the blood of Jesus. If one **has faith, he has already** passed from death to life. (John 5:24).

Objection: But isn't it true that many times, when "all" is used in the Bible, it does not really mean "all" but is using hyperbole to make a point? There are literally hundreds of examples of this. Here are some common usages as such by the Apostle Paul.

Romans 3:12 **All** have turned aside; together they have become worthless; no one does good, not even one."

Romans 10:21 But of Israel he says, "**All** day long I have held out my hands to a disobedient and contrary people."

Romans 15:14 I myself am satisfied about you, my brothers, that you yourselves are full of goodness, filled with **all** knowledge and able to instruct one another.

1 Corinthians 3:21 So let no one boast in men. For **all** things are yours,

1 Corinthians 6:12 "**All** things are lawful for me," but not all things are helpful. "**All** things are lawful for me," but I will not be dominated by anything.

Answer: But these words **ARE** at certain times very much all encompassing. Consider the following:

Psalm 8:6 You have given him dominion over the works of your hands; you have put all things under his feet,

2 Samuel 14:20 In order to change the course of things your servant Joab did this. But my lord has wisdom like the wisdom of the angel of God to know all things that are on the earth."

Psalm 138:2 I bow down toward your holy temple and give thanks to your name for your steadfast love and your faithfulness, for you have exalted above <u>all things</u> your name and your word.

Isaiah 44:24 Thus says the LORD, your Redeemer, who formed you from the womb: "I am the LORD, who made <u>all things</u>, who alone stretched out the heavens, who spread out the earth by myself,

Jeremiah 10:16 Not like these is he who is the portion of Jacob, for he is the one who formed <u>all things,</u> and Israel is the tribe of his inheritance; the LORD of hosts is his name.

Matthew 19:26 But Jesus looked at them and said, "With man this is impossible, but with God <u>all things are possible.</u>"

Luke 10:22 <u>All things</u> have been handed over to me by my Father, and no one knows who the Son is except the Father, or who the Father is except the Son and anyone to whom the Son chooses to reveal him."

John 1:3 <u>All things</u> were made through him, and without him was not any thing made that was made.

John 3:35 The Father loves the Son and has given <u>all things</u> into his hand.

These are but a few of the many passages in which ALL means ALL. I don't know of anyone who would deny that in these passages ALL means ALL.

Objection: This passage written by Paul states:

This is good, and it is pleasing in the sight of God our Savior, who **desires all people to be saved** and to come to the knowledge of the truth. (1 Timothy 2:3-4)

Isn't this passage best understood as people **of all types** will be saved? Also, doesn't it say that God **desires all people** to be saved? It does **not say** that all people are saved.

Answer: God is indeed **Sovereign. WHAT GOD WANTS, OR WILLS, HE GETS.** Would anyone dare to say that God's will is not going to be accomplished? Notice the passage below:

> Job 42:2 "I know that You can do **ALL THINGS,** And that **NO PURPOSE** of Yours can be **THWARTED.**

1 Timothy 2:3-4 is a powerful passage with a clear context, and is very much applicable to this question. The King James is the best rendition of this in this particular case. Notice the words as we read through verse 6.

> For this is good and acceptable in the sight of God our Saviour; Who **WILL HAVE ALL** men to be saved, and to come unto the knowledge of the truth. For there is one God, and one mediator between God and men, the man Christ Jesus; Who gave himself a ransom **for ALL,** to be testified **IN DUE TIME.** (1 Timothy 2:3-6)

The Greek word for will in this passage is θελει. The root word is θελω , which means "to determine." Thus, we could translate this passage to say: "**who determines all men to be saved.**

Dare we say that what God has determined will be thwarted? Not according to Job 42:2 as quoted above.

Objection: What about 1 John 2:2? It could not actually mean everyone because it runs counter to other passages. It reads:

> 1 John 2:2 He is the propitiation for our sins, and not for ours only but also for the sins of the whole world.

This could not mean exactly what it says, could it? Isn't it true that it only means that everyone in the world **COULD be saved or benefit by** the fact that he died on the cross? To say this actually means the whole world is contrary to the most famous passage:

> John 3:16 "For God so loved the world, that he gave his only Son, that **whoever believes in him** should not perish **but have eternal life.**

So, doesn't this mean that salvation is **available** for the whole world—**BUT** only those who put their faith in Jesus receive it?

Answer: This would be the best outcome! We help people come to knowledge of Christ. But those who do not accept Christ in this life **will indeed eventually** accept him. Is that not the meaning of **Philippians 2:9-11**? Note the words:

> Therefore, God has highly exalted him and bestowed on him the name that is above every name, so that at the name of Jesus **EVERY KNEE** should bow, **in heaven and on earth and under the earth,** and **EVERY TONGUE** confess that Jesus Christ is Lord, to the glory of God the Father.

Only a **heartfelt confession** would bring glory to God the Father, and this is the only confession of faith that the Father would accept! But this is definitely not a free pass to those who have rejected him in this life.

For no one can lay a foundation other than that which is laid, which is Jesus Christ. Now if anyone builds on the foundation with gold, silver, precious stones, wood, hay, straw— each one's work will become manifest, for the Day will disclose it, because it will be **revealed by fire,** and **THE FIRE** will test what sort of work each one has done. (1 Corinthians 3:11-13)

Objection: What about this passage:

John 12:32 And I, when I am lifted up from the earth, will draw all people to myself."

Doesn't the "all people" in this passage need to be qualified? If not, doesn't this negate the doctrine of justification? What about the following?

Romans 3:24 and are justified by his grace as a gift, through the redemption that is in Christ Jesus,

Romans 3:28 For we hold that one **is justified by faith** apart from works of the law.

Romans 5:1 Therefore, since we have been **justified by faith**, we have peace with God through our Lord Jesus Christ.

Romans 5:9 Since, therefore, we have now been **justified by his blood**, much more **shall we be saved** by him from the wrath of God.

Galatians 3:24 So then, the law was our guardian until Christ came, in order that we might be **justified by faith**.

Answer: There is no contradiction here. There is not a hint of anything in these passages that would require "qualifying." It is **only by grace through faith** in Jesus Christ that we are justified. But I would like you to notice carefully what is said here. Jesus said:

And I, when I am lifted up from the earth, will draw (ελκυσω) **all people** to myself." (John 12:32)

The Greek word for draw literally means "**to drag.**" So, Christ has determined to make this happen **even if he has to drag people to him.** This was reiterated by Paul when he proclaimed, "Every knee will bow, and every tongue confess Jesus is Lord." If this confession is to be heartfelt, it means that some must suffer remedial punishment first. Only a Dictator would demand a confession that was not heartfelt. Then they will see clearly that Jesus is Lord, and will **want to** bow before him.

Objection: Isn't it true that there will be many who call him Lord **that will still** be rejected?

"Enter by the narrow gate. For the gate is wide and the way is easy that leads to destruction, and those who enter by it are many. For the gate is narrow and the way is hard that leads to life, and those who find it are few. (Matthew 7:13-14)

Matthew 7:21 "Not everyone who says to me, 'Lord, Lord,' will enter the kingdom of heaven, but the one who does the will of my Father who is in heaven.

Answer: In Matthew 7:13-14 and Matthew 7:21, Jesus gave those listeners the Sermon on the Mount, especially the religious leaders present, a precursor to the judgment of the Jewish system of worship in AD70 with the destruction of Jerusalem, the temple, and the entire system of sacrificial worship. He is speaking of what would happen at the judgment of Israel at the end of the generation, a prophecy which was fulfilled in its entirety. This passage **does not** refer to life after death.

Objection: What about the unforgivable sin? (Mark 3:28-29). Isn't this committed by one who continually rejects Christ?

Answer: Here is that passage in Young's Literal Translation.

`Verily I say to you, that all the sins shall be forgiven to the sons of men, and evil speakings with which they might speak evil, but whoever may speak evil in regard to the Holy Spirit hath not forgiveness--to the age, but is in danger of age-during judgment;' (Mark 3:28-29)

When this passage is read here, there is a totally different tone. They will be in danger of an age-enduring punishment by God. But once the punishment is over, there will be reconciliation.

Objection: What about the everlasting destruction spoken of in the first Chapter of 2 Thessalonians?

Answer: This chapter is eschatological of a specific age, and speaks of the destruction of Jerusalem and those Jewish persecutors of the Christian church.

Objection: Surely these passages must reject the doctrine of Universal Reconciliation:

Eternal fire for those cursed cannot be reconciliation (Matthew 25:41). The wrath of God against unrighteousness cannot be reconciliation (Romans 1:18). The fiery lake of burning sulfur cannot be reconciliation (Revelation 21:8). Resisting or betraying Jesus is said to lead to a curse worse than if he had never been born (Mark 14:21). Such a curse cannot be reconciliation. The "road to destruction" cannot be reconciliation (Matthew 7:13-14).

Answer: These passages convey the meaning of something as being eternal. The error of this type of thinking is the assumption that these things are eternal. As already noted, the Greek word used in these passages does not mean eternal.

The word translated as "eternal" in these passages has as its root the Greek words αιων (pronounced **aion**). This word has been properly translated as "age," and αιωνιος **(aionios)** as **age-abiding or age-enduring.**

Rotherham's Emphasized Bible translates these words:

Matthew 25:41 Then, will he say unto those also, on his left hand: Depart ye from me, accursed ones! **Into**

the age-abiding fire, which hath been prepared for the adversary and his messengers;

In a fiery flame; holding forth vengeance—against them that refuse to know God, and them who decline to hearken unto the glad-message of our Lord Jesus, Who, indeed, a penalty, shall pay—**age-abiding destruction** from the face of the Lord and from the glory of his might— (2 Thessalonians 1:8-9)

Matt 25:46   And, these, shall go away, into, age-abiding, **correction,** but, the righteous, into, **age-abiding,** life.

The word translated as "eternal" in our modern translations is the Greek word αιωνιος (**aionios,**) which means age-abiding. This means that God sets the time limit for the age. There is a **different Greek word for eternal** and that word is αιδιος (**aidios.**)

Notice how Young's Literal Translates Matthew 25:41, and 2 Thessalonians 1:8-9

Matthew 25:41   Then shall he say also to those on the left hand, Go ye from me, the cursed, to the fire, the **AGE-DURING,** that hath been prepared for the Devil and his messengers;

in flaming fire, giving vengeance to those not knowing God, and to those not obeying the good news of our Lord Jesus Christ; who shall suffer justice-- destruction **AGE-DURING**--from the face of the

Lord, and from the glory of his strength, (2 Thessalonians 1:8,9)

There is a good reason for this. Consider the following concerning punishment:

The root word for punishment in the Greek as used in Matthew 25:46 is κολασις. This is defined in Thayer's Greek-English lexicon as correction, punishment, penalty.

As John W. Hanson notes in his book:

The word translated punishment means improvement. The word is κολασιν. It is thus authoritatively defined, "chastisement, punishment." "The trimming of the luxuriant branches of a tree or vine to improve it and make it fruitful." "The act of clipping or pruning – restriction, restraint, reproof, check, chastisement." "The kind of punishment which tends to the improvement of the criminal, is what the Greek philosophers called kolasis or chastisement." "Pruning, checking, punishment, chastisement, correction." "Do we want to know what was uppermost in the minds of those who formed the word for punishment?[66]

But **what is just as important** to consider here are the words for punishment **which were not used by Jesus.**

Jesus **did not** use either of these two Greek words (from Thayer's Greek Lexicon):

---

[66] Hanson, John (2011-09-30) Aion-Aionios (Kindle locations 2263-2265) Tentmaker Ministries & Publications, Inc. Kindle Edition.

τιμωρεω – (English timoreo) – to be the guardian or avenger of honor; to take vengeance on one, to punish.[67]

In the case of the first (timoreo), the punishment is made for the sake of honor, or **to avenge.**

The Apostle Paul used this word in Acts 22:4-5 when speaking of a retributive punishment of those who were going against the Jewish law covenant. Note the usage below:

> I persecuted this Way to the death, binding and delivering to prison both men and women, as the high priest and the whole council of elders can bear me witness. From them I received letters to the brothers, and I journeyed toward Damascus to take those also who were there and bring them in bonds to Jerusalem **to be punished.** (Acts 22:4-5)

Jesus also **did not** use the word timoria. From Thayer's Greek Lexicon we find:

τιμωρια - (English timoria) – vengeance, penalty, punishment[68]

In the sake of the second (timoria), the punishment is **purely for the purpose of retribution.**

The writer of Hebrews used this word when he noted that this would be used to punish the one who "has profaned the blood of the covenant by which he was sanctified, and has

---

[67] Thayer's Greek Lexicon, Eleventh Printing, Feb 2014 p. 624
[68] Ibid p. 624

outraged the Spirit of grace?" (Hebrews 10:29) This would be the judgment of those ones that occurred at the destruction of Jerusalem which Jesus promised would occur within the same generation of his speaking. (Matthew 26:62-64)

But it is a fact that Jesus **did not use either one of these words.** Instead he used the word **kolasis** in Matthew 25:46 which is corrective punishment. This would accomplish a dual purpose, that being to deter others from wickedness and provide a refining effect on the sinner.

As for the thought of "everlasting punishment" we are confronted with the Greek word αιωνιον, the root word of which is αιων which means "age" or a specified period of time, usually meaning a long period of time.

There is another word for eternal which is αιδιος. This word is defined by Thayer's Greek English Lexicon as "eternal, everlasting." This is not the word used by Jesus in Mathew 25:46.

From all of this, is it possible that the meaning of Matthew 25:46 is that the punishment would be for an "age of discipline, correction, or purification," because, Heb 12:29 "for our God is a consuming fire?"

Make no mistake about it, those who reject Christ in this life will suffer in the age-enduring fire of purification. But even though **the place may be eternal**, the time spent there **is not**. It is punishment, which means that at some point it will be over and the final result will be that it will be reconciliatory. As Paul said, in the end they will "confess that Jesus Christ is Lord, to the glory of God the Father."

This confession will not be an arm-twisting event. They will actually be reconciled to God and will see in their heart that "God is Love."

Objection: What about the wrath of God? Notice what Paul wrote to the church at Rome:

but God shows his love for us in that while we were still sinners, Christ died for us. Since, therefore, **we have now been justified by his blood, much more shall we be saved by him from the wrath of God.** (Romans 5:8 -9)

Answer: There is no question that those who are not justified by faith will have to face the wrath of God. What is missed by most people is that God's punishment is made with a view to reconciliation. Even the Greek word for punishment indicates a positive outcome. The word is κολασιν. It is thus authoritatively defined, "chastisement, punishment". (See Hanson's comments above.)

Notice the qualities of our Lord as mentioned in his Word:

He is "kind to the ungrateful and the evil." (Luke 6:35)

He is the "Lamb of God, who takes away the sin of the world" (John 1:29).

He is "the light of the world" (John 8:12)

He is " the propitiation for our sins, and NOT FOR OURS ONLY but also for the sins of the whole world" (1 John 2:2)

He is "the Savior of ALL people" (1 Timothy 4:10)

There is no "ignoring the wrathful side of God" in the doctrine of Christian Reconciliation.

Yes, those who do not accept Christ WILL HAVE TO SUFFER. They will be judged according to the Law of Moses. God stands by his principle as set out in the Old Covenant:

Deuteronomy 19:21 Your eye shall not pity. It shall be life for life, eye for eye, tooth for tooth, hand for hand, foot for foot.

Those who consider God to be just and loving must answer the following question:

Is there anywhere in the Old Law Covenant where we see anything about a punishment that goes on forever? **NO!** Just as in the Old Covenant, the punishment must fit the crime. This is a principle of the justice of God. **God does not change!**

We must honestly ask: Is this compatible with the character of our loving Savior, who said of the men who nailed him to the cross: "Father, forgive them, for they know not what they do?" (Luke 23:34)

The punishments of God are just. The punishments of God have a purpose. All will be reconciled to God.

1 John 2:2 He is the propitiation for our sins, and not for ours only but also for the sins of the whole world.

Objection: Isaiah 66:24 speaks of a place of eternal torment where the worm does not die and the fire is not quenched. This must mean that there is a place of eternal torment.

Isaiah 66:24 "Then they will go forth and look On the corpses of the men Who have transgressed against Me. For **their worm will not die** And their fire will not be quenched; And they will be an abhorrence to all mankind."

Answer: This chapter of Isaiah, along with chapter 66 speaks of the rejection of the Jews to accept the gospel message of Christ. This would eventually result in the destruction along with over a million Jews. But regarding the nature of the "worm that dieth not" commentator Albert Barnes had this to say:

This figure is taken from Isa 66:24. See the notes at that passage. In describing the great prosperity of the kingdom of the Messiah, Isaiah says that the people of God "shall go forth, and look upon the carcasses of the men who have transgressed against God." Their enemies would be overcome. They would be slain. The people of God would triumph. The figure is taken from heaps of the dead slain in battle; and the prophet says that **the number would be so great that**

their worm - the worm feeding on the dead - **would not die**, would live long - **as long as there were carcasses to be devoured**; and that the fire which was used to burn the bodies of the dead would continue long to burn, and would not be extinguished until they were consumed. The figure, therefore, denotes great misery, and certain and terrible destruction.

This in fact is what occurred at the destruction of Jerusalem. This verse speaks of living people looking at dead bodies. Historian Josephus said that the bodies were piled so high in the city that people walked over them like they were nothing.

Objection: Daniel 12:2 states: "And many of those who sleep in the dust of the earth shall awake, some to everlasting life, and some to shame and everlasting contempt."

Answer: The word translated here as everlasting is the word *olam* in the Hebrew. Notice how it is used in Exodus:

> Exodus 40:15 and anoint them, as you anointed their father, that they may serve me as priests. And their anointing shall admit them to a *perpetual priesthood throughout their generations*." (ESV)
>
> (KJV) And thou shalt anoint them, as thou didst anoint their father, that they may minister unto me in the priest's office: for their anointing shall surely be

an *everlasting priesthood throughout their generations.*
(GNB) Then anoint them, just as you anointed their father, so that they can serve me as priests. This anointing will make them priests *for all time to come.*"
(Rotherham) and shalt anoint them as thou didst anoint their father, and they shall minister as priests unto me,—so shall their anointing remain to them for an *age-abiding priesthood, to their generations.*
(YLT) and anointed them as thou hast anointed their father, and they have acted as priests to Me, and their anointing hath been to be to them for a priesthood *age-during, to their generations.*'

Which of these translations make the most sense? To say that the Jewish Priesthood is *perpetual or everlasting* does not mean the same as that it lasts *throughout their* generations (a shorter time). This is a contradiction in terms.

Let's look at one more set of comparisons. This will entail Daniel 12:2,3, which speaks of the resurrection. First notice how this passage is translated in the English Standard Version:

And many of those who sleep in the dust of the earth shall awake, some to *everlasting life*, and some to shame and *everlasting contempt*. And those who are wise shall shine like the brightness of the sky above; and those who turn many to righteousness, like the stars *forever and ever*. (Daniel 12:2,3)

Now notice how it is translated in the Rotherham's Emphasized Bible:

and, many of the sleepers in the dusty ground, shall awake,—these, shall be to *age-abiding life*, but, those, to reproach, and *age-abiding abhorrence*; and, they who make wise, shall shine like the shining of the expanse,—and, they who bring the many to righteousness, like the stars to times *age-abiding and beyond*. (Daniel 12:2,3)

Now notice Young's Literal Translation of this passage:

And the multitude of those sleeping in the dust of the ground do awake, some to life *age-during*, and some to reproaches--to *abhorrence age-during*. And those teaching do shine as the brightness of the expanse, and those justifying the multitude as stars to *the age and forever*.

The difference becomes especially apparent in the Rotherham and Young's translations at the end of verse three. Notice the words:

like the stars to times *age-abiding and beyond*. (Rotherham)

the multitude as stars to *the age and forever*. (Young's)

Do you notice the difference between the words used? Rotherham's describes it as *age-abiding*, and then adds *and beyond*! This shows that age-abiding **does not** mean forever!

Objection: Matthew 18:6-9 and Mark 9:43-48 are parallel passages that make reference to a place of eternal torment.

Answer: These are a direct reference by Jesus to the words of Isaiah 66:24 as explained above. While it is true that he mentioned the place called Gehenna several times in Scripture (which has been translated as hell by many translators) he does not say anything concerning the duration of the punishment. The closest thing we have is the following passage from the King James Version:

> And if thy hand offend thee, cut it off: it is better for thee to enter into life maimed, than having two hands to go into hell, into the fire that never shall be quenched: Where their worm dieth not, and the fire is not quenched. And if thy foot offend thee, cut it off: it is better for thee to enter halt into life, than having two feet to be cast into hell, into the fire that never shall be quenched: Where **their worm dieth not**, and the fire is not quenched. And if thine eye offend thee, pluck it out: it is better for thee to enter into the kingdom of God with one eye, than having two eyes to be cast into hell fire: Where their worm dieth not, and the fire is not quenched. (Mark 9:43-48)

Commentator William Barclay explains the meaning of this passage.

> The Jewish Rabbis had sayings based on the way in which some parts of the body can lend themselves to sin. "The eye and the heart are the two brokers of sin." "The eye and the heart are the two handmaids of sin." "Passions lodge only in him who sees." "Woe to him

who goes after his eyes for the eyes are adulterous." There are certain instincts in man, and certain parts of man's physical constitution, which minister to sin. This saying of Jesus is **not to be taken literally**, but is a vivid eastern way of saying that there is a goal in life worth any sacrifice to attain it.

Objection: The book of Jude makes reference to eternal damnation in two places. What about these passages:

Jude 1:7 just as Sodom and Gomorrah and the surrounding cities, which likewise indulged in sexual immorality and pursued unnatural desire, serve as an example by undergoing a punishment of **eternal** fire. Jude 1:13 wild waves of the sea, casting up the foam of their own shame; wandering stars, for whom the gloom of utter darkness has been reserved **forever**.

Answer: Once again we need to look at the root words. The root words used above for eternal and forever are αιων (aion) and αιωνιος (aionios). These passages convey the meaning of something as being eternal. The error of this type of thinking is the assumption that these things are eternal. As already noted, the Greek word used in these passages **does not** mean eternal, but have a variable meaning **which could reach up to** perpetuity, **but does end at some point.**

The word translated as "eternal" in these passages has as its root the Greek words αιων (pronounced **aion**). This word has been properly translated as "age," and αιωνιος **(aionios)** as **age-abiding or age-enduring.** There is a **different Greek word for eternal** and that word is αιδιος (**aidios**). Notice the translation from the Rotherham Emphasized Bible:

Jude 1:7 As, Sodom and Gomorrah, and the cities around them, having in like manner to these given themselves over to fornication, and gone away after other kind of flesh, lie exposed as an example, a penalty of **age-abiding fire**, undergoing.
Jude 1:13 Wild waves of sea, foaming out their own infamies, wandering stars, for whom the gloom of darkness **age-abiding** hath been reserved.

Thus, an "age" is a period of time determined by God, and **does have an end.**

Objection: What about Revelation 14:10-11. These also speak of eternal torment. Also, Revelation 20:10, and 14-15 make such a reference.

Revelation 14:10 he also will drink the wine of God's wrath, poured full strength into the cup of his anger, and he will be tormented with fire and sulfur in the presence of the holy angels and in the presence of the Lamb.
Revelation 14:11 And the smoke of their torment goes up forever and ever, and they have no rest, day or night, these worshipers of the beast and its image, and whoever receives the mark of its name."
Revelation 20:10 and the devil who had deceived them was thrown into the lake of fire and sulfur where the beast and the false prophet were, and they will be tormented day and night forever and ever.

Revelation 20:14 Then Death and Hades were thrown into the lake of fire. This is the second death, the lake of fire.

Revelation 20:15 And if anyone's name was not found written in the book of life, he was thrown into the lake of fire.

Answer: This passage speaks of the "beast" of Revelation and those who worship the beast. In my book, ***God's promise of Redemption, a story of fulfilled prophecy,*** I show conclusive evidence that this beast is identified in the first century as Caesar Nero and those who worship him. But the verse also states that this beast would be tormented in the presence of the holy angels and the lamb, so it could not be referring to hell. Hell is a place of separation from God. Additionally, it does not say they are tormented to the ages of ages, but that "the smoke of their torment doth go up to ages of ages."

A better translation of this is Young's Literal Translation which reads:

Revelation 14:10 he also shall drink of the wine of the wrath of God, that hath been mingled unmixed in the cup of His anger, and he shall be tormented in fire and brimstone before the holy messengers, and before the Lamb,

Revelation 14:11 and the smoke of their torment doth go up to ages of ages; and they have no rest day and night, who are bowing before the beast and his image, also if any doth receive the mark of his name.

Revelation 20:10 and the Devil, who is leading them astray, was cast into the lake of fire and brimstone,

284

where *are* the beast and the false prophet, and they shall be tormented day and night--to the ages of the ages.
Revelation 20:14 and the death and the hades were cast to the lake of the fire--this *is* the second death;
Revelation 20:15 and if anyone was not found written in the scroll of the life, he was cast to the lake of the fire.

The fact that it uses the term "ages" in the plural shows that this term cannot mean eternal. Remember that an age is a period of time with an end. It is similar to the use Paul makes of "ages" in Eph. 2:7.

From the standpoint of Annihilationism

Objection: The following passages show that the wicked perish. How can you say that this does not mean complete destruction?

Psalm 1:6   for the LORD knows the way of the righteous, but the way of the wicked will perish.
Psalm 37:20 But the wicked will perish; the enemies of the LORD are like the glory of the pastures; they vanish—like smoke they vanish away.
Psalm 69:28 Let them be blotted out of the book of the living; let them not be enrolled among the righteous.
Isaiah 1:28-31 But rebels and sinners shall be broken together, and those who forsake the LORD shall be consumed. For you shall be like an oak whose leaf withers, and like a garden without water. And the strong shall become tinder, and his work a spark, and

both of them shall burn together, with none to quench them.

Obadiah 1:16 For as you have drunk on my holy mountain, so all the nations shall drink continually; they shall drink and swallow, and shall be as though they had never been.

Malachi 4:1 "For behold, the day is coming, burning like an oven, when all the arrogant and all evildoers will be stubble. The day that is coming shall set them ablaze, says the LORD of hosts, so that it will leave them neither root nor branch.

John 3:16 "For God so loved the world, that he gave his only Son, that whoever believes in him should not perish but have eternal life.

Romans 6:23 For the wages of sin is death, but the free gift of God is eternal life in Christ Jesus our Lord.

Philippians 3:19 Their end is destruction, their god is their belly, and they glory in their shame, with minds set on earthly things.

2 Thessalonians 1:9 They will suffer the punishment of eternal destruction, away from the presence of the Lord and from the glory of his might,

1 Corinthians 3:17 If anyone destroys God's temple, God will destroy him. For God's temple is holy, and you are that temple.

2 Corinthians 2:15 For we are the aroma of Christ to God among those who are being saved and among those who are perishing, ago is not idle, and their destruction is not asleep.

Answer: The word "perish" is taken from the Hebrew words kawrath, and abad, with both basically meaning:

to destroy, to be void of, to lose, abolish, put an end to, **to ruin, to lose.**

Notice some of the ways this word is used in the Bible.

1. Genesis 41:36 That food shall be a reserve for the land against the seven years of famine that are to occur in the land of Egypt, so **that the land may not perish** through the famine."

Did the land actually perish? Or was it just temporarily unusable because of the famine.

2. Numbers 17:12 And the people of Israel said to Moses, "**Behold, we perish**, we are undone, we are all undone.

Did these people actually perish?

3. Deuteronomy 8:20 Like the nations that the LORD makes to perish before you, so shall you perish, because you would not obey the voice of the LORD your God. Yahweh sent the Chaldeans into Judah to destroy it.
   2 Kings 24:1-2 In his days, Nebuchadnezzar king of Babylon came up, and Jehoiakim became his servant for three years. Then he turned and rebelled against him. And the LORD sent against him bands of the Chaldeans and bands of the Syrians and bands of the Moabites and bands of the Ammonites, and sent them against Judah to destroy it, according to the word of the LORD that he spoke by his servants the prophets.

But in these cases, were they permanently destroyed, or were they **temporarily destroyed, i.e. brought to ruin?**

But notice what the book of Isaiah also states concerning the term "perish:"

4. Isaiah 57:1 The righteous perish, and no one lays it to heart. Merciful men are taken away, and no one considers that the righteous is taken away from the evil.

The righteous perish? Really? Permanently? I don't think so. Does this not indicate that the meaning of perish in the above passages is temporary?

And Jesus himself proclaimed:

John 12:24 Most certainly I tell you, unless a grain of wheat falls into the earth and dies, it remains by itself alone. But if it dies, it bears much fruit.

Did the grain that died really die a complete destruction? If so, how could it bear "much fruit?"

We see in the book of Hebrews that after we die, we perish from the earth, we go to the judgment.

Hebrews 9:27 And just as it is appointed for man to die once, and **after that comes judgment,**

So, if we look at this passage, it indicates that **we only die once.** So, in effect we only perish in human bodily form. According to the annihilationist scenario, it would be necessary for the individual to **die twice,** once **before the**

judgment, and then again **after the judgment**. But as Paul stated, with this judgment comes corrective punishment for those who do not believe. Notice his words:

who shall suffer justice—destruction age-during— from the face of the Lord, and from the glory of his strength, (2 Thessalonians 1:9 YLT)

The word for destruction used in this passage is ολεθρος (olethros) which means a loss of a life of blessedness after death (for the age enduring period). As Thayer's Lexicon shows, it also means the destruction of the flesh whereby the lusts of the flesh are subdued and destroyed[69]

Objection: What about the following passage? This shows the finality of the destruction.

Revelation 20:10 and the Devil, who is leading them astray, was cast into the lake of fire and brimstone, where *are* the beast and the false prophet, and they shall be tormented day and night--**to the ages of the ages**.
Revelation 20:14 and the death and the hades were cast to the lake of the fire--this *is* the second death;
Revelation 20:15 and if anyone was not found written in the scroll of the life, he was cast to the lake of the fire. (YLT)

Answer: We must remember that the death that Adam was sentenced to was spiritual death. We know this is true because God told Adam:

---

[69] Thayer's Greek Lexicon (eleventh printing February 2014) p. 443

Genesis 2:17 but of the tree of the knowledge of good and evil you shall not eat, for **in the day that you eat of it you shall surely die.**"

Adam did die that very day, spiritually . . . no more walks in the garden with God. He was separated from God from that day forward. When he did die physically, he did not "perish" but went to Sheol (or Hades in the Greek), which was the realm of the dead.

Later, as Jesus noted, there were two compartments for this place. One was Paradise, and the other was a place of darkness and separation. Even though death was defeated at the cross, which included the resurrection of Christ, Hades remained operative throughout the New Testament.

Now regardless of when you believe the Parousia (sometimes called the "Second Coming") did occur, or will occur, this is when death and Hades are thrown into the Lake of fire. I believe this has already occurred when Christ kept his promise and came in judgment in the generation that saw the destruction of Jerusalem.

The fact that it uses the term "ages" in the plural in verse 10 shows that this term cannot mean eternal. Remember that **an age is a period of time with an end**. It is similar to the use Paul makes of "ages" in Ephesians 2:7: "so that in the coming ages he might show the immeasurable riches of his grace in kindness toward us in Christ Jesus."

Thus, while it is possible that the worst of the worst of sinners may have to suffer for a very long period of time, I still believe that **there will be ultimate victory**

through Christ the Lord. As Paul wrote under the inspiration of the Holy Spirit:

> 1Tim 4:10 For to this end we toil and strive, because we have our hope set on the living God, **who is the Savior of all people**, especially of those who believe.

Appendix II

The Resurrection

When we think of the resurrection of the dead, we automatically think of dead bodies physically coming up out of the ground, do we not? And of course, we know that Jesus **was** resurrected **bodily. Upon this resurrection we pin our hope**! The Bible also shows accounts of several others that were resurrected. But there is much more to the resurrection that this. Before we begin, let me show you a picture given by the Apostle Paul which perfectly describes the nature of the resurrection. How many of you believers, have been baptized?

I will hold my hand up on that one, but I also realize that some may have determined from your studies that a baptism in water is not necessary. This is an entirely different discussion, which is out of the scope of this thesis. The apostle Paul gives us concerning Baptism, and how it relates to resurrection. It is found in Romans Chapter 6 and it reads:

> Do you not know that all of us who have been baptized into Christ Jesus were baptized into his death? **We were buried therefore with him by baptism into death, in order that, just as Christ was raised from the dead by the glory of the Father, we too might walk in newness of life.** For if we have been united with him in a

death like his, we shall certainly be united with him in a resurrection like his. We know that our old self was crucified with him in order that the body of sin might be brought to nothing, so that we would no longer be enslaved to sin. For one who has died has been set free from sin. Now if we have died with Christ, we believe that we will also live with him. (Romans 6:3-8 ESV)

So, the apostle said here that we were baptized into His death. But I want to look again at verse four. Notice that in verse four is this beautiful picture of our death and resurrection – **Buried with Christ, raised to walk in the newness of life!**

Do you see the profound significance of this passage? I did NOT see it for many years. I remember when I was baptized in water well over 30 years ago. As I was going down into the water, the Pastor said those very words: "buried with Christ." Then when I was coming up out of the water he said: "raised to walk in the newness of life." The implication by those words in Romans 6:4 are that since we were being buried with Christ, **we must have been dead in some manner.**

But to get the full understanding of this, we must begin with the question: What is death? This requires that we go back to the book of Genesis. Remember that God told Adam that *on the day* he ate of the forbidden fruit of the "tree of knowledge" that he would die. This promise was made to him in Genesis chapter 2. But if you look at the chronological record in Genesis you find that Adam lived over 900 years! So how do we reconcile this? When Adam was placed in the garden he was in perfect spiritual fellowship with God. His most important assignment was to obey God. When he disobeyed God, **he died that day, spiritually**. He was then separated from God....... no more walks in the Garden together, and no more discussions together. It was over. But physically, he lived for over 900 years. Here is the passage:

> And the LORD God commanded the man, saying, "You may surely eat of every tree of the garden, but of the tree of the knowledge of good and evil you shall not eat, for *in the day that you eat of it you shall surely die.*" (Gen 2:16-17 ESV)

So, the question is: Did God keep his word or not? *YES, He did!* On that day, Adam and Eve **lost their relationship** with their heavenly father. The death that they suffered was not physical death, but **spiritual death**. The account of this is recorded for us in Genesis 3:

> But the serpent said to the woman, "You will not surely die. For God knows that when you eat of it *your eyes will be opened, and you will be like God*, knowing good and evil." So when the woman saw that the tree was good for food, and that it was a delight to the eyes, and that the tree was to be desired to make one wise, she took of its fruit and ate, and she also gave some to her husband who was with her, and he ate. Then the *eyes of both were opened*, and they knew that they were naked. And they sewed fig leaves together and made themselves loincloths. (Gen 3:4-7 ESV)

Yes! The opening of their eyes in this manner signified their **death to God spiritually speaking**. By disobedience to God (*sin*), they were separated spiritually from God in "death." The record in Genesis tells us that because of this, God cast them out of the garden, with no opportunity to eat of the tree of life. Notice the words in Genesis:

> Then the LORD God said, "Behold, the man has become like one of us in knowing good and evil. Now, lest he reach out his hand and take also of the tree of life and eat, and live forever—" therefore the LORD God **sent him out from the garden** of Eden to work the ground from which he was taken. He drove out the man, and at the east of the garden of Eden he placed the cherubim and a flaming sword that turned every way to guard the way to the tree of life. (Gen 3:22-24 ESV)

From this we can see that the relationship between God and Adam ended . . . no more beautiful garden, no more chance to eat from the tree of life. But there was still hope for mankind due to the promise which God made. Here was the promise:

> The LORD God said to the serpent, "Because you have done this, cursed are you above all livestock and above all beasts of the field; on your belly you shall go, and dust you shall eat all the days of your life. I will put enmity between you and the woman, and between your offspring and her offspring; **he shall bruise your head, and you shall bruise his heel.**" (Gen 3:14-15 ESV)

From these words by God, there was hope. But the meaning of this passage was that there would arise one who would later be called the "son of man" who would crush Satan, who was the serpent. But for now, the relationship between Adam and God had been destroyed due to man's disobedience. Thus, this spiritual death spread to all of Adam's seed. Centuries later, Jesus himself referred to those who were dead in a similar manner. On the occasion when one of His disciples wanted to delay following him, note Jesus words:

> As they were going along the road, someone said to Him, "I will follow You wherever You go." And Jesus said to him, "The foxes have holes and the birds of the air have nests, but the Son of Man has nowhere to lay His head." And He said to another, "Follow Me." But he said, "Lord, permit me first to go and bury my father." But He said to him, "Allow **the dead** to bury their own dead; but as for you, go and proclaim everywhere the kingdom of God." (Luke 9:57-60 NASB)

It is perfectly clear that Jesus was not speaking of someone who was physically dead burying their dead. Notice how 18th Century Bible Commentator Adam Clark describes this:

> "This does not mean any of the twelve, but one of those who were constant hearers of our Lord's preaching; the name of disciple being common to all those who professed to believe in him, John 6:66. Bury my father: probably his father was old, and apparently near death; but it was a maxim among the Jews, that, if a man had any duty to perform to the dead, he was, for that time, free

296

from the observance of any other precept or duty. The children of Adam are always in extremes; some will rush into the ministry of the Gospel without a call, others will delay long after they are called; the middle way is the only safe one: not to move a finger in the work till the call be given, and not to delay a moment after."[i]

The Apostle Paul confirmed this line of thinking in the book of Romans when he writes:

Wherefore, as by one man sin entered into the world, and death by sin; and so **death passed upon all men, for that all have sinned**: For until the law sin was in the world: but sin is not imputed when there is no law. Nevertheless **death reigned from Adam to Moses**, even over them that had not sinned after the similitude of Adam's transgression, who is the figure of him that was to come. (Rom 5:12-14)

This raises some questions, but first let's look at what Paul said to the church at Colossae:

And you, who were *dead in your trespasses* and the uncircumcision of your flesh, God made alive together with him, having forgiven us all our trespasses, by canceling the record of debt that stood against us with its legal demands. This he set aside, nailing it to the cross. (Col 2:13-14 ESV)

Did you notice how Paul defines death in this passage? He said they were **dead in their trespasses**, but God made them alive with Christ. Were they physically dead? Of course not; It is obvious that Paul was speaking of going from **spiritual death to spiritual life.** So now, the question has to be, if death reigned from Adam to Moses, as Paul said earlier, did Moses solve the problem of death? Man has continued to die physically even to this day after Moses came, so we know that this does **not speak of physical death**. So, what did this mean?

With Moses came the Old Covenant. The purpose of that Old Covenant was to show man the utter impossibility of keeping the covenant due to his inherited sin. So, in effect, what it did was to show man the impossibility of his ability to keep the law. But at the same time, the Old Law Covenant pointed to the Messiah who would actually provide redemption for the sins of man. Paul stated it in this passage to the Roman church:

> Therefore, as **one trespass led to condemnation for all men**, so **one act of righteousness leads to justification** and life for **all** men. For as by the one man's disobedience the many were made sinners, so by the one man's obedience the many will be made righteous. Now **the law came in to increase the trespass, but where sin increased, grace abounded all the more,** so that, as sin reigned in death, grace also might reign through righteousness leading to eternal life through Jesus Christ our Lord. (Rom 5:18-21 ESV)

Thus, we see that sin and death are inseparable. Verse 20 shows us that when the law entered, the effect of sin increased to an even greater extent. But physical death did not get any worse in terms of its severity. So, the reference here is to spiritual death. This is clearly shown by what Paul later said in Romans 7:

I was once alive apart from the Law; but when the commandment came, sin became alive **and I died;** and this commandment, which was to result in life, proved to result in **death for me;** for sin, taking an opportunity through the commandment, deceived me and through **it killed me.** So then, the Law is holy, and the commandment is holy and righteous and good. Therefore did that which is good become a cause of death for me? May it never be! Rather it was sin, in order that it might be shown to be sin by effecting my death through that which is good, so that through the commandment sin would become utterly sinful. (Romans 7:9-13 NASB)

Do you see the profound significance of this? It is obvious that since Paul **had not yet died physically**, he **had to be** speaking of spiritual death. This is **the death which all men experience when they sin against God**. But this death is not something which cannot be reversed. Paul also wrote:

> For as in Adam **all** die, even so in Christ shall **all** be made alive. (1 Cor 15:22 ESV)

Did you notice how Paul worded this verse? **Paul did not say**, "even so in Christ all **have been** made alive." He said "even so in Christ shall all be made alive." He explains why he said it this way in the next verse. Note his words:

> But each in his own order: Christ the first fruits, after that those who are Christ's **at His coming** (1 Cor 15:23 ESV)

This will not happen in the physical realm. If the death that Adam experienced **was spiritual death**, then **the life that Christ brings is spiritual life!** This is what occurred at the Parousia. Spiritual life for all man was finally and completely restored. So, if the Parousia has not happened, then our salvation is not complete. This is confirmed in Hebrews 9 where it says:

> so Christ, having been offered once to bear the sins of many, will appear a second time, not to deal with sin **but to save those who are eagerly waiting for him.** (Heb 9:28 ESV)

We must remember that physical death is not our enemy. Even Paul said that he longed to "go and be with the Lord." When he did go, he was immediately "in Paradise" as was the thief on the cross who professed Christ. He would then go to heaven at the Parousia, because at that time according to Hebrews 9:28 his salvation was complete. Just like Adam, we all die through sin (spiritually). Thus, we can be made alive spiritually through Christ. Paul also confirmed this when writing to the church in Ephesus:

> And you were **dead in the trespasses and sins** . . . But God, being rich in mercy, because of the great love with which he loved us, even when **we were dead in our trespasses**, made us alive together with Christ—**by grace you have been saved** — and **raised us up with him and seated us with him in the heavenly places** in Christ Jesus, so that in the coming ages he might show the immeasurable riches of his grace in kindness toward us in Christ Jesus. (Eph 2:1,4-7 ESV)

When Paul spoke to the Ephesian Church, he made it clear that these first century Christians **were made alive** in Christ because of their being saved. They had been raised from spiritual death! But Paul was just echoing the words spoken to him by Jesus. For these words of our Lord were recorded by the Apostle John:

> Truly, truly, I say to you, if anyone keeps my word, **he will never see death**. (John 8:51 ESV)

The Jews did not understand that He was speaking of spiritual death either! Notice what they say in response to Jesus:

> The Jews said to him, "Now we know that you have a demon! **Abraham died**, as did the prophets, yet you say, 'If anyone keeps my word, he will never taste death.' (John 8:52 ESV)

Then later Jesus once again confirmed His words:

> Jesus said to her, "**I am the resurrection and the life**. Whoever believes in me, though he die, yet shall he live, and everyone who lives and believes in me **shall never die**. Do you believe this?" (John 11:25-26 ESV)

Do you see the contrast here? Obviously, people have continued to die physically! But by trusting and believing in Him while yet alive, we are raised to spiritual life through Him and will never die! Paul also confirmed this in Romans 6:23:

For the wages of sin is death, but the free gift of God is eternal life in Christ Jesus our Lord. (Romans 6:23 ESV)

Paul made it clear that this was also **spiritual death and spiritual life.** Make no mistake about it, each one of us will die physically, but once we become believers, and put our trust in Christ, we are made alive in the spirit at the very moment we accept him! The Apostle John confirms this with these words:

And this is the testimony, that God gave us eternal life, and this life is in his Son. **Whoever has the Son has life**; whoever does not have the Son of God **does not** have life. I write these things to you who believe in the name of the Son of God that you may **know that you have eternal life**. (1 John 5:11-13 ESV)

Do you see the incredible significance of this? If you believe, you have life **NOW!** Just as the Jews in that day were focused on physical death, so are most people today. But this was about spiritual death and spiritual life. Now let's focus on another aspect of this that will look at this from another perspective, and that is that the resurrection was the hope of Israel. This was the original teaching of the prophets. Paul confirmed this in the book of Acts. Paul was teaching what the prophets taught:

But this I confess to you, that according to the Way, which they call a sect, I worship the God of our fathers, **believing everything laid down by the Law** and written in the Prophets, having a **hope in God**, which these men themselves accept, that there will be a **resurrection of both the just and the unjust**. (Acts 24:14-15 ESV)

What did the prophets say about this? Let's look at a few examples:

He will swallow up death forever, And the Lord GOD will wipe away tears from all faces; The rebuke of His people He will take away from all the earth; For the LORD has spoken. And it will be said in that day: "Behold, this *is* our God; We have waited for Him, and He will save us. This *is* the LORD; We have waited for Him; We will be glad and rejoice in His salvation." (Isa 25:8-9 ESV)

I will ransom them from the power of the grave; I will redeem them from death. O Death, I will be your plagues! O Grave, I will be your destruction! Pity is hidden from My eyes. (Hos 13:14 NKJV)

Daniel shows that the timing of this would be for the last days of the nation of Israel. First of all, he predicts that the Messiah would come to put an end to sin, and bring in everlasting righteousness:

Seventy weeks are determined for your people and for your holy city, To finish the transgression, **To make an end of sins**, **To make reconciliation** for iniquity, **To bring in everlasting righteousness**, To seal up vision and prophecy, And **to anoint the Most Holy**. (Daniel 9:24 NKJV)

Then in chapter 12 we confirm the timing of this:

> At that time Michael shall stand up, The great prince who stands *watch* over the sons of your people; And there shall be a time of trouble, Such as never was since there was a nation, *Even* to that time. And **at that time your people shall be delivered**, Every one who is found written in the book. **And many of those who sleep in the dust of the earth shall awake, Some to everlasting life, Some to shame *and* everlasting contempt.** (Daniel 12:1-2 NKJV)

This was the promised resurrection. Next, we see the exact timing:

> Then I heard the man clothed in linen, who *was* above the waters of the river, when he held up his right hand and his left hand to heaven, and swore by Him who lives forever, that *it shall be* for a time, times, and half *a time;* and **when the power of the holy people has been completely shattered, all these *things* shall be finished.** (Daniel 12:7 NKJV)

The power of the Holy people was shattered at the destruction of Jerusalem and the temple! This ended the Old Covenant and allowed the New Covenant to stand on its own alone. This was the time of the resurrection. Now that we know the timing of this, let's look at what Paul said concerning the resurrection hope of Israel. Let's start with Romans 8:

> And not only the creation, but we ourselves, who have the first fruits of the Spirit, groan inwardly as

we wait eagerly for adoption as sons, the redemption of our bodies. For in this hope we were saved. Now hope that is seen is not hope. For who hopes for what he sees? But if we hope for what we do not see, we wait for it with patience. (Romans 8:23-25 ESV)

This was the hope of Israel. Paul confirms this in Romans 9:

I am speaking the truth in Christ—I am not lying; my conscience bears me witness in the Holy Spirit—that I have great sorrow and unceasing anguish in my heart. For I could wish that I myself were accursed and cut off from Christ for the sake of my brothers, my kinsmen according to the flesh. *They are Israelites, and to them belong the adoption*, the glory, the covenants, the giving of the law, the worship, and the promises. To them belong the patriarchs, and from their race, **according to the flesh**, is the Christ, who is God over all, blessed forever. Amen. (Romans 9:1-5 ESV)

The adoption that Paul is speaking of here is the promise of the resurrection *made to Israel*. But even though this was made according to the flesh, it does not mean that it was fulfilled in a fleshly manner. This is because when Christ was raised from the dead, even though he was raised from the dead bodily, this body was now somehow changed. Actually, **He was raised into the spirit realm** as shown by Peter in this passage:

For Christ also suffered once for sins, the righteous for the unrighteous, that he might bring us to God, being **put to death in the flesh** but **made alive in the spirit**, (1 Peter 3:18 ESV)

Thus, our Lord, upon His resurrection was **not going** to fulfill these things in the realm of the flesh, but **He would fulfill these** in the realm of the spirit.

From now on, therefore, we regard no one **according to the flesh**. Even though we once regarded Christ according to the flesh, **we regard him thus no longer**. (2 Cor 5:16 ESV)

This means that **they regarded Him as in the spirit** in terms of His mode of existence. Paul confirmed the meaning of this in Romans 8 when he said:

Those who are in the flesh **cannot please God**. (Rom 8:8 ESV)

Does this mean no one alive can please God? Of course not! Notice how he continues in the next verse.

You, however, **are not in the flesh but in the Spirit**, if in fact the Spirit of God dwells in you. Anyone who does not have the Spirit of Christ does not belong to him. (Rom 8:9 ESV)

So, from this we can see unequivocally that he was speaking of these people who, since they were believers, were living in physical bodies who were alive in the spirit. And we also know that since Christ was the first one raised into the realm of the spirit; he was the "first fruits" of those who have fallen asleep. This is a concept that deals with the harvest in Israel. This is what Paul is saying to the Corinthian church:

But now Christ is risen from the dead, *and* has become the firstfruits of those who have fallen asleep. (1 Cor 15:20 NKJV)

This idea of the first-fruits is a concept that deals with the harvest in Israel, and subsequently, the harvest had to do with the end of the Old Covenant age in Israel. How do we know this? We can determine this from a parable that Jesus gave in Matthew 13:24-30. In this parable, Jesus spoke of an enemy coming in and sowing tares among the wheat in the field, and that they should be gathered up and separated at the harvest, which would occur at the end of the age. When Jesus interpreted this to the disciples, He told them that the wheat was a reference to the true believers, and the tares were those wicked ones sown in among them by the enemy to disrupt the faith.

Therefore as the tares are gathered and burned in the fire, **so it will be at the end of THIS age**. The Son of Man will send out His angels, and they will gather out of His kingdom all things that offend, and those who practice lawlessness, and will cast them into the furnace of fire. There will be wailing and gnashing of teeth. (Matt 13:40-42 NKJV)

The end of the age that Jesus was speaking of was the **end of the age Jesus was living in**, the Jewish age, or the end of the Old Covenant age, in which the city of Jerusalem, the temple, and the entire system of Levitical worship would be destroyed. We can confirm the timeframe as being the end of the Jewish age **because the Christian age in which we are now living has no end:**

> Now to Him who is able to do exceedingly abundantly above all that we ask or think, according to the power that works in us, to Him *be* glory in the church by Christ Jesus **to all generations, forever and ever.** Amen. (Eph 3:20-21 NKJV)

This is the age WITHOUT END, the Christian age. Then Jesus said:

> Then the righteous will shine forth as the sun in the kingdom of their Father. He who has ears to hear, let him hear! (Matt 13:43 NKJV)

This is a direct quote from Daniel 12:3. Notice Daniel's words:

> Those who are wise shall shine Like the brightness of the firmament, And those who turn many to righteousness Like the stars forever and ever. (Daniel 12:3 NKJV)

Remember what we saw earlier concerning the timing of this? The prophet Daniel explicitly told when this would happen:

> Then I heard the man clothed in linen, who *was* above the waters of the river, when he held up his right hand and his left hand to heaven, and swore by Him who lives forever, that *it shall be* for a time, times, and half *a time;* and **when the power of the holy people has been completely**

shattered, all these *things* shall be finished. (Daniel 12:7 NKJV)

The time **when the power of the holy people has been completely shattered** was none other than at the end of the Old Covenant age, or at the destruction of the temple, and the holy city in AD 70. Paul confirmed that this resurrection was to happen **at that time**:

> And *do* this, knowing the time, that **now *it is* high time** to awake out of sleep; for now **our salvation *is* nearer than when we *first* believed**. The night is far spent, the day is at hand. Therefore let us cast off the works of darkness, and let us put on the armor of light. (Romans 13:11-12 NKJV)

Paul also confirmed this would happen soon when he said:

> And the God of peace will **crush Satan under your feet shortly**. The grace of our Lord Jesus Christ *be* with you. Amen. (Rom 16:20 NKJV)

Thus, the spiritual death brought on by Satan was now about to be crushed. The resurrection was to occur at the end of the Jewish age. Jesus said:

> Do not think that I came to destroy the Law or the Prophets. I did not come to destroy **but to fulfill.** For assuredly, I say to you, **till heaven and earth pass away**, one jot or one tittle will by no means pass from the law **till all is fulfilled**. (Matt 5:17,18 NKJV)

The term "heaven and earth" was a description of the temple. The Most Holy represented heaven where God alone dwelled, and the rest represented earth, where man was. The Law that He was speaking of was the Old Testament Law.

Do you see the profound significance of this statement?

That law **had to be completely fulfilled** to become obsolete, and **that law had to fulfill all of those references to the resurrection** within the law and that written by the prophets, including those in the writings of the Major Prophets we have mentioned. Thus, the resurrection is spiritual, not physical. It occurs at the time of being "born again." Once again, I will refer to the picture painted by the Apostle Paul. He describes this perfectly in Romans chapter 6 when he says:

> Or do you not know that as many of us as were baptized into Christ Jesus were **baptized into His death?** Therefore we were buried with Him through baptism into death, that **just as Christ was raised from the dead** by the glory of the Father, **even so we also should walk in newness of life**. (Romans 6:3-4 NKJV)

The newness of life that Paul spoke of was that they were no longer separated from God in their sins, but they were now alive in the spirit, having been resurrected from the spiritual death passed down from Adam. The timing of this is crucial. The fact that this would happen soon is **emphasized by Christ himself** when He said:

> Truly, truly, I say to you, **an hour is coming, and is now here**, when the dead will hear the voice of the Son of God, and those who hear will

live. For as the Father has life in himself, so he has granted the Son also to have life in himself. And he has given him authority to execute judgment, because he is the Son of Man. Do not marvel at this, for an hour is coming **when all who are in the tombs will hear his voice and come out**, those who have done good to the resurrection of life, and those who have done evil to the resurrection of judgment. (John 5:25-29 ESV)

This was not something which was to happen thousands of years later. Those who were spiritually dead would hear His voice and would live, and all those in the tombs would soon be resurrected, to either life, or judgment. When would this happen? As we found earlier, **Daniel the prophet unequivocally gave a proclamation of the exact timing:**

And **many of those who sleep in the dust of the earth shall awake, some to everlasting life, and some to shame and everlasting contempt** . . . And I heard the man clothed in linen, who was above the waters of the stream; he raised his right hand and his left hand toward heaven and swore by him who lives forever that it would be for a time, times, and half a time, and that **when the shattering of the power of the holy people comes to an end all these things would be finished.** (Daniel 12:2,7 ESV)

There is no question that the power of the Holy people was shattered at the time of the destruction of Jerusalem, the temple, and the entire Levitical system of worship. This occurred at the hands of the Romans in AD 70.

1 Corinthians 15

Now let's look at what Paul said concerning this resurrection. First, we will look at 1 Corinthians 15. In the first eleven verses of this chapter, we find that Paul speaks of the resurrection of Christ, and confirms the fact that it happened, and was witnessed by Peter, James, and over 500 others. Paul mentions that Christ also appeared to him, and he was called into service. The Corinthian church knew that Christ was raised from the dead, but there seemed to be some here who were questioning the concept of the resurrection. Paul's argument was that since they know Christ was raised, it thus must follow that there is a resurrection from the dead. Note what he says:

> Now if Christ is proclaimed as raised from the dead, how can some of you say that there is no resurrection of the dead? But if there is no resurrection of the dead, then not even Christ has been raised. And if Christ has not been raised, then our preaching is in vain and your faith is in vain. We are even found to be misrepresenting God, because we testified about God that he raised Christ, whom he did not raise if it is true that the dead are not raised. For if the dead are not raised, not even Christ has been raised. And if Christ has not been raised, your faith is futile, and you are still in your sins. Then those also who have fallen asleep in Christ have perished. If in Christ we have hope in this life only, we are of all people most to be pitied. (1 Cor 15:12-19 ESV)

Paul's argument is clear. There **is a resurrection from the dead**, and the resurrection of Christ was the beginning. In another letter to the church at Colossae he said: "He is the beginning, the firstborn from the dead, that in everything he might be preeminent." (Col 1:18) Notice how he brings this together.

> But in fact Christ has been raised from the dead, the firstfruits of those who have fallen asleep. For as by a man came death, by a man **has come** also the resurrection of the dead. For as in Adam all die, so also in Christ **shall all be made alive**. But each in his own order: Christ the firstfruits, then at his coming those who belong to Christ. (1 Cor 15:20-23 ESV)

This illustration of the first fruits was in accordance with Jewish Law. Notice the command:

> "Speak to the people of Israel and say to them, when you come into the land that I give you and reap its harvest, **you shall bring the sheaf of the firstfruits of your harvest to the priest**, (Lev 23:10 ESV)

Thus, the **first fruits and the harvest occurred at the same time**. The first fruits were presented; Christ had already been resurrected from the dead as the first fruits. **That means that the harvest of resurrected ones was about to begin.** But now your question might be, "How can this be since the resurrection of Christ was bodily? There were no bodies coming up out of the graves." You are right! But if you will recall, the Jews always required a sign. Jesus told them the only sign they would receive was the sign of Jonah. What did that mean? He told them:

For just as Jonah was three days and three nights in the belly of the great fish, so will the Son of Man be three days and three nights in the heart of the earth. (Matthew 12:40 ESV)

Jesus rose from the dead so that people living at that time could witness it, and without question they did. And when Christ rose from the dead, He became the "first-fruits" of the harvest. After His ascension to heaven, He did not stay in the same form. That body of a Jewish man was no longer present. But He was as described as John recorded in Revelation chapter one:

The hairs of his head were white, like white wool, like snow. His eyes were like a flame of fire, his feet were like burnished bronze, refined in a furnace, and his voice was like the roar of many waters. In his right hand he held seven stars, from his mouth came a sharp two-edged sword, and his face was like the sun shining in full strength. (Rev 1:14-16 ESV)

Jesus had returned to His spiritual body, the body of the son of God, and one with the father. Now as we return to 1 Corinthians, we notice the wording of the verse. As Paul emphasizes in verse 21 the resurrection of the dead **has come (present tense).** There was **not to be a gap** of thousands of years between the first fruit and the final harvest. When Paul wrote this to the church in Corinth, it was only about 15 years away. Once again remember that Daniel said: **"when the shattering of the power of the holy people comes to an end all these things would be finished**." (Daniel 12:7). The power of the holy people was shattered completely when Jerusalem, the temple, and the entire Levitical system of worship was brought to an end in AD 70. Although Paul knows this is about to occur, he did not know the exact timing. This is the end that he speaks of in the next verse.

> Then comes the end, when he delivers the kingdom to God the Father after destroying every rule and every authority and power. For he must reign until he has put all his enemies under his feet. The last enemy to be destroyed is death. For "God has put all things in subjection under his feet." But when it says, "all things are put in subjection," it is plain that he is excepted who put all things in subjection under him. When all things are subjected to him, then the Son himself will also be subjected to him who put all things in subjection under him, that God may be all in all. (1 Cor 15:24-28 ESV)

Just prior to His ascension into heaven, Jesus said: "All authority in heaven and on earth has been given to me." (Mat 28:18) But after His ascension to heaven, He went into the Holy of Holies in heaven to present His blood of the sacrifice. As the writer of Hebrews noted:

> It was indeed therefore necessary for the glimpses of the things in the heavens with these to be purified; but, the heavenly things themselves, with better sacrifices than these. For, not into a Holy place made by hand, entered Christ,—counterpart of the real Holy place ; but, **into the heaven itself, NOW**, to be plainly manifested before the face of God in our behalf;— (Hebrews 9:23-24 Rotherham)

Thus, from this we see that at the ascension, all authority was given to Christ, but when He went into the Most Holy in heaven and presented the blood of His sacrifice, the prophecy given by the Apostle Paul came true when he said: "The God of peace will **soon crush Satan** under your feet."(Romans 16:20) So then at the Parousia, when Christ came as He promised; and through the use of the Roman armies, He completely destroyed the city of Jerusalem, the temple, and the entire system of Levitical sacrifice and worship. Yes, with this, Satan was "crushed." This system and those who posed the most severe opposition to them would be finally crushed. Satan's authority over them would end. Additionally, the last enemy, which was the "death" which Adam experienced in the garden, was destroyed. Now, because of the precious blood of Christ being presented in the Holy of Holies in heaven, man could once again have a restored relationship with God. Now as we return to 1 Corinthians, in verse 29 we see that Paul made a very obscure statement:

> Otherwise, what do people mean by being baptized on behalf of the dead? If the dead are not raised at all, why are people baptized on their behalf? (1 Cor 15:29 ESV)

Commentator Adam Clarke said of this verse: "This is certainly the most difficult verse in the New Testament; for, notwithstanding the greatest and wisest men have labored to explain it, there are to this day nearly as many different interpretations of it as there are interpreters."

Remember that **Paul is speaking in the present tense**. He is not speaking of a future event. So, let's just think about this for a moment in the light of what Paul has said in the past. We know that in Romans chapter 5 Paul said:

> Yet death reigned from Adam to Moses, even over those whose sinning was not like the transgression of Adam, who was a type of the one who was to come . . . For if, because of one man's trespass, death reigned through that one man, much more will those who receive the abundance of grace and the free gift of righteousness reign in life through the one man Jesus Christ. (Rom 5:14,17 ESV)

The presence of the Old Covenant was a stop gap measure to cover the sin of the people and give them a relationship with God, based on the future blood of Christ. The act of baptism symbolized the spiritual death of the believer, and the coming up out of the water symbolized a new life in Christ. So, their status changed from being dead in Adam to being made alive in Christ. Of course, this **would not be complete until the Parousia.**

As the writer of Hebrews said:

> so Christ, having been offered once to bear the sins of many, **will appear a second time**, not to deal with sin **but to save those who are eagerly waiting for him**. (Hebrews 9:28 ESV)

Without a doubt, the writer of Hebrews made his point. The Parousia is the **completion of salvation** for the believer. So, in looking at verse 29 once again we realize that perhaps Paul was answering a question or misconception posed regarding this by one of the believers in Corinth in the first half of the verse, in relationship to this. But whatever was meant, the statement is meant to show another proof that those who are spiritually dead are raised. Let us continue:

> Why are we in danger every hour? I protest, brothers, by my pride in you, which I have in Christ Jesus our Lord, I die every day! (1 Cor 15:30-31 ESV)

Paul was continually being exposed to death. But he was proud of the faith of his Corinthian brothers. He was emphasizing that this is the cross that they must bear, the possibility of being killed for the sake of Christ.

> What do I gain if, humanly speaking, I fought with beasts at Ephesus? If the dead are not raised, "Let us eat and drink, for tomorrow we die." Do not be deceived: "Bad company ruins good morals." Wake up from your drunken stupor, as is right, and do not go on sinning. For some have no knowledge of God. I say this to your shame. (1 Cor 15:32-34 ESV)

Paul was once again emphasizing the point he made earlier concerning the resurrection of Christ. If there is no resurrection from the dead, there is no point to our faith. We might as well live it up for otherwise we have nothing. But NO, quit associating with those ones who would deny the resurrection, and the existence of God. They are ruining your faith and will cause you to sin with them.

> But someone will ask, "How are the dead raised? With what kind of body do they come?" You foolish person! What you sow does not come to life unless it dies. And what you sow is not the body that is to be, but a bare kernel, perhaps of wheat or of some other grain. But God gives it a body as he has

chosen, and to each kind of seed its own body. (1 Cor 15:35-38 ESV)

If the resurrection of those who have died physically was a bodily resurrection of the same type that goes into the ground, there would be **no purpose for Paul to go into the seed analogy** as he did in this passage. The body that dies and goes into the ground is like a seed. Therefore, the body that comes out of the ground is a different body, suited for the purpose which is chosen by God.

> For not all flesh is the same, but there is one kind for humans, another for animals, another for birds, and another for fish. There are heavenly bodies and earthly bodies, but the glory of the heavenly is of one kind, and the glory of the earthly is of another. There is one glory of the sun, and another glory of the moon, and another glory of the stars; for star differs from star in glory. (1 Cor 15:39-41 ESV)

Continuing with his seed analogy, Paul gives some examples of different types of bodies; each one is individually suited for its own purpose. Additionally, even with the heavenly bodies, each body type has its own glory. For example, the sun has a magnitude of glory that is far greater than the moon.

> So is it with the resurrection of the dead. What is sown is **perishable; what is raised is imperishable.** It is sown in dishonor; it is raised in glory. It is sown in weakness; it is raised in power. **It is sown a natural body; it is raised a spiritual body**. If there is a natural body, there is also a spiritual body. (1 Cor 15:42-44 ESV)

This passage sounds simple, but it must be understood in the context of what the rest of the Scriptures say about the resurrection. Now I want you to **look closely** to what I am about to say. It gets a little complex. Revelation 20:4-5 tells us that there are two groups who participate in the first resurrection. Notice what it says:

> Then I saw thrones, and seated on them were those to whom the authority to judge was committed. Also I saw **the souls of those who had been beheaded for the testimony of Jesus** and for the word of God, and those who had not worshiped the beast or its image and had not received its mark on their foreheads or their hands. They came to life and reigned with Christ for a thousand years. **The rest of the dead did not come to life until the thousand years were ended**. This is the first resurrection. (Rev 20:4-5 ESV)

Upon first reading verse 5, it seems very confusing. It appears that there have been two separate and distinct groups being mentioned here, which we would think indicates two resurrections. The above is the verse as translated in the English Standard Version. Now notice the difference between this and the New International Version:

> (The rest of the dead did not come to life until the thousand years were ended.) This is the first resurrection. (Rev 20:5 NIV)

Do you see the difference?

- In the ESV, the passage **must be taken as follows**: "The rest of the dead (in Christ) did not come to life until the thousand years were ended." (This makes them a part of the first resurrection.)

- In the NIV, the presence of the parentheses is an indication that those words in parentheses are a side note. (In other words, these ones are not a part of the first resurrection but belong to the second resurrection.)

This passage has to be taken in one of these two ways in order to make sense. Otherwise we have to separate verse 5 as a second resurrection, which is contrary to what it says. As such, there would have to be a third resurrection, but this does not agree with how the verse is written.

I believe that the ESV has translated it correctly, and here is why.

Now in order to put this in perspective, we must remember the prophecy of Daniel 12:1-7 which tells us when the resurrection would occur. Let's read this again:

> "At that time shall arise Michael, the great prince who has charge of your people. And there shall be a time of trouble, such as never has been since there was a nation till that time. But at that time your people shall be delivered, everyone whose name shall be found written in the book. **And many of those who sleep in the dust of the earth shall awake, some to everlasting life, and some to shame and everlasting contempt.** (Daniel 12:1-2 ESV)

This is the resurrection.

> And those who are wise shall shine like the brightness of the sky above; and those who turn

many to righteousness, like the stars forever and ever. But you, Daniel, shut up the words and seal the book, until the time of the end. Many shall run to and fro, and knowledge shall increase." Then I, Daniel, looked, and behold, two others stood, one on this bank of the stream and one on that bank of the stream. And someone said to the man clothed in linen, who was above the waters of the stream, "How long shall it be till the end of these wonders?" And I heard the man clothed in linen, who was above the waters of the stream; he raised his right hand and his left hand toward heaven and swore by him who lives forever that it would be for a time, times, and half a time, and **that when the shattering of the power of the holy people comes to an end all these things would be finished.** (Daniel 12:3-7 ESV)

Did you notice how specific this verse was. It specifically says: **"when the shattering of the power of the holy people comes to an end ALL these things would be finished." This had to be at the destruction of Jerusalem in AD 70.** This was the complete end of the Old Covenant and the Jewish Levitical system of worship. The power of God's heretofore holy people was completely shattered. This system of worship was no longer possible! **It also had to be the end of the Millennium**, because Rev. 20:5 plainly states that those dead in Christ did not come to life **"until the thousand years were ended."** Also, we must realize that Revelation 20:4 tells us that this resurrection includes not only:

- The saints who were beheaded, but also,

- Those who had not worshiped the beast or received the mark. Therefore, these are people who are still alive.

If the resurrection included both those dead at the time, and those alive, then we know that **it meant that all believers** were resurrected at that time, both those who were physically dead, and those who were physically alive. Thus, the first resurrection is by nature a spiritual resurrection, but at AD 70 it included those who were removed from "paradise" in Hades and were taken to heaven. This was the resurrection that Paul was speaking of in the passage in 1 Corinthians 15:42-44. Thus, **we as believers are a part of the first resurrection.** The picture Paul painted in Romans 6:4 applies to us. **We were buried with Christ.** This put away our sin. **Then we were resurrected to walk in the newness of life! We are already part of the first resurrection!** What a blessing! As Rev 20:6 says, **the second death has no authority over us,** and this is in harmony with what Paul said:

> But God, being rich in mercy, because of the great love with which he loved us, even when we were dead in our trespasses, made us alive together with Christ—**by grace you have been saved—** and **raised us up with him and seated us with him in the heavenly places** in Christ Jesus, so that in the coming ages he might show the immeasurable riches of his grace in kindness toward us in Christ Jesus. For by grace you have been saved through faith. And this is not your own doing; it is the gift of God, (Ephesians 2:4-8 ESV)

Do you see the powerful significance of what Paul said? Those saints who **were still alive on earth** were also seated "**with Him in the heavenly places.**" Their **resurrection from spiritual death was complete,** and the second death now had no power over them.

> Thus it is written, "The first man Adam became a living being"; the last Adam became a life-giving spirit. But it is not the spiritual that is first but the natural, and then the spiritual. The first man was from the earth, a man of dust; the second man is from heaven. As was the man of dust, so also are those who are of the dust, and as is the man of heaven, so also are those who are of heaven. Just as we have borne the image of the man of dust, we shall also bear the image of the man of heaven. (1 Cor 15:45-49 ESV)

When Adam was placed in the garden he was in perfect spiritual fellowship with God. His most important assignment was to obey God. When he disobeyed God, **he died that day, spiritually**. He was then separated from God .... no more walks in the Garden together, and no more discussions together. It was over. But physically, he lived for over 900 years. When Jesus died on the cross, he died physically as well, but just as man did, **he also suffered spiritual separation from God**. Paul would later tell the Corinthian church:

> For our sake **he made him to be sin who knew no sin**, so that in him we might become the righteousness of God. (2 Cor 5:21 ESV)

As the Apostle John noted:

And as Moses lifted up the serpent in the wilderness, so must the Son of Man be lifted up, **that whoever believes in him may have eternal life.** "For God so loved the world, that he gave his only Son, that whoever believes in **him should not perish but have eternal life.** (John 3:14-16 ESV)

The fact of the matter is that if Jesus came to the earth to suffer physical death so that we did not have to die physically, **then this death was ineffective.** Why? Because men have continued to die without ceasing! But Jesus experienced the same alienation from God as man did when He died on that Cross. As Paul said, "**he made Him to be sin who knew no sin**, so that in Him we might become the righteousness of God." The only way for the man to be restored to that right relationship with God was for Him to also die to the flesh. This is done by belief in Christ as Lord and Savior. It is pictured perfectly by the baptism analogy . . . **buried with Christ . . . raised to walk in the newness of life.** (Romans 6:3-4) That new life is a spiritual one. When we accept Christ as Savior, we begin a new spiritual life with Christ, and we will never die again (spiritually). That is what Jesus meant when He said:

Jesus said to her, "**I am the resurrection and the life**. Whoever believes in me, though he die, yet shall he live, and **everyone who lives and believes in me <u>shall never die</u>**. Do you believe this?" (John 11:25-26 ESV)

Now as we continue with 1 Corinthians we read:

I tell you this, brothers: flesh and blood cannot inherit the kingdom of God, nor does the perishable inherit the imperishable. Behold! I tell you a mystery. We shall not all sleep, but we shall all be changed, in a moment, in the twinkling of an eye, at the last trumpet. For the trumpet will sound, and the dead will be raised imperishable, and we shall be changed. For this perishable body must put on the imperishable, and this mortal body must put on immortality. When the perishable puts on the imperishable, and the mortal puts on immortality, then shall come to pass the saying that is written: "Death is swallowed up in victory." (1 Cor 15:50-54 ESV)

The words used by Paul in verse 50 makes it clear that the Kingdom of God is not primarily a physical kingdom. It is a spiritual kingdom. We inherit this kingdom spiritually when we become believers. Thus, when we die physically, we do not actually die, but are changed in the twinkling of an eye. Our spirit still lives, and we will receive a spiritual body, as we read earlier in verse 44, **"It is sown a natural body; it is raised a spiritual body**." Since Paul included himself in with those who would "not sleep," we know that Paul was expecting the return of the Lord at any time. What Paul was emphasizing in verses 51-53 is that soon, at the Parousia (the last trumpet), this would be finalized. Not everyone would die at that time, but would be changed in a moment, in the twinkling of an eye **to complete spiritual life**. Thus, they would never die. This is in harmony with what the writer of Hebrews stated:

so Christ, having been offered once to bear the sins of many, will appear a second time, not to deal with sin **but to save those who are eagerly waiting for him**. (Heb 9:28 ESV)

This event where Christ appeared "a second time," is called the Parousia, and as stated above, it finalized the salvation for the believer. Did you notice the wording at the end of the verse? They were **eagerly awaiting** this event. The death of Adam, that is, spiritual death, was swallowed up forever. It is as Jesus said:

Truly, truly, I say to you, whoever hears my word and believes him who sent me has eternal life. He does not come into judgment, **but has passed from death to life**. (John 5:24 ESV)

As we conclude the passage in 1 Corinthians 15, we read:

"O death, where is your victory? O death, where is your sting?" The sting of death is sin, and the power of sin is the law. But thanks be to God, who gives us the victory through our Lord Jesus Christ. Therefore, my beloved brothers, be steadfast, immovable, always abounding in the work of the Lord, knowing that in the Lord your labor is not in vain. (1 Cor 15:55-58 ESV)

It is no wonder that Paul breaks out in praise here. By the accomplishment of being finally changed to complete spiritual life, those alive at that time would never die, and **those believers who had died physically** would be raised from the "paradise" side of Hades, to life in heaven, and would receive their spiritual body. But it is true of both groups that they would always be with the Lord. What a great chapter of encouragement to those to whom Paul wrote. Praises to our Lord and Savior forever!

Scripture Index

Genesis

2:9	58
2:15	23
2:16	23,294
2:17	23,290,294
3:4-7	294
3:14	295
3:15	202,295
3:22-24	295
4:4-5	189
6	195
12:1-3	25,184,245
12:3	184,245
13:2-6	26
13:12	27
14:18-20	27
15:1	232
15:4-6	27
19	195
25:8	85
25:23	190
41:36	287

Exodus

4:21	190,196
10:20	194
10:27	194
12	195,196
12:24	148
14:17	190
15:6	244
19:5-6	36
19:9	36
19:7-8	36
22:20	110,246
40:15	144,148,278,279

Leviticus

3:17	148
6:13	148
23:10	313
24:17	39
24:17-20	193

Deuteronomy

2:30	194
8:20	287
9:29	244
15:17	148
19:21	276
23:3,6	148
28:24	110,246
28:45-51	118
33:27	135,136

Joshua

14:9	148

Judges

6:11-12	189

Ruth

2:10-12	231

1 Samuel

23:10-13	244
26:22-25	239

2 Samuel

12	196
14:20	2,263

Scripture Index

1 Kings

8:13	148
8:16	189
14	196

2 Kings

5:27	148
19	196
24:1-2	118,287

1 Chronicles

16:34	50
16:36	133
29:11	244

2 Chronicles

16:9	229,235
28:1-3	87

Nehemiah

9:5	133
9:7	188

Job

1:8	190
1:12	190
23:10	244
37:16	244
41:4	148
42:2	265,266

Psalms

1:6	285
8:6	263
9:17	84
36:7	109
37:7,20,34	111,246,285

Psalms (continued)

37:9-10	110
41:13	133
55:15	84
68:11	227
69:13	109
69:28	285
78:33-35	236
78:34	236
78:68	189
80:8	101
86:6	55
90:2	134
103:1-6,9	64
103:10-13	65
103:17	134
106:48	134
138:2	263
139:1-4,7-10	244
147:5	244

Proverbs

3:5,6	3,329

Ecclesiastes

3:11	228

Isaiah

1:28-31	285
9:6-7	30
25:8-9	303
26:14	10
30:18	259
34:9-10	102,148
36	172
37	172
40:1-5	206
41:21-25	170
44:24	264

Scripture Index

Isaiah (continued)

45:23-25	131,177,237
55:7-9	179
55:10-11	82,179
57:1	118,246,288
66:24	204,277,281

Jeremiah

1:5	245
2:21	101
7:30-35	52,77,87,88
7:30-31	246
10:16	264
18:1-6	183
23:23-24	244
29:10-13	37
48:47	149
49:6	149

Ezekiel

20:5	189

Daniel

4:27-37	254
4:29-33	173
4:34-37	174,258
9:24	303
12:1-2	304,321
12:1-7	321
12:2	278,279,311
12:2-3	145,146,280
12:3	308
12:3-7	322
12:7	304,309,311, 314

Hosea

10-1	101
13:14	303

Obadiah

1:16	286

Jonah

2:5-6	146

Micah

7:18	109

Malachi

3:6	39,244
4:1	286

Matthew

5:11-12	232
5:17-18	309
5:19-21	236
5:22	89
5:29	89
5:30	89
5:43-44	50
5:46	232
6:1-2	233
6:4-6	233
6:16-18	233
7:13-14	40,76,268, 269,270
7:15-20	41
7:21-23	41,268,269
8:25-26	104
10:28	89,112,115, 116,139,247,254
10:29-30	117
11:28	197

Scripture Index

Matthew (continued)

12:40	314
13:24-30	304
13:40-43	307,308
18:6-9	281
18:9	89
18:10-14	9,66
18:20-22	70
19:26	197,264
19:29	240
22:43	111
23:15	89
23:33	42,51,90
24	42,93
24:34	150
24:34-38	43
25:30	94
25:41	142,270,271 269
25:43-46	138
25:46	94,95,149, 150,153,155, 224,248,255 271,272,274
26:62-64	153,274
27:52-53	212
28:18	39,197

Mark

3:28-29	269
9:43	90
9:43-50	203,281
9:49-50	193,205,258
9:45	90
9:47	90
13	93
13:26	36
14:21	270

Luke

1:32-33	149
2:3-6	29
2:13-14	201
3:2-6	207
3:6	30,34,196
3:7-9	31
3:10-15	32
3:16	32
3:17	33
3:21-22	33
5:37	120
6:35	50,154,249, 259,275
6:35-36	180
9:57-60	296
10:22	197,264
12:5	90,102,192
14:1	234
14:12-14	235
15:4	120
15:8-9	66
15:11-19	62
15:11-32	66
15:20-22	62
15:24	121
15:47	66
16:19-24	95
18:29-30	140-143
21	93
23:34	276

John

1:3	264
1:14-17	55
1:29-36	13,197,275
3:12-17	207

Scripture Index

John (continued)

3:13	99
3:14-16	111,325
3:16	121,266,286
3:35	264
3:36	14
5:22	197
5:22-24	158,287
5:22-27	122
5:24	14,262,327
5:25-29	311
5:26	123
6:35	13
6:39	197
6:39-40	208
6:44	253
6:47	14
6:65	253
6:66	296
8:12	273
8:31-32	11,15
8:44	49
8:51	13,301
8:52	301
10:9	13
10:11	13
11:25	13
11:25-26	301,325
12:24,32	119,267,288
12:37-41	195
13:34-35	50
14:6	13
15:1	13
15:19	189
17:1-2	209
17:2	197

John (continued)

17:7	197
17:7-10	12
17:10	197
17:10	197
17:17	15
17:24	245

Acts

2:29-30	111
4:8-12	22
4:13	22
16:31	3
17:10-11	11,244,248
20:28	125
22:4-5	152,153,273
24:14-15	303

Romans

1:18	270
1:20	135,136,137
3:9-12	125
3:12	263
3:11-12	309
3:21-24	126
3:24	267
3:28	267
5:1-2	159,267
5:3-5	159
5:6	38,45,245
5:8	38,45,245,275
5:9	267,272
5:10-12	160
5:12	34
5:12-14	297
5:13-14	161,297
5:14,17	317

Scripture Index

Romans (continued)

5:15-17	162
5:18	34,124,128
	163,209,261
5:18-19	154
5:18-21	298
5:19	163
5:20-21	166
6:3-4	310,325
6:3-8	293
6:4	290,293,323
6:23	286,301,302
7:9-13	299
8:8-9	306
8:23-25	305
8:37-39	53
8:28	249
9:1-5	305
9:21-23	253
10:21	263
11:26-27	131
11:26-29	164
11:29-32	125,126
11:30-31	165
11:32	127,128,129,
	209,255,261
11:32-36	260
11:33-36	166,181
11:36	209
12:3	230
13:11-12	309
14:8-9	39,46,245
14:9-11	171
15:14	263
16:20	309,316

1 Corinthians

3:8	229
3:11-13	267
3:17	286
3:21	263
6:12	263
15:12-19	312
15:20	307
15:20-23	313
15:21-22	164
15:22	127,128,255
15:22-28	218,256
15:21-23	164,299
15:24-28	255,315
15:29	316
15:30-31	318
15:32-34	318
15:35-38	319
15:39-41	319
15:42-44	319,323
15:45-49	324
15:50-54	326
15:55-58	327

2 Corinthians

2:15	286
5:10	228
5:16	306
5:17-19	229
5:20-21	161
5:21	324
12:9	242

Galatians

3:24	267
3:24-29	38

Scripture Index

Ephesians

1:3-6	185,187,188
1:4	245
1:7-10	217
2:1	161
2:1,4-7	300
2:4-5	161
2:4-8	323
2:4-9	56
2:7	285,290
2:8-9	59,161,239
3:20-21	308

Philippians

2:9-11	131,169,175
2:9-11	209,266
3:19	284

Colossians

1:16	171,209
1:18	313
1:19-20	129,254
1:20	171,209,262
2:13-14	297

1 Thessalonians

5:21	11,86

2 Thessalonians

1:8-9	271,272
1:9	139,286,289
1:11-12	230

1 Timothy

2:3-4	210,264

1 Timothy (continued)

2:3-6	129,130,155, 191,192,210, 255,265
2:4-6	251
4:10	276,291
6:15-16	111,122,123

Titus

2:11-15	124
2:13	3,7,127

Hebrews

4:12	107
9:11-12	159
9:23-24	315
9:27	20,121,129 157,169,176, 247,288
9:28	300,317,327
10:29	153,274
11:9-10	26
12:29	274

James

1:17	244
2:17	60
3:6	90

1 Peter

1:20	24,245
3:18	306

1 John

2:2	266,276
4:8	53,109,259
4:8-11	180
4:8-14	79

Scripture Index

1 John (continued)

4:10	110
4:14-16	79
4:16	53
5:11-13	302

Jude

1:6	135,137
1:7	282,283
1:13	282,283

Revelation

1:7	254
1:14-16	314
2:4-6	58,317
2:7	58,59
14:9-11	99
14:10	283,284
14:11	100,283,284
14:18-19	101
20:4-5	320
20:5	322
20:10	49,283, 284
20:14	284,289
20:15	284,285,289
21:8	270
22:12	229

ABOUT THE AUTHOR

D. Robert Pike (Rob) is a retired Engineer and husband of his beloved wife Ida. He holds a Bachelor of Science degree from Indiana Wesleyan University, a Master of Arts Degree from Webster University, and Ph.D. in Theology at Trinity College and Seminary.

He is the author of four previous books:

1. **God's Promise of Redemption, a story of fulfilled prophecy**
2. **The Lamb of God Victorious, the keeping of the Revelation Promise**
3. **Jehovah's Witnesses, Modern Day Arians or Not**
4. **The Great American Divide, How we got here and what we can do about it**

All of Rob's Books are available at Amazon.com, or by order at your favorite book store.

Rob is a member of Gideon's International and lives with his wife of 37 years in Southwest Florida in the winter, and central Indiana in the summer. His life verse is Proverbs 3:5,6:

> "Trust in the LORD with all your heart, and do not lean on your own understanding. In all your ways acknowledge him, and He will make straight your paths."

Be sure to visit Rob's website at: www.truthinliving.net.

If you have questions concerning this book, send an email to Rob at robpike@truthinliving.net.

———————————

Made in the USA
Monee, IL
09 December 2022

20560107R00187